The Little
PC Book
Windows XP Edition

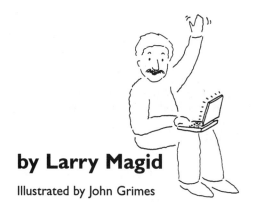

by Larry Magid

Illustrated by John Grimes

⦿ **Peachpit Press**

The Little PC Book, Windows XP Edition
by Larry Magid

Peachpit Press
1249 Eighth Street
Berkeley, CA 94710
800/283-9444
510/524-2178
510/524-2221 (fax)

Find us on the World Wide Web at www.peachpit.com

Peachpit Press is a division of Addison Wesley Longman.

Editor: Whitney Walker
Illustrator: John Grimes
Production coordinator: Connie Jeung-Mills
Copyeditor: Kate McKinley
Compositor: Jan Contestable
Cover design: TMA Ted Mader + Associates
Interior design: Chuck Routhier

3 3113 02142 3688

ISBN 0-201-75470-3

9 8 7 6 5 4 3

Printed and bound in the United States of America

To Clarence and Lucille Regehr for helping me
to understand the value of a loving family.

Acknowledgments

Many thanks to Whitney Walker for editing the manuscript and shepherding the project. It would never have seen the light of print were it not for Whitney.

I'm also indebted to John Grimes for his creative, funny, and informative cartoons. This is the fourth time John and I have worked together and it keeps getting better.

Thanks to copyeditor Kate McKinley and proofreader Tracy Brown for making sure that everything in this book actually makes sense. And to production coordinator Connie Jeung-Mills and compositor Jan Contestable for making it look so good.

Nancy Ruenzel, publisher of Peachpit Press, has long been a source of support and advice. Becky Morgan, Nancy Davis, and Rebecca Ross of Peachpit's editorial team provided invaluable input and assistance for this edition.

Finally, special thanks to my family—Patti, Katherine, and William—for reminding me that some things in life are far more important than computers.

Preface

This, the fourth edition of The Little PC Book, *is the most ambitious rewrite to date. That's because it's based on a completely new operating system, and although Windows XP draws some of its inspiration from its predecessors, it is also remarkably different.*

Previous versions of this book were aimed primarily at novice PC users, and though novices will still have no trouble understanding the book, this edition is aimed at a much broader audience—those who are new to Windows XP. And that, of course, is just about everyone. So even if you're an old hand at Windows 98, Windows Me, or Windows 2000, read on. There are plenty of new things to learn.

The Little PC Book is divided into four parts:

Part 1: Getting Oriented introduces you to the world of PCs. Here you'll learn just what people mean when they talk about "Windows," "IBM compatible," and "applications."

Part 2: Working with Windows XP gives you the rules of using Windows XP, Microsoft's new operating system. You'll learn how to give commands, open applications and files, create multi-user accounts, and carry out the other basic tasks that will help you control your PC and get your work done.

Part 3: Cool Things You Can Do with Your PC tells you how to use your PC to do all kinds of great stuff: play and record digital music and movies, edit digital photographs, create greeting cards, pay your bills online, play games, and choose the software that's right for you.

Part 4: Exploring the Internet shows you how to use Internet Explorer and other tools included in Windows XP for surfing the Web. (If you have earlier versions of Windows, don't worry, you can explore the Net, too.) This section covers email, Internet security, America Online, and a tour of the World Wide Web.

The book is designed to make finding the information you need as easy as possible. To make it easy to learn the jargon that clutters the world of computers, I've boldfaced new terms as they're introduced. Any time you see a boldface term, you can look it up in the glossary at the end of the book.

Now, before you go any further, take note: This book covers Windows-based PCs, not Macintoshes. (If you want to know the difference, go to Chapter 2.) If you've gotten this book by accident and want to know about Macs instead, you can return the book to Peachpit Press and exchange it for a copy of *The Little Mac Book* (Peachpit's address is on the copyright page).

You should also know that I've assumed that the readers of this book will be using Windows XP or upgrading from an earlier version of Windows. (If you don't know what that means, turn to Chapter 4.)

Ready? OK, let's get started.

Table of Contents

Part I / Getting Oriented   **3**

1	Why I Wrote This Book and Why You Need It	4
2	Types of Computers	6
3	Where to Get Help	8
4	The Windows Operating System: What's Inside Your PC	19
5	Introducing Windows XP: A House No Longer Divided	22
6	What Do You Call That Thing, Anyway?	28
7	Where to Buy a PC	30
8	Should You Get a Laptop PC?	34
9	Choosing the Right Computer	40
10	The CPU: The Computer's Brain	43
11	Memory: The Electronic Workspace	46
12	The Hard Disk: The Computer's Filing Cabinet	49
13	Removable Disk Drives: The Computer's Front Door	52
14	Connectors: Plug In and Move Up	55
15	Expansion Slots: Room to Grow	59
16	Monitors and Display Adapters: The Face of the Computer	62
17	The Keyboard: Talking to Your Computer	68
18	Mice and Other Pointing Devices: Making Quick Moves	73
19	Printers: Putting Your Work on Paper	76
20	Modems: Dial-Up, Broadband, and Fax	82
21	Getting the Picture: Scanners, Digital Cameras, Camcorders	88
22	Accessories: Making Yourself Comfortable	94
23	Putting It All Together	98
24	Setting Up Your Workplace	104

Part 2 / Working with Windows XP   109

25	Starting Your Computer	110
26	The Windows XP Desktop	112
27	The Start Menu: Gateway to Windows XP	115
28	Giving Commands in Windows	123
29	Using the Taskbar	132
30	Windows Control Panel	134
31	The Help and Support Menu	145
32	Working with Files	149
33	File Naming Conventions	154
34	Working with Folders	159
35	Working with Programs	166
36	Windows Accessories	177
37	Networking	183
38	Preventing and Recovering from Disasters	191
39	Shutting Down, Standing By, and Logging Off	203

Part 3 / Cool Things You Can Do with Your PC   209

40	Stocking Up on Software	210
41	Where to Get Software	216
42	Installing and Uninstalling Software	222
43	Digital Music and DVD Movies	224
44	Creating Digital Video	234
45	Digital Photography	239
46	Greeting Cards and Other Creative Projects	245
47	Personal Finances	248
48	Games	252

Part 4 / Exploring the Internet   259

49   Internet Basics   260
50   Getting Online   265
51   Safety, Privacy, and Security   271
52   Email, Instant Messaging, and Online Chatting 281
53   Internet Explorer   288
54   Surfing the World Wide Web   294
55   Using Microsoft.net   299
56   My Favorite Sites   302

Glossary   321

Index   351

Whether you're new to personal computers or just new to Windows XP, there's always more to explore. This section will get you started with a basic introduction (for some, a re-introduction) to PCs and a first look at Windows XP. You'll find out how to choose the right computer for you and learn all about the components that go along with it. By the time you're finished with this section, you'll be up and running on a new computer, or at least that much more knowledgeable about the one you've already got.

Getting Oriented
one

1 Why I Wrote This Book and Why You Need It

This is the fourth edition of this book. The first edition, published in 1993, came out just as people were starting to flock to the personal computer, or PC. Today, while there are still those with little or no PC experience, an increasing number of people around the globe consider themselves at least somewhat computer literate.

However, plenty of folks who use PCs still feel they have a lot to learn, and since you picked up this book, you're probably one of them. After all, unless you're a PC hobbyist or work in the PC industry, your life simply doesn't revolve around computers. Let's face it, these machines can be frustrating and unreliable, and just because things go wrong when you're using the computer doesn't mean you're stupid (or a "dummy").

I'll let you in on a little secret. I've been using personal computers since the late '70s and have written numerous books and thousands of articles about them—and I still have problems! There are times when I want to scream at my PC (or do something worse to it). Even I have to get on the phone with tech support because no matter how hard I try, I can't figure out how to use some product. Like the rest of the world, I don't always get through to a competent techie and I, too, have to sit on hold or get stuck in voice mail hell in an attempt to find help.

Still, over the years I have picked up some pointers on how to make using PCs easier, and that's exactly what I want to share with you. You might need this book if:

- You are new to computers.
- You are sometimes frustrated by PCs.
- You are in the process of buying a new PC.
- You are upgrading your operating system to Windows XP.
- You want a refresher.

It's Not As Tough As You Think

You don't need to know how a computer works; you just need to learn how to use it. It's like a radio, TV, VCR, movie projector, or any other piece of equipment. When you turn on your TV, you don't think about picture tubes, vertical hold, or broadcast frequencies. If you want to, you can learn about the those things, but you don't need to in order to enjoy your favorite show.

Like a TV, the PC is just the box that plays the programs. With a VCR, you play videotapes. With a PC, you play **application programs** or **software** and access the **Internet.**

With a computer, you need to know just enough about your system to buy one, set it up, turn it on and off, and play the software. You should also learn about the different kinds of software and how to buy what you want. You'll probably want to use your computer to do some cool projects and surf the Internet, too. This book will tell you all those things—and no more, because that's everything you really need in order to buy and use a computer.

Admittedly, PCs aren't quite as simple as TVs, stereos, or even VCRs, but they're a lot more powerful and versatile. In fact, today's PCs are stereos as well as movie players, audio recorders, and much, much more. Don't worry—just because your PC has tons of uses, that does not mean you have to learn them all at once. If you're new to PCs, start off by learning how to turn it on and explore the Web browser, email, and word processor. Later, you can try out some more features and before you know it, you'll be a whiz kid and your friends will be calling you a nerd. Just don't put tape on your glasses.

Of course, someday you may want to write your own software or put up your own Web page. But in the meantime, this book will give you a good start and provide basic reference information that you can come back to down the line.

2 Types of Computers

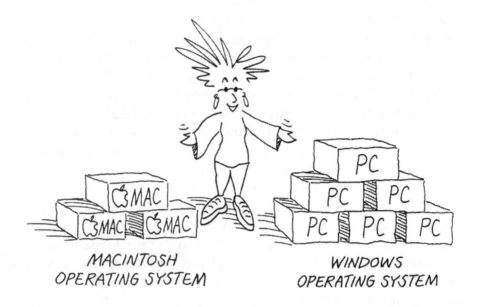

MACINTOSH
OPERATING SYSTEM

WINDOWS
OPERATING SYSTEM

When you go into a computer store, you'll see machines
of all sizes and shapes, from many different manufacturers.
You'll see desktops and laptops from Toshiba, IBM, Dell,
Hewlett-Packard, and other companies. Don't worry about it.
There are really only two kinds of personal computers: those
designed to run the Windows operating system (or "PCs")
and those designed to run the Macintosh operating system
(or "Macs").

Technically, both Macs and Windows-compatible computers are
PCs—personal computers. When most people say "PC," though,
they're referring to Windows machines (as I am in this book).

More than 90 percent of today's personal computers are
designed to run various versions of Windows. These machines
used to be called IBM compatibles because they run the same
type of software as personal computers from IBM do. Industry

insiders sometimes call them **Wintel** machines (short for Windows and Intel) because they run Windows and have an Intel or Intel-compatible microprocessor inside of them. But these days, they're more likely to just be called PCs.

No matter who the manufacturer is, all these computers work the same way and run the same software because they have one important thing in common: They're all based on the same type of **processor** (sometimes called the **central processing unit,** or **CPU**). PCs are based on processors made by Intel or by Advanced Micro Devices (AMD), which has developed Intel-compatible CPUs. All machines sold today have some version of Intel's **Pentium** processor or a chip from AMD that's compatible with the Pentium. Older CPUs that you might hear about include the 486, 386, and so on.

The other personal computers on the market today are **Macintoshes,** made by Apple Computer. They use entirely different processors and require software made especially for them.

You may also have heard of a **network computer.** That's a general term that refers to a device that doesn't use either the Windows or Macintosh operating system. But it still lets you access the Internet, or when installed at an organization, your company's **local area network (LAN).** Network computers have been around for a few years, but so far they're not very popular.

Much more trendy these days are hand-held computers, or **palmtops,** that run the Palm Operating System or Microsoft's PocketPC operating system. You may also see devices, including WebTV and some video game consoles, that offer Internet access from a television set. Although they aren't called computers, they basically are—but they aren't covered in this book, because most people who are serious about using the Web or doing work are going to get a PC or a Macintosh.

Now, assuming you've settled on a Windows PC and not a Macintosh, let's get on with the book.

3 Where to Get Help

The first thing you should know when you set out to learn about computers is that you're not on your own. Help is out there, though sometimes you have to ferret it out. My main advice is to speak up when you're confused and not to worry about "stupid" questions. I often hear from readers who are embarrassed because they think their questions are silly, but some of those inquiries turn out to be quite challenging.

The Manual and the Help Command

Most pieces of hardware (computer) or software (applications) come with a manual, or user's guide, that is designed to be your first resource. Some programs now come with onscreen instructions instead. It's always a good idea to read the manual (or at least glance at it) before you call for help. If you have a problem, pay special attention to the troubleshooting guide that's typically at the end of the manual. But be aware that manuals rarely answer every possible question, so there's a good chance you'll eventually have to look beyond the documentation for further help.

The Help and Support Menu on Windows XP

Sometimes a program doesn't come with a manual because all of its instructions are listed in the Help menu, a built-in help feature that calls up information about the program's commands right on screen. Press the F1 key or pull down the Help menu any time and get help. Help with Windows itself is available from the Help option on the **Start menu** in the lower-left corner of your desktop.

The XP Start menu.

A Quick Guide to Software Manuals

Over time, a standard, effective organization for manuals has evolved. Assuming the software you buy has a manual, look for these sections:

System requirements. The minimum hardware and software you need in order to use the program are listed right up front in the user's guide, often in the installation instructions. Sometimes this information is also on the outside of the box.

Installation instructions. These are usually near the front of the user's guide or in a separate booklet, and they lead you step by step through installing the software.

Tutorial. Also generally near the front of the user's guide, the tutorial leads you through a practice session with the software.

Reference guide. Use this alphabetical listing of commands when you want to know how a particular command works.

Troubleshooting. In most manuals, there's some list of common problems you might run up against and how to solve them. Of course, no troubleshooting section lists every possible problem, but it's the first place to look when you hit a snag.

Quick-reference card. This summarizes the commands you're most likely to need.

The Internet and AOL

Virtually all hardware and software companies have Web sites, and most have some type of online help. If you don't know the Web address of the company, you can guess. Dell is www.dell.com, Compaq is www.compaq.com, and so on. If that doesn't work, try using an Internet search engine like Google (www.google.com) to look up the company by name. When you get to the Web site, look for a Support option. Some Web sites have search features where you can enter a question. Also look for a list of "Frequently Asked Questions" (often referred to as a "FAQ"), which may answer your inquiry before you have to ask it. Finally, Web sites sometimes have forums where customers ask each other questions or get answers from company staff.

Also, all of the computer magazines have Web sites and those sites are often great places to turn to for information. In most cases, they publish the full text of all their articles online, and they usually have a search option that lets you look for articles on any subject.

Newsgroups

A **newsgroup** is just another word for a "forum" or "bulletin board" where people exchange information about products. You can't always be sure that everyone in a newsgroup actually knows what they're talking about, but it's still a good place to get opinions. You can access newsgroups with the newsgroup reader that comes with Microsoft Outlook Express, but the easiest way is by going to www.deja.com, where you can type in any subject and find a newsgroup. Don't be too specific. Your best bet is to type in the name of whatever product you're inquiring about.

Finding Drivers and Software

As you work with PCs, you'll hear a lot about **drivers.** It doesn't refer to someone who drives your computer for you. It refers to special software that is generally used to help Windows work with hardware, such as a graphics board, a sound card, or a modem. When you buy a PC, the drivers come preinstalled for all the hardware on the machine. When you buy a new device, the drivers are usually on the CD-ROM. Sometimes, however, you need to locate the drivers on the Internet. This is also the case when the manufacturer releases new, revised drivers or when you misplace or damage your CD-ROM. In almost every situation, you can find the drivers you need at the manufacturer's Web site. There is usually a search box on the Web site where you can enter the model number or name of the hardware. It may also ask you what operating system you're using, as there are often different drivers for different operating systems.

Upgrader's Tip

Unlike previous versions of Windows, Windows XP has a feature that automatically updates drivers, even from companies other than Microsoft. You can access this feature from the Add/Remove Programs icon in the control panel. For more on this, see Windows Update in Chapter 31.

In addition to the manufacturer's site, there are Web sites that specialize in helping you find drivers. These are a few of the best known:

- **Virtual Dr.** (www.virtualdr.com) offers information about hardware, software, and operating systems as well as drivers.

- **DriverGuide.com** (www.driverguide.com) provides software and hardware drivers as well as a help forum.

- **Download.com** (www.download.com) supplies drivers and utilities along with all sorts of other software.

In addition to all the sites operated by magazines and PC companies, there are lots of other handy Web sites that can help you find software or learn more about your computer. (See the sidebar on page 13 and Chapter 50 for more on how to get online access to such resources.)

Friends, Relations, and Gurus

You know who I'm talking about. That person down the hall who seems to know everything there is to know about computing. Your niece, your dad, your brother-in-law. Whoever it is, they're your best resource for helping you solve that little problem that has you stuck. Most people are really glad to help. They're honored—flattered even—to be asked to show off their knowledge, even if their level of accomplishment is only a month or two beyond your own. One note of caution: Some people can be a bit arrogant about computers, especially which brand to buy. I'm not saying that you shouldn't listen to their advice, but realize that there are people who, for reasons I don't totally understand, get all emotional about PCs. This is especially true if you start talking about PCs versus Macs. For some, the choice of a computer becomes almost a religious issue.

Tech Support Lines

Most hardware and software manufacturers have a support line you can call when you need help with their products. Some have toll-free numbers, but others require you to make a long-distance call. A few charge your credit card when you call for help.

Before you call tech support, try to find the information on the company's Web site—assuming, of course, that your machine is working and that you have access to the Web. When you call tech support, make sure you know which version of Windows you're using. (If you don't know, right-click on My Computer and select Properties.) You'll also need the version number of the program and the exact name of the hardware you're using it on, especially how much **memory** your computer has and what **expansion boards,** if any, you have installed. (You can usually tell the version number and the amount of memory installed on your PC by selecting the About option from the program's Help menu. Sometimes you'll need the serial number of your program or computer. With software, you can often find the serial number or product ID in the About option, but you'll almost always find it in the manual, on the box, or on the registration card. With hardware, it's usually on a label on the back or bottom of the unit. If you don't know the serial number, call anyway. Most tech support people are very understanding.

A Bunch of Tech Support Numbers

Listed below are phone numbers and Web site addresses for popular software and hardware companies. If the number you need isn't listed here, check the manual.

HELLO, COMPUTER HELP LINE.
THERE'S NO SUCH THING AS
A SILLY QUESTION.

SORRY, SIR —
THAT'S A NEW ONE...

SOFTWARE COMPANY	PHONE	WEB SITE
Adobe Systems	206-675-6304	www.adobe.com
Broderbund Software	319-247-3333	www.broderbund.com
Corel	613-274-0500	www.corel.com
Disney Interactive	818-841-3326	www.disney.com/DisneyInteractive
Humongus Entertainment	425-486-9258	www.humongous.com
Intuit	650-944-6000	www.intuit.com
Microsoft	425-882-8080	www.microsoft.com
Symantec & Norton Computing	408-517-8000	www.symantec.com

HARDWARE COMPANY	PHONE	WEB SITE
Compaq	800-OKCOMPA	www.compaq.com
Dell	800-624-9896	www.dell.com
Epson America	800-922-8911	www.epson.com
Gateway	800-846-2301	www.gateway.com
Hewlett-Packard	208-323-2551	www.hp.com
IBM	800-237-5511	www.ibm.com
Toshiba	800-457-7777	www.csd.toshiba.com

Upgrader's Tip

The tech support provider will often try to walk you through a solution over the phone, so make sure you're sitting at your computer (and that it's turned on) when you call. Also, have a good book handy because you'll probably be on hold for a while. Once you get through the first time, ask the person to advise you on the best time to call back if you need more help.

User Groups

User groups are organizations formed by people who use a particular type of computer or software. Most user groups have meetings once or twice a month so members can ask each other questions and see new product demonstrations. Some have newsletters, Web sites, and "special interest groups" aimed at novices, too.

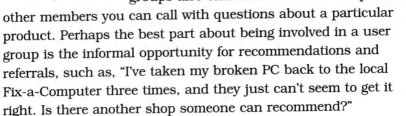

Typically, user groups don't charge for their help, but if you want to get the newsletter, you might be asked to pay a small membership fee. Often, membership gives you access to a library of free or low-cost software, plus special discounts on products. Many groups also offer their own list of experts— other members you can call with questions about a particular product. Perhaps the best part about being involved in a user group is the informal opportunity for recommendations and referrals, such as, "I've taken my broken PC back to the local Fix-a-Computer three times, and they just can't seem to get it right. Is there another shop someone can recommend?"

As in most volunteer groups, a handful of stalwart souls ends up doing most of the work. If you have the time to pitch in for some of the chores, your efforts will be heartily appreciated. (You volunteer to bring refreshments one week, and the next week you find out you've been nominated for a two-year term as group secretary.) Pitching in is more than courteous, though. If you get involved, you'll find you're on the inside track for all sorts of information. Whatever you do, make friends with the newsletter editor. He or she can always use more help and may be able to get you free software—as long as you're willing to test it and write a review. You can find a local user group by visiting the Association of PC User Groups on the Internet at www.apcug.org.

Your Local Computer Store

Chances are you live within driving distance of a computer store— hopefully one staffed by people who know a lot about computers and are happy to share that information. Maybe yes, maybe no. Though some computer and software salespeople are very knowledgeable, others just act as if they are.

With this caveat in mind, it's still a good idea to become friends with the folks who work at the computer store. Once you've latched on to one or two of these people, milk them for all they're worth. Call them up with questions, ask their advice. Flatter their egos. And, when you need some hardware or software, make sure you buy stuff from them, too. I'm encouraging you to use these people—not exploit them.

Magazines and Newsletters

There are several magazines devoted to personal computing, and a few of them can be understood by beginners. All of these publications carry software reviews written by professional computer journalists with educated opinions. The magazines are a good place to start when you want to find out about a particular program. They are all available at any good newsstand and by subscription.

PC Magazine is a great place for encyclopedic data on anything you might consider buying.

PC World also has reviews and useful tips. It's targeted primarily at business users but offers plenty of useful information to home users, too.

Computer Shopper is mostly a compendium of advertisements for computer hardware and software. It's a good place to find bargains.

Yahoo Internet Life focuses primarily on the Internet. It's a good place to learn about Web sites, Net strategies, service providers, and Internet culture.

Resources

PC Magazine
800-365-2770
www.pcmag.com

PC World
800-234-3498
www.pcworld.com

Computer Shopper
www.zdnet.com/
computershopper

Yahoo Internet Life
www.yil.com

Some communities have free computer newspapers, like *MicroTimes* and *Computer User.* These papers often have some very good articles, including reviews and tips. They often bring you a local angle, and they're a good place to find out about user group meetings, training classes, and other local resources.

Several software companies also publish newsletters—and in some cases, magazines—devoted to providing tips and current information on their software packages. Virtually all manufacturers have Web sites with plenty of great information.

Books

Computer books can be a great way to learn about computers in general or about a particular piece of software. The first place you should look for any book is at your local bookstore. If you're confused by the array of computer books, just ask the clerk for a recommendation. Even if they don't have the one you need, they can probably order it for you, especially if you know the title and the name of the author or publisher. You might also be able to find good computer books at your public or college library—but be sure that the book covers the latest version of the software or hardware you're using.

A Pocket Guide to Computer Books

Any trip to the computer section of a bookstore will overwhelm you with books that range from beginning to advanced, in topics from the general to the very specific. You can narrow down your search with these guidelines.

Beginner books are generally slimmer volumes that sell for about $20 and have titles like ABCs of..., Introduction to..., ...Made Easy, ...For Dummies, The Little..., and so on. You're reading one now.

Quick-reference books generally cost less than $10 and provide only brief explanations of the various commands or menu options of a program. They're better for looking up an occasional piece of information than for learning a program.

Tutorials walk you through classroom-style exercises.

Interactive tutorials come with a CD that leads you through lessons on your own computer.

Advanced books often have titles like ...Tips & Tricks or Supercharging... to make it clear that they are for people who already know a program and want to get better at it.

Reference books tend to be the super-fat tomes, seemingly sold by the pound. Once you know the basics of a program, they're useful for looking up features.

You can also buy computer books online at the usual places, such as Amazon (www.amazon.com) and Barnes & Noble (www.bn.com). FatBrain (www.fatbrain.com), which is owned by Barnes & Noble, specializes in computer books. Of course, I urge you to check out Peachpit's Web site (www.peachpit.com), but, like that Macy's Santa who won friends for the store by sending customers elsewhere, I have to admit that you'll also find some excellent computer books from competing publishers. The "Dummy" books are published by Hungry Minds (www.hungryminds.com). You'll find a wide variety of titles at Osborne/McGraw Hill (www.osborne.com), as well as Macmillan USA (www.mcp.com), where you'll find links for Que, Sams, and the Idiot's Guides.

Courses

Of course, for personalized help, there's no substitute for a live instructor. Computer courses are available everywhere. Start by perusing the offerings at a local community college. Many private companies also offer computer training. Check your local Yellow Pages under "training" or "computers." For online, CD-ROM, or video-based tutorials, check out ElementK (www.elementk.com), PlanetLearn (www.planetlearn.com), Computer Training Network (www.comptrain.net), and Learn2University (www.learninguniversity.com/fd/luonlinesn.asp).

Experiment

Last but not least, don't be afraid to experiment. You should know that no matter what you do on a computer, it's all but impossible to actually damage the hardware (unless you directly assault the machine or try to use it in the bathtub). The worst you can possibly do is lose some data and waste some time. Pull down the menus and see what's there. Try out any unfamiliar commands. Watch what happens and you'll learn about your computer in no time.

The Windows Operating System: What's Inside Your PC   4

The hardware is the physical machine that you can see and touch. The software is the set of instructions that make the computer do the things you want it to do. There are basically two kinds of software: the operating system and application software. An operating system is the basic computer software that makes your PC work. An application program is the software you use for specific tasks, like word processing, playing games, paying bills, and so forth.

The operating system is basically the computer's traffic cop: It helps determine the way the hardware and software interact. Just about everything that the machine does—from saving files to the disk or displaying text and graphics on the screen—is controlled by the operating system. It's the intermediary between the machine's hardware and its application software. In the old days, an operating system was pretty basic. It mainly controlled how programs would write to the disk or interact with the computer's memory, and it was used to issue some basic system commands.

But Microsoft changed all that when it introduced Windows. Windows is really a combination of an operating system and a set of basic programs that do lots of other things. Today's Windows operating system comes with a host of programs, including Microsoft Internet Explorer for surfing the Web, Windows Media Player for listening to music or watching videos, and Outlook Express for sending and receiving email. Not to mention software for backing up your hard drive, sending and receiving faxes, and often much more.

In fact, the integration of new features to the operating system is one of the things that got Microsoft into trouble with the Justice Department and a federal judge in 1998. A lot of other software companies complained that Microsoft was putting them out of business by bundling too many features with Windows. The Justice Department agreed and used that argument as a focus for its antitrust case. I'm not sure what will ultimately happen (maybe you'll know by the time you read this). But I do know that Microsoft will continue to be a dominant player and that no matter what Microsoft's competitors and the Justice Department think, Windows XP will emerge as a significant product.

Several versions of Microsoft Windows are currently in widespread use. The newest—and the one I've focused on in this book—is called Windows XP, but plenty of machines run Windows 2000, Windows Me, Windows 98, Windows 95, or even the comparatively ancient Windows 3.1 from 1992.

For the past several years, Microsoft has been shipping two types of PC operating systems. One version, collectively referred to as "Windows 9x," started with Windows 95, which as you might expect, was released in 1995. Three years later, Microsoft came out with **Windows 98** followed by Windows 98 Second Edition. Then, in 2000, the company published **Windows Millennium Edition** (Windows Me), which was a minor refinement of Windows 98.

Windows Me was clearly positioned as a home operating system, but at the same time Microsoft was developing a separate operating system for businesses. It started as **Windows NT**, but was pretty much replaced with **Windows 2000**. Unlike Windows 9x, Windows NT and Windows 2000 were based on an entirely new code. They were much more reliable and robust and had a higher level of security than Windows 9x. But they were also a bit harder to use and configure and were considerably more expensive.

5 Introducing Windows XP: A House No Longer Divided

With Windows XP, Microsoft is no longer selling separate operating systems for home and business. XP is for everyone.

Although the two operating systems look a bit different, under the hood, Windows XP has a lot in common with Windows 2000. That's a good thing, because Windows 2000 is a very reliable operating system. First, neither XP nor 2000 is likely to crash (stop running) simply because a program crashes. That's important since there will always be programs that, for one reason or another, simply stop functioning. In theory, Windows 9x had a way for you to shut down a misbehaving program and keep on working, but it often failed to function properly and you'd sometimes wind up having to restart the machine. Now that shouldn't be necessary: The operating system isolates crashed programs in their own "memory space" and allows everything else to continue running.

Also like Windows 2000, XP uses your PC's memory better. Other versions of Windows sometimes caused "memory leak," allowing programs to eat up PC resources even after you stopped using them. With Windows XP, as soon as you stop using a program, the memory becomes available for other programs to use.

But Windows XP also differs from Windows 2000 in some significant ways, and that's also a good thing. It's more user-friendly and is compatible with more programs that people use at home. Games were not especially compatible with Windows NT and Windows 2000, and neither were some printers, scanners, and other devices that had been designed for Windows 9x.

The good news for you is that Microsoft has been putting pressure on hardware and software companies to update their products so that they are compatible with Windows XP. Of course, not every manufacturer will comply, but the vast majority are smart enough to realize that they have to work with XP if they are going to survive. In fact, a lot of companies have already provided updates so their products work with Windows 2000, and with a

Should You Upgrade to Windows XP?

Choosing whether or not to upgrade is an important decision. Although Microsoft has made upgrading a bit easier than it was in the past, it's never 100 percent foolproof. Also, upgrading takes time, so don't do it unless you have a few hours to spare.

It's always a good idea to back up all of your important data, but it's especially important to do so before you upgrade to a new operating system. If all goes according to plan, all your data and software will be intact after you upgrade, but there is always a chance that something could go wrong and you'll be very glad of that backup. Just in case, be sure you have copies of all the installation CDs for your software. For more on backing up, see Chapter 38.

Be sure to check that your machine meets the necessary system requirements to upgrade. Windows XP takes up more disk space, uses more memory, and requires a somewhat faster CPU than other versions of Windows.

Before you upgrade, make sure your PC has

- At least 128 MB of memory

- At least a 300 MHz Pentium Celeron, or equivalent CPU from AMD

- At least 2 GB of free disk space

To see if your machine can handle XP, visit www.pcanswer.com/xpupgrade.htm.

Even if your machine meets the system requirements, you should still consider whether upgrading will significantly improve your current operating system. If you're already using Windows 2000, then you might be better off staying where you are. Although Windows XP has a different interface and more features than Windows 2000, it isn't any more stable. Both operating systems are relatively robust and unlikely to give you too many problems.

That said, there are still plenty of reasons to upgrade to Windows XP. I personally like XP better than Windows 2000—and a lot better than Windows 95, 98, and Me. Although it took me a couple of weeks to get used to it, I now find the XP user interface friendlier than the Windows 2000 interface, which was designed for professionals. Even pros will appreciate how much easier it is to find commands, features, and programs in XP.

Because XP is much more stable than Windows 98 or Windows Me, it's worthwhile upgrading from those versions. If you're running one of them now, you'll enjoy the new features and benefit from an upgrade.

But even if you're on an old operating system, if everything is working OK—well, if it ain't broke, don't fix it. Also, an upgrade CD will cost you about $100 ($200 for the professional edition), which may or may not be worth it to you. Eventually, when you get a new computer, it will have Windows XP or whatever the operating system du jour is then.

few exceptions, most products that work with Windows 2000 also work with Windows XP. And in any case, like Windows 98 and Windows Me, XP has a "compatibility mode" that will run some of your older programs.

"Users are always taken aback whenever you change something. And for the first couple of hours people try XP, they will be delighted by the new things they find there, and also a little bit disconcerted. The Start menu is quite different in XP than it's been before. Also, the color scheme and the way the dialogue boxes look is quite different."
—Bill Gates in an interview with Larry Magid, March 2001

All in all, Microsoft is putting a lot of muscle behind Windows XP and when Microsoft flexes its muscles, the rest of the industry (not to mention the United States Department of Justice) takes notice. Microsoft wants everyone to use a version of XP: Windows XP Home Edition for home users and Windows XP Professional for businesses. But frankly, even Bill Gates doesn't get his way all the time. Plenty of people still use Windows Me and Windows 98 and a lot of businesses still use Windows 2000. But if you buy a new PC today it will probably come with Windows XP, so that's the operating system we're concentrating on.

Getting XP on a New Machine

To be honest, the easiest and most reliable way to get Windows XP is to buy a new machine. New machines are designed with XP in mind, and when manufacturers install XP, they make sure it has all the drivers and other software it needs to work with your new hardware.

If you do buy a new PC, chances are pretty good that it will come with Windows XP. But, just to be sure, ask the salesperson or check the company's Web site to see what comes with the machine.

What's New in Windows XP

Besides the increased reliability imparted by the Windows 2000 code, XP has several new features as well as improvements to some of the older features from Windows Me and Windows 2000.

One new feature is a redesigned look and feel. While some experienced users will jump for joy over a sleeker, less cluttered, and more user-friendly Windows, I have to admit that when I first started using XP, I felt a bit lost. Some of the familiar icons and menu items were gone and there were new options that I hadn't heard about. Some of the ways that I used to look at files and folders no longer worked. In fact, that was one of the things that inspired me to write this book. I realized that if I—someone who has been using Windows from the beginning—was confused, a lot of other people would be, too.

Multi-user Capability

Windows XP has a multi-user function designed to be shared among family members or co-workers. Everyone who shares a computer can have his or her own "account," with an individualized workspace, a personalized welcome screen, and customized system settings. Of course, it's really the same machine, but Sally's version could look very different from the one that John uses. A more limited form of multi-user access has been available in previous generations of Windows, but one nice new feature is the ability to "log off," switching from one user to another without shutting down programs. When you log back on, your system looks just as it did before. (I'll have more on multi-user features in Chapter 30, including a discussion on how to set up additional "accounts.")

The Desktop

For experienced Windows users, the most noticeable new feature of the XP desktop is that there isn't much on it. Many of the program icons that used to be on the desktop are now located in the newly designed Start menu. You can still use the desktop to store shortcuts for programs and files, but it is no longer the default location.

The XP desktop looks pretty different from earlier versions of Windows. All of the programs and files are now stored in the Start menu.

The Start menu

The most important piece of real estate on your Windows XP desktop is a small green rectangle in the lower-left corner called the Start menu. You'll notice that it's a bit bigger than it was in previous versions of Windows—and it's even more important now.

All Programs. The Start menu is where you literally start all your programs. If you left-click it, you may see some of your programs already listed. If you don't see the one you want to run, click the green All Programs icon for a complete listing of all your software.

Special folders. In addition to programs, the Start menu is the gateway to your documents. You'll notice folders called My Documents, My Pictures, and My Music.

Although folders that contain documents can be given any name, the one called My Documents is generally the default folder for the documents you save in Microsoft Word and other text programs. My Pictures and My Music have very special attributes, which I'll cover in Chapter 27.

My Computer. The My Computer icon opens a window that allows you to explore everything on your disk drives. It also displays a menu (on the left) that you can use to access the Control Panel and to perform other tasks, such as adding or removing programs or viewing system information. Most of these functions can also be accessed from other parts of Windows, so the main function of My Computer is that it lets you explore the files on your drives. (I'll have more on My Computer in Chapter 27.)

6 What Do You Call That Thing, Anyway?

A desktop PC system is made up of many parts. When you buy a PC, you could buy just the main system unit, but these days most people buy a complete system—CPU, keyboard, monitor, mouse, and modem—or at least everything but the monitor. (Sometimes printers, scanners, and other peripheral devices come with a PC, but they are typically bought separately.)

Buying a complete system makes your choices easier, of course, but if you pick and choose separate components, you can get exactly what you want. In any case, here are the basic parts that make up a full PC system. Each one is explained in detail in the chapters that follow.

The **speakers** let you hear sounds coming from your PC. That includes MP3 music files downloaded from the Internet and music from a standard audio CD in your CD drive, as well as all the beeps, whirls, and other sounds coming from your software or the Internet. The speakers plug directly into the **sound card** at the back of your PC. For more on sound cards and speakers, see Chapter 14.

The **printer** puts the documents you create onto paper. For more on printers, see Chapter 19.

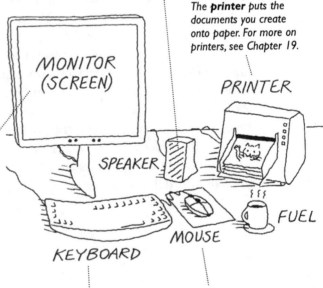

The **monitor** (sometimes called the **display** or the **screen**) is the main way your computer communicates with you. This is where the computer shows you what your system is doing and what your files contain. There are generally two types of screens: Cathode ray tube (CRT) screens have large picture tubes in them, and the more modern liquid crystal display (LCD) screens are flatter and easier on the eyes, but more expensive. See Chapter 16 for more on monitors.

The **keyboard** is one way you communicate with the computer. You use it to issue commands and enter words and numbers. Its layout is similar to that of a standard typewriter keyboard. See Chapter 17 for more on keyboards.

The **mouse** is used to move a **pointer** around your monitor's screen. The pointer lets you to show the program where you want your next action to apply. For more on mice, see Chapter 18.

This box, called the **system unit,** contains the guts of your computer. It holds the central processing unit (CPU), the memory (RAM, or random-access memory) chips, and all the other electronic components that make your computer do what it does. For more about CPUs and memory, see Chapters 10 and 11.

The **hard disk** (which is inside the system unit) stores most of your data. Hard disks are measured by the amount of data they store, expressed in **gigabytes,** abbreviated as GB (1 GB is about 1,000 MB or just over a billion bytes). For more about hard disks, see Chapter 12.

Most computers have some type of optical drive. These drives used to be called **CD-ROM drives** but now there are lots more options, including DVD drives and recording CD drives.

The **floppy disk drive** holds disks on which you can store programs and data that you want to get into or out of your computer. For more about floppy drives, see Chapter 13.

A **modem** connects your PC to the Internet using a standard phone line. Most PCs have a built-in modem that typically operates at 56 Kbps. Modems can also be used to send and receive faxes. Some PCs don't have modems. Instead, they connect to the Internet over a "broadband" connection such as DSL or a cable modem. For more about modems, see Chapter 20.

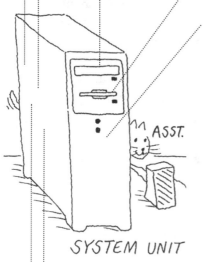

ASST.

SYSTEM UNIT

Some PCs now have an **Ethernet card** or **network card** that provides a high-speed connection to the Internet or a local network. In Chapter 14, I'll describe alternative types of network adapters including regular Ethernet, wireless network adapters, and adapters that use standard phone lines to connect PCs within the home.

The **expansion slots,** or **ports,** are slots that let you plug in extra equipment and expansion boards that enhance the machine's capabilities. Expansion boards (sometimes known as **cards** or **adapters**) can add features such as TV tuners or a network adapter. For more on expansion slots and expansion boards, see Chapter 15.

CD-ROM Drives

CD-ROM drives can read a standard CD-ROM or audio CD.

CD-RW (CD-rewritable) drives can not only read a CD-ROM but can write one as well, on special blank CDs. They can be used to backup data, copy PC or audio CDs, or create your own audio CDs that can be played in standard audio systems.

DVD-ROM drives can read standard CD-ROMs as well as DVDs that have movies on them. If you have such a drive, you can buy or rent a regular movie on DVD and watch it on your PC. Theoretically, you can get software on DVD, but—at least so far—very few software titles come out on DVD. Some DVD movies do have special software features that can only be played on a PC. You wouldn't even know about them if you only played the movie in a regular TV DVD player.

DVD/CD-RW combo drives are DVD drives that can also be used to write CD-RW discs.

DVD-R drives are combination drives that play and write both DVDs and CDs. If you get the right one, you can save your home movies on a DVD and watch them on a TV set with a DVD player. As this book was being written, these drives were just coming out and were pretty expensive. If you get a DVD-R drive, find out whether it's compatible with standard TV DVD players, because some aren't.

7 Where to Buy a PC

*It used to be you bought a computer at a computer store.
You still can, of course, but now you can also buy a computer
at warehouse stores like Costco, at home electronics stores
like Circuit City, or online. I haven't seen them for sale at
7-Eleven yet, but that day may come. I'll describe the
advantages and drawbacks of each option here.*

Computer Stores

Computer specialty stores are able to give you special attention.
If you buy from one of those stores, you can ask a service person
to preinstall the software and check to see that everything works
together before you take it home. Some stores will even deliver the
computer and set it up for you, and many offer extensive technical
support, so you have the right to expect someone to answer all
your questions. Some specialty stores offer their own "house
brand" machine, which, in some cases, is built right there in the
store. Those systems are generally cheaper than brand-name
systems and, if well built, can be just as reliable.

Discount Stores and Department Stores

If you know exactly what you want, you can get a pretty good deal
by buying your computer at buyers' clubs like Costco and Sam's
Club or superstores like Computer City, Best Buy, or CompUSA.
You'll even find PCs at department stores like Sears and Wal-Mart.
You're not likely to get much hand-holding at those places, but
you can always call the manufacturer's technical support if you
have a problem.

Stereo and Home Electronics Stores

An increasing number of stereo and home electronics stores now
carry computers right along with DVD players, TV sets, and boom
boxes. You take potluck when it comes to help on the sales floor.
The guy or gal who knows all about hi-fidelity won't necessarily

be all that helpful if you have a technical question about computers. You may find a good deal at one of those stores, but if you decide to buy from a stereo store, make sure you get a name-brand machine from a company that offers a national warranty and a toll-free technical support line.

Over the Web or by Phone

Configuring and ordering a PC over the Web can sometimes be frustrating, but it can also be very enlightening. Most PC companies let you "build your own" PC. You select every component and the Web site prices the system accordingly. It's a great way to comparison shop and find out what your options are. You can also play "what if" games with various components or specifications that you are considering. Technically speaking, "mail-order" sales really aren't by mail. You usually contact the company over the phone or order from the Web site (have your credit card handy), and your computer is shipped by UPS or Federal Express. Companies like Compaq Computer, Dell Computer, IBM, and Gateway have proven that quality and value can coexist in an online or mail-order shopping environment. These companies will build your custom machine and send it to you within a week or two, if not overnight.

The best way to find out if a company is on the level is by word of mouth. Ask other people where they bought their computers and whether they were satisfied. Also look at ads in computer magazines. If a company advertises for several months (or years) in a row, chances are, it's a reasonably substantial business. At least it has stayed in business and paid its advertising bills.

One disadvantage to buying online is that you can't walk in to return items, get repairs, or ask questions. Some companies offer attractive service contracts with 24-hour on-site repairs or free pickup and delivery for repairs off site. Most of the major mail-order firms at least offer toll-free telephone technical support. This is critical. Test them before you buy. Your first call shouldn't be to the sales department but to the technical support group. Ask some questions and see how responsive they are. Did you get through on the first call? Were you kept on hold? If they had

When to Buy: Now or Later?

One frequently asked question is, "Should I buy a PC now, or should I wait until the price comes down or the technology improves?" It doesn't matter when you ask the question, the answer is always the same. If you really want a computer now, buy it now, even though you can get a better and faster machine for less money in a year or so. The technology is continually evolving. Whatever you buy today will be outclassed by what comes on the market tomorrow. And what you buy tomorrow will be superseded by something introduced after that. If you worry about that, though, you'll never buy a new system, so go ahead and take the plunge.

to call you back, did they get back to you quickly? Are the people patient and friendly? Also check the technical support section of the company Web site. It should have plenty of information as well as places where you can download the latest "drivers" (required software).

If you do buy mail order, it's a good idea to use a credit card. That way, if you have a beef with the PC vendor, you can withhold payment and send a detailed letter to the credit card company describing your problem. The credit card com-pany will suspend the bill while it investigates. That won't necessarily protect you from buyer's remorse, but it can protect you from fraud.

New, Used, or Refurbished

Most people buy new computers, but if you're looking for a bargain, consider buying a used one. Unlike a car, a PC isn't likely to break down just because it's old. Quite the contrary. Although it might be out of date now, the PC you bought five years ago should be just as good as the day you bought it. In fact, there are still some of the original, vintage 1981 IBM PCs in use, though if they're able to run Windows, they've been updated with modern components.

Before buying a used computer, make sure it can run today's software. Don't buy a machine with anything less than a Pentium CPU because it won't be able to run Windows XP or even do a decent job with Windows 98 or Me. (For more on CPUs, see Chapter 10.) If you want to upgrade an out-of-date PC, find out

Companies Selling Refurbished Computers

COMPANY	WEB SITE
Compaq Works	www.compaqworks.com
Dell	www.dell.com and click on Refurbished Systems
IBM	www.ibm.com/products/ and click on Refurbished
Used Computer Mall	www.usedcomputer.com

what the upgrade will cost and compare that to the price of a modern machine. You may be better off buying a new one.

Some of the major vendors sell refurbished equipment, machines that were sold and returned for one reason or another, and have been given a good once-over to make sure they're still up to factory specifications. Refurbished machines can be just as good as new ones and often come with a pretty good warranty. If you're paying extra for software on a used machine, make sure you're getting legal copies that you can register in your own name. Insist on documentation and original disks or CDs.

8   Should You Get a Laptop PC?

The first decision you need to make when considering a PC is whether to get a laptop or a desktop machine. Before you decide, consider your needs carefully. Laptops are great—for some people.

LAPTOP POSITIONING

Laptop vs. Desktop

Laptop or **notebook** PCs combine all of a system's components into a single, portable unit. They look different, but they have essentially the same components as desktop machines—just smaller. There was a time when the term "notebook PC" referred to a lighter portable PC, and the term "laptop" to a slightly heavier unit. But machines keep getting lighter and you won't find too many of those bigger machines around anymore, so the terms are pretty interchangeable now.

Lots of people like the idea of a laptop computer, because they can take it with them wherever they go. You can carry it from your office to your home, take it on trips, and even use it on planes and commuter trains. People who work by themselves look forward to working at the beach, in the park, or in the neighborhood cafe. And yes, all that is possible. Even though I wrote most of this book on my desktop PC, I worked on parts of it on planes, in hotel rooms, and from a local coffee shop, thanks to my notebook PC.

Given all those advantages, why get a desktop PC? Well, desktop PCs can't really be hauled around, but they do have some advantages over laptops. For one, they are generally a lot cheaper. Feature for feature, a portable PC will usually cost you more than a comparable desktop machine. So if you have a certain amount of money to spend on a computer, you can generally get a better one—faster and loaded with more options—if you get a desktop machine.

Another possible disadvantage with a portable computer is that you're pretty much stuck with what you get. With a desktop machine, you can just swap out the keyboard or monitor if you decide you need something better; not so with a portable. Laptops are also less "expandable" than desktop machines. Even the most common ways of upgrading an older machine—adding memory or upgrading to a larger disk drive—can be difficult and expensive on a portable, because the parts aren't as interchangeable as they are on desktop machines.

Perhaps most important, if you're usually going to be working at a desk anyway, a desktop machine can be a lot more pleasant to work on. The keyboards are larger and generally more comfortable to use. The monitor can be set at the height that works best for your chair and desk. Lots of people find that a mouse is much easier to use than the electronic touchpad or other pointing device used on laptops.

If you do a lot of business traveling and expect to need your computer, a laptop may really be the best option for you, and it could be worth the extra money and other trade-offs to get a portable machine. If you don't travel a lot, though, it's easy to overestimate just how much you're going to use your computer away from your desk.

If You're Buying a Laptop Computer

If you decide to get a portable PC, you'll face the same decisions about its components as you would when buying a desktop machine—and a few more. In this section, I'll run down some of the special considerations for notebooks. If any of them don't make sense to you yet, read what I say about each item in the other chapters in this section, then come back here when you're actually considering a purchase. And remember, these issues are more critical for laptops, because once you've bought the machine it's much more difficult to upgrade the components of a laptop than with a desktop system.

Keyboard. Some notebook machines, especially the subnotebook and ultralight models, save on size and weight by reducing the size of the keys, the distance between the keys, or the "travel" (how far you can depress the keys). Be sure you're comfortable with the keyboard, especially if you're a touch typist.

Screen. Most notebook PCs come with **active matrix screens** (sometimes called "thin film transistor" or "TFT" screens), but you may still find some with passive matrix screens. The active matrix screens produce better color and cost more than passive matrix ones. Unlike passive matrix, active matrix screens can be viewed from almost any angle; you can only see the images on a passive matrix screen if you're staring directly at it.

Notebook vs. Ultralight

These days, the two terms that float around are "notebook PC" and "ultralight." An ultralight, as its name implies, is an even lighter notebook PC, typically weighing less than 4 pounds. Ultralight machines don't usually have an internal floppy drive or CD (or DVD) drive. Also, their keyboards and screens are sometimes slightly smaller than normal. Some come with external drives (and if not, you can buy one separately), but in order to use the drive, you have to plug it in or insert the machine into an expansion chassis. Ultralights can be very handy if you think you'll be carrying your machine around with you during the day, or if you frequently travel by air. If you mostly carry the machine

The Best of Both Worlds

DON'T WAIT UP.

If money isn't tight, there is a way to get the best of both worlds. Most portable computers let you plug in external monitors, keyboards, mice, and other **peripherals** so you can get all the comfort of working at a desktop machine while you're at your desk. Then you can just unplug the peripherals when you want to take your computer on the road.

Some notebook machines make this easier (if more expensive) by offering a **docking station.** The docking station holds the ports for the external keyboard, mouse, monitor, printer, and other devices. You can keep all the devices plugged in to the docking station, and just slide the notebook PC from the docking station when you're ready to hit the road.

between home and work, you're probably better off with a standard notebook PC. Besides having internal drives, larger screens, and keyboards, they're typically a bit cheaper than ultralights.

Peripherals and Expandability
Any portable computer you buy should have at least one **PC card slot** (a slot that lets you plug in credit card–size expansion boards, such as a LAN connector or a wireless modem), and two is even better. Virtually all PCs—including laptops—have USB ports that will let you plug in extra devices, such as external drives or digital cameras.

But there are other ports you might want to add with a PC card. For example, if you're going to connect your laptop to a network or a high-speed Internet connection, you may need an Ethernet card. Or you might need a FireWire card to connect external hard drives, video cameras, and other peripherals that require a high-speed connection. Also, be sure there's a place to plug in an external monitor, printer, modem, and keyboard or mouse, either directly into the notebook or using a docking station (see the sidebar "The Best of Both Worlds" on page 37). An external monitor port is especially important if you plan to use your portable computer to give presentations, because you may want to connect it to an overhead projector that plugs into that port. Some laptops also have standard RCA plugs that you can use to connect video monitors or TV sets. Finally, you can now find machines with built-in adapters for wireless networks. The technology, known as "802.11b" or "WiFi," lets you connect to a network without an Ethernet card. If your laptop doesn't come with an 802.11b card, you can always add one. (I'll have more on this in Chapter 37.)

Battery life. A portable PC won't do you any good if the battery dies halfway between Chicago and Seattle. Look for a laptop with a nickel–metal-hydride battery or (even better) a lithium battery. The machine should be able to run three to four hours between battery charges. And if you plan to take it on long trips, consider buying an extra battery for backup.

Hard drive and memory. Today's laptops can be configured with a fair amount of memory and high-capacity hard drives, but they don't always come that way. Be sure you get a system that has ample hard disk space and memory. The machine may be smaller than a desktop model, but the software you'll run on it is just as big, so get at least 128 MB of RAM (preferably 256 MB) and at least 10 GB of hard disk space.

Pointing device. You can plug a mouse into any laptop, but you don't really want to have to carry one everywhere you go. All portable machines have a built-in pointing device, but the type varies. Many have an electronic touchpad which senses the movement of your fingers. You move your finger around the pad just as you would move a mouse around on a mouse pad. Some people love touchpads, while others find them hard to use. It's really a matter of personal preference.

My favorite pointing device, found on machines from IBM, Toshiba, and some other companies, looks like the tip of a pencil eraser that sticks up between the G, H, and B keys. You don't have to take your hands off the keyboard to position the cursor. A trackball, which is like an upside-down mouse that you roll around with your fingers, used to be popular but you don't see them much any more. Whatever type of pointing device you use, try it before you buy it, because in most cases you're stuck with what you get.

9 Choosing the Right Computer

Once you've made the choice between desktop and laptop, you still have a few more decisions to make, but they're pretty easy ones. Aside from peripheral devices such as the monitor, there are three major things that make one PC different from another. The first is the machine's central processing unit (CPU). The second is the hard disk. And the third is the amount of memory it has.

Once you've figured out what you need in these three areas, your selection will still be wide. That's when you start thinking about the "extras," such as the number of expansion slots the system has, the type of keyboard and mouse, whether it has a FireWire port, and the quality of the components. Other considerations include the quality of the case and whether the controls and switches are in a convenient position. Does it fit into your work environment? Will it fit on (or under) your desk? Is it quiet? (Some PCs have very noisy fans.) You get the idea.

You Don't Need a Brand Name

Does the brand name make a difference? There was a time when I would have told you to stay away from "no-name brands," but those days are over. To be good, a PC company doesn't have to be big. It's now possible for a neighborhood PC dealer to assemble a quality computer that stands up against those from the likes of IBM, Dell, Gateway, Compaq, and other big-name companies.

The advantages of dealing with well-established companies usually (but not always) include a nationwide guarantee, telephone support, and the peace of mind of that comes from knowing that you're dealing with a stable company. My advice is not to get too hung up on the name, but to judge each computer on its qualities and on how well its manufacturer backs it up.

One thing I like to do when evaluating a PC company is to divide the warranty by the price to determine the "worst case" cost of ownership. Say you spend $1,000 for a PC from a reputable company that offers a three-year warranty. In the unlikely event your computer fell apart the day after the warranty expired, your total cost of ownership would be only about 91 cents a day ($1,000 divided by 1095, which is 365 times 3). Not a bad deal.

It's the Components That Count

Although the name of your PC's manufacturer might not make all that much difference, the companies that make the components do. I wouldn't worry about components if you buy a name-brand PC, but if you buy a no-name PC, make sure it's built from quality components. You don't have to worry too much about the stuff inside the box—just be sure that all disk drives, memory chips, and other components are up to snuff. What you mainly have to worry about is the monitor, the keyboard, the mouse, and other accessories.

As general advice, it's not necessary to buy the latest, greatest, and fastest PC around, but it's also not a good idea to buy the bottom of the line. My rule of thumb is to go for a machine whose specifications were state-of-the-art maybe three to six months ago. That will still be plenty good enough for almost anything you plan to do for the next two or three years, but a lot cheaper than today's top of the line.

Earlier editions of this book contained a chart showing exactly how much disk space I recommend, what CPU to get, how much memory you need, and that sort of thing. I took the chart out of this edition because, frankly, the chart was out of date even before the ink was dry on the book. Hardware systems evolve all the time and it's hard to know what will be best for you even a few weeks from now. When I started writing this edition, for example, machines with an Intel Pentium 4 CPU typically cost several hundred dollars more than systems with a Pentium III CPU, but then Intel lowered its prices dramatically and all that changed.

My advice is, when you're ready to buy, find out what is state-of-the-art and what is "entry level" (cheapest). Then avoid both extremes. The highest-grade systems will almost always be overpriced relative to those that were state-of-the-art only a month or two earlier. And the bottom-end machines are typically about to drop off the tree, so to speak, so if you can afford a bit more, it's worth it.

You can get a pretty good idea of what's hot and what's middle-of-the-road from the pages of *PC Magazine* or *PC World*, or by looking at www.cnet.com or www.pcmag.com, or even just by perusing computer ads or PC vendor Web sites like www.cdw.com or www.pcwarehouse.com. Check the Resources section of www.littlepcbook.com for even more information.

The CPU:
The Computer's Brain

10

THE "SYSTEM BOARD" OR "MOTHERBOARD" HOLDS THE BRAINS OF THE COMPUTER.

IT'S CALLED THE "MOTHERBOARD" BECAUSE IT DOES MOST OF THE WORK.

The central processing unit, or CPU, is the part of the computer that does the main computing work. It sits on the computer's system board (sometimes called the motherboard), along with other chips. It's not very big, but when you talk about the computer, that's what you're talking about. The rest of the machinery is just a way of getting data to and from that chip.

As I explained in Chapter 2, having a processor based on Intel's technology is what makes a computer an "IBM-compatible." The processors in the earliest IBM PCs were called 8088 chips. Later, more-powerful versions were called, in order, the 80286, 80386, and 80486, later shortened to just 386 and 486. Intel's next chip after the 486 didn't have a number; instead it had a name: Pentium. The one after that was called the Pentium II, followed by Pentium III and Pentium 4 (don't ask me why the Pentium 4 isn't the Pentium IV). Intel also makes a CPU called the Celeron, which is similar to a Pentium but not quite as powerful.

The speed of a CPU is, in many ways, like the horsepower in your car. In the 1950s, people were nuts about horsepower and

Intel Inside: Is It Important?

Intel has been conducting an expensive marketing campaign to convince consumers that it's important to have a PC with "Intel Inside." The ads suggest that Intel chips are the only ones fully compatible with today's software. It's good marketing, but that's all it is. Fact is, Intel's major competitor, AMD, makes great chips, too. If you buy a machine from a major PC maker such as Compaq, IBM, Toshiba, Gateway, or Dell, you really don't need to worry about who made your CPU. Major PC companies put their machines through a great deal of testing and stake their reputations on the fact that their machines can run the current version of Windows and all Windows programs.

automakers bragged that their cars had bigger and faster engines. By the '70s, consumers and car manufacturers started to wise up: Just about any car is plenty fast for the average driver on public roadways. So instead of worrying about horsepower, car buyers started to concentrate on more important features, like economy, safety, and comfort.

The same thing is becoming true in computing. Back in the '80s and early '90s, people had to wait for their PCs to perform tasks, so the industry kept coming up with faster and faster processors. The industry is still coming out with faster CPUs, but today most CPUs from Intel and its competitors are more than fast enough to run typical home and office applications. Faster chips are being developed for two reasons: Because people are willing to buy them, and because they enable software developers to come . up with new and even more complex programs. But for ordinary use, you don't need a superfast processor.

Cache Memory

Another factor in your computer's speed is whether or not it has **cache memory**. This is high-speed memory on the system board or built into the CPU that runs much faster than the computer's regular memory. Cache memory speeds up the operation of some programs by storing the most recently used information, which generally will be needed again soon.

All chips since the 486 have had at least some cache memory built in. Cache memory that is internal to the CPU is called the L1 (level one) cache. Cache memory that is external to the CPU (on the motherboard) is called L2 (level two). But all types of cache memory are different from the computer's main memory, or RAM, which is covered in Chapter 11.

Two Kinds of Cache

Don't confuse cache memory with disk cache. A **disk cache** uses your computer's regular RAM to speed up hard disk performance by copying recently used data from the disk to a portion of your RAM. Since RAM is faster than a disk, data in the cache can be accessed more quickly than data on the disk.

Many computer companies increase the disk cache by adding external high-speed cache memory. It's not uncommon to see ads for 128 K, 256 K, or even 512 K of cache memory. A larger cache does improve performance, but there's a point of diminishing returns. The slight extra difference in performance between 256 K and 512 K of cache hardly justifies the extra expense.

A Faster Bus

If you hang around PCs long enough, you'll hear somebody talking about a "bus." A **bus** is basically a collection of circuits or tiny wires within a computer through which data travels. To my mind, it's misnamed: When I think of a bus, I envision a vehicle that travels over a highway. But in the computer world, the bus is actually the highway. Like all highways, the number of lanes helps determine how fast you can drive. So a bigger bus is like a wider highway.

Some busses are faster than others. The bus on the Pentium 4, for example, is faster than that on the Pentium III. Don't get too hung up on this, though—like all other specifications, it's only part of the story. But if you hear about a bus, just remember that they're like highways and the bigger the highway, the faster you can go.

11 Memory:
The Electronic Workspace

The computer's RAM (random access memory) holds the programs and data that you have open at the moment. The more memory you have, the more programs and files you can keep open at once.

More memory also makes your computer run faster. Many programs can work with a limited amount of RAM by keeping only the most often used parts of the program in memory. When you want a less often used part, the program needs to stop and load that data from the hard disk, which takes a bit of time. If you have more memory, the computer can load more of the data all at once, so that it's right there when you need it.

Don't even think about using a computer with less than 128 MB of RAM. But if you want the best performance with Windows XP, you're better off with 256 MB. More than that probably won't make much of a difference unless you're running specialized software that requires extra memory.

Recommended RAM for Windows XP

MINIMUM	BETTER	ROOM TO SPARE	USUALLY OVERKILL
128 MB	256 MB	384 MB	512 MB

Units of Measurement: Bits and Bytes

Computer data is measured in special units called bits and bytes. These terms (and certain variations on them) are used to describe the size of files, memory, and hard disks, and the speed at which data is transferred. Here are some of the most common terms:

A bit, the smallest unit, is one-eighth of a byte.

A byte, the next unit up on the ladder, is made up of 8 bits. It takes 8 bits to store a single character, such as the numeral 1 or the letter J, so the word the, for example, is 3 bytes long.

A kilobyte (KB) is approximately 1,000 bytes (1,024, to be exact). It's equivalent to about a page of double-spaced text.

A megabyte (MB) is a tad more than 1 million bytes (OK, 1,048,576), about as much text as in the average novel.

A gigabyte (GB) is just over a billion bytes (1,073,741,824 to be exact) or 1,024 MB.

Memory comes in units called **SIMMs, DIMMs,** or **RIMMS.** (The *S* stands for *single*, the *D* stands for *dual*, the *R* stands for *Rambus*, and *IMM* stands for *in-line memory module*.) They're all strips with preinstalled memory chips. To add memory to your computer, you plug one or more of these modules into your computer's system board.

Here are some general types of memory, listed in order of the slowest speed to the fastest:

- **DRAM** (dynamic random-access memory) is an older type of memory that's still used in some machines.

- **SD-RAM** (synchronous dynamic random-access memory) is used in many machines.

Windows XP requires more memory than Windows 98 or Me. Microsoft recommends at least 128 megabytes.

- **DDR** (double data rate) is a faster memory based on SD-RAM.
- **RD-RAM** (Rambus random-access memory) is a very fast type of memory developed by a company called Rambus; it's used in some Pentium 4 and a few Pentium III machines.

Like everything else in computing, memory usage changes. Whatever might be hot at the moment, be aware that memory should be matched to other system components. Installing super-fast memory in an otherwise slow machine is a waste of money. The price of memory chips change all the time, so check with a local computer dealer or search the Internet for companies that sell memory, like Alpha Memory or Kingston. Last time I checked you could get a 32 MB SIMM for about $80. When you buy a PC, ask your dealer to preinstall as much memory as you think you'll need to start with. Later, if you find you need more memory, you just buy more and install it yourself—it's easy, as long as you don't mind taking the case off.

Resources

Alpha Memory
956-618-3323
www.memory.com

Kingston Memory
800-337-8410
www.kingston.com

The Hard Disk: The Computer's Filing Cabinet

The hard disk is where your computer keeps all of the programs you use and the files you create—sort of like a filing cabinet. Unlike RAM, hard disks hold their information even when the computer is turned off, because the information is physically recorded on the disk's magnetic surface.

You probably won't ever see your hard disk: It's buried in the system unit of your computer. What you will see is a blinking light on the front of the system unit that indicates when the hard disk is in use.

Hard disks are like closets. You think you have plenty of room when you first move in, but it doesn't take long for things to get cramped. So how much storage do you need? The rule of thumb is simple. Estimate what you think you'll need, double it, then go for the next size up.

Today's machines typically come with a hard disk that stores anywhere from 6 to 100 GB. You might find one with less, and you might even be able to get a machine that stores more.

Windows takes up a lot of space, as do many of the programs you'll want to run. I recommend that you get at least 20 GB, but I think you'll be more comfortable if you go with 40 or more. A larger hard drive doesn't cost all that much more, and it's a lot better to have too much room than too little.

When you're looking for a hard disk, you might hear the terms IDE (integrated drive electronics) and SCSI (small computer systems interface, pronounced "scuzzy"). They describe different ways that the hard disk connects to your computer (sometimes called an **interface**). For PC hard drives, an **IDE** interface is the most popular method because it's the least expensive. You can have up to two IDE hard drives on a single machine without having to buy a new interface card.

The biggest advantage with a **SCSI** interface is that you can connect several devices (hard drives, CD-ROM drives, scanners, and so on) to a single controller board. Unfortunately, it doesn't always work as it should because not all companies that make SCSI devices follow the same standards. Frankly, I would avoid SCSI because you'll find it a lot easier to add extra drivers with FireWire. If you run out of room on your internal hard disk, you can replace it with a larger-capacity disk or, even more conveniently, add another hard disk drive. Another option is to connect a removable high-capacity drive such as a FireWire drive. Hard disks are the primary type of disk storage for most computers, but they aren't the only kind. In the next chapter I'll discuss **floppy disks** and some other kinds of removable storage that are used for different purposes.

Out of Memory

Why Does My Computer Say I'm Out of Memory When I've Got Plenty of Space on My Hard Disk?

A lot of people confuse memory (RAM) and storage (the hard disk). Maybe it will help to remember it this way: Storage (the hard disk) is your computer's filing cabinet, where you keep everything you may ever need to use again; memory (RAM) is like a desktop, where you keep just the things you happen to be working on at the moment.

Information stays in RAM (on the desktop) as long as the computer is on, but once you turn the power off, that information is erased. In order to keep that data when the computer is off, you need to file it away on the disk, where it is physically written to magnetic platters that keep the information intact until it's needed again.

If your computer tells you you're out of disk space, you have to delete some files from it; closing some of the programs that you have open won't help. If you're out of memory, you have to close some programs; deleting files from your hard disk won't solve the problem.

THINK OF "STORAGE" ("DISK SPACE") AS A FILING CABINET FOR LONG-TERM INFORMATION....

....WHILE "MEMORY"("RAM") IS LIKE THE DESK WHERE YOU KEEP JUST THE STUFF YOU'RE WORKING ON.

13 Removable Disk Drives: The Computer's Front Door

On the front of your computer's system unit, you'll usually find two slots. The smaller one is for floppy disks, and the larger one is for CD-ROMs or DVDs. Some computers have both a DVD drive and a CD-RW drive. Both can read software and music on CD-ROMs, but you can use the CD-RW drive to create your own CDs and the DVD drive to play movies on DVDs.

You can use both floppy disks and CD-ROMs for storage. Floppy disks work pretty much the same way your hard disk works (described in Chapter 12): They store information on magnetic media that keep the data intact even after you turn off the computer. Unlike hard drives, though, floppies (and CDs) are removable storage devices that separate the storage medium

When a Floppy Isn't Big Enough

Floppy disks and CD-ROMs are the most common forms of removable storage, but there are lots of other types.

For example, you can buy an external hard drive that connects to either the USB port or a FireWire port. FireWire is a lot faster, but USB is much more common. The next generation of USB (2.0) will be about as fast as FireWire, but it's not clear when that will become widely available. (See Chapter 14 for more on FireWire and USB.)

There was a time when Iomega's Zip Disk was a virtual standard for backing up and moving data from one PC to another. Those little disks, which typically cost about $7.50, were perfect back in the days when 100 MB was a lot of data. But with all the large multimedia files available today, 100 MB doesn't go as far as it used to. Iomega has since introduced a 250 MB Zip drive, which was met with resounding yawns from most PC users, especially now that many PCs come with CD-RW drives that let you back up your data onto cheap, 700 MB CDs that can be read by any CD-ROM drive.

If you still need more storage room, there are some reasonably priced ways to add external storage to PCs. Several companies, including QPS, Maxtor, and LaCie, make external hard drives that can connect to a PC using either a USB port or a FireWire port. Both USB and FireWire make it easy to add a drive.

I have a 20 GB QPS Que M2 hard drive plugged into the FireWire port of my desktop machine. LaCie makes similar drives that connect to the USB port. Iomega also offers the Peerless external hard drive, which uses removable cartridges to store data. Although not quite as fast as most internal IDE drives, the Peerless is much faster than a CD, Zip Disk, or floppy, and is suitable for storing both data and software.

(the disk itself) from the drive (the mechanism that reads the data). That way, you can buy as many inexpensive floppy disks or CDs as you need, without also investing in an expensive new drive mechanism.

Floppy disks store a maximum of 1.44 MB of data, and these days, that's just a handful of text files—not much at all. Consequently, floppies aren't used for very much anymore, though they're handy if you want to share a relatively small file with a friend or colleague. To store a bunch of photos or MP3 music files, you need to use a CD-RW drive or some other, larger form of storage.

Upgrader's Tip

Windows XP has built-in software for writing data to a CD-ROM. However, this software isn't as powerful as some third-party programs.

Larger Storage Media

- **CD-ROMs,** which look just like audio CDs, store about 690 MB. They're used to distribute software that takes up a lot of room on disk, such as complicated applications, games, and electronic encyclopedias.

- **DVD** drives look exactly like CD drives but they hold DVD discs that can store up to 17 GB of data, or a full-length movie.

- **CD-RW** drives can both read and write CDs. You can use them to back up and make copies of audio CDs or software programs. You can also use a CD-RW to create your own music CDs.

  CD-RWs drives use two types of discs. A **CD-R** disc can only be written to once, but CD-RW discs can be modified, or erased and reused. CD-RW sounds better, but they cost more, are a bit more of a hassle to use, and they're not always necessary. Because CD-R discs are so cheap (last time I checked they were less than 50 cents each), you can just keep adding more every time you back up your files. In fact, there is something to be said for having non-erasable discs for backup. Also, a CD-R disc works in just about any type of PC and you don't need any special software to run it. Windows XP has built-in software for recording CD-R discs, though there are other programs (like Roxio's Easy CD Creator) that have more features.

- **Tape cartridges** look like giant cassette tapes, and in fact, they work in pretty much the same way. As with audio and VCR tapes, the disadvantage of tape cartridges is that you can't go directly to the track you need; you have to rewind or fast forward to get to the part you want. This makes them too slow to use for the files you work with every day, but they're OK for backups and archives, because they're relatively cheap.

Connectors: Plug In and Move Up

14

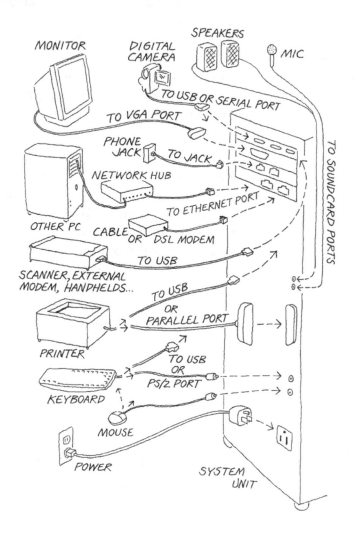

MONITOR

DIGITAL CAMERA

SPEAKERS

MIC

TO USB OR SERIAL PORT

TO VGA PORT

PHONE JACK

TO JACK

NETWORK HUB

TO SOUNDCARD PORTS

TO ETHERNET PORT

OTHER PC

CABLE OR DSL MODEM

TO USB

SCANNER, EXTERNAL MODEM, HANDHELDS...

TO USB OR PARALLEL PORT

PRINTER

TO USB OR PS/2 PORT

KEYBOARD

MOUSE

POWER

SYSTEM UNIT

Look at the back of any laptop or desktop PC and you'll see a bunch of connectors. You could also call them plugs, sockets, outlets, or ports. Whatever you call them, they're basically holes in the machine designed to accommodate different types of cables. Here are some of the different types of ports in your PC.

Serial Port

Virtually all PCs have a **serial port** that you can use to connect your computer to an external modem, some types of printers, and handheld devices such as Palm organizers, among other things. Before USB came along a few years ago, the serial port was a vital link to the outside world. But these days, many devices can plug into a USB port instead of a serial port. Given a choice, I'd opt for USB because it's faster and easier to manage.

USB Port

All PCs built in the last few years also come with a **USB (universal serial bus)** port. A single USB port can be used to connect up to 127 devices, because you can "daisy chain" USB devices by plugging one device into another. You can also buy a USB hub to add more ports, so you never have to worry about running out. USB can be used for mice, printers, keyboards, and lots of other devices and is in the process of replacing the serial and parallel ports (see below). USB might just eliminate the need to take a computer apart to add components. All versions of Windows since Windows 98 fully support USB. So does the Macintosh, which is a good thing because companies can now make devices that connect to both PCs and Macs, though they need different driver software.

Parallel Port

A **parallel port** is mainly used to connect a printer, but it can also be used for other devices designed to transfer data from one PC to another. These days, many printers support USB, which is really a better choice than parallel because it's easier to manage.

VGA Port

This connects your monitor to your computer. It's built into a video card installed inside your PC. All CRT monitors and most LCD monitors use the same type of VGA connector. However, some LCD monitors use a special digital connector that's shaped differently. See Chapter 16 for more on VGA.

USB 2.0

As I write this book, PCs that support USB 2.0 are just starting to roll out. USB 2.0 is fully compatible with the original USB, but it's much faster. Instead of running at 12 Mbps, it's up to 480 Mbps, which means it's fast enough for video cameras, hard drives, and other high-speed devices.

PS/2 Ports

Most PCs have two small round connectors that look alike. One is for a keyboard, the other for a mouse. These are called **PS/2 ports** because they were originally used on IBM's PS/2 computer back in the 1980s. On some PCs, the mouse and keyboard are plugged into the USB ports instead.

Sound Card

Whether you have a laptop or a desktop PC, your computer has either a **sound card** or sound chips built into it. Either way, there are some connectors at the back of your machine for speakers (or headphones) and a microphone. Some PCs have extra **line in** connectors for plugging in an external sound source like a CD-player. Some have extra **line out** ports (for an amplifier) or a digital line out port for digital sound systems. Even if your system doesn't have a special line in or line out connector, you can still use the headphone (speaker) jack to send sound to a stereo system. You may also be able to use the microphone jack as a line-in connector. However, if you do use these jacks, be sure you set your sound levels appropriately.

Phone Jack for Built-in Modem

Most desktop and notebook PCs have an internal modem with a connector. If the connector looks familiar, that's because it's the same kind (called an RJ-11) that's used to plug your phone into the wall. You connect the modem to the phone line with a standard phone cord.

Ethernet

Some, but not all, PCs have an Ethernet connector that is used to plug the PC into a LAN, or connect it to a DSL modem, cable modem, or other high-speed Internet connection. An Ethernet cord looks like a fat telephone cord. The connector is called an RJ-47.

FireWire or IEEE 1394

Apple developed FireWire, a high-speed method for connecting computer peripherals. After Apple made the technology available to other companies, the Institute of Electrical and Electronics Engineers (IEEE) adopted it as an industry standard with the official and more boring moniker "IEEE 1394." Sony then came up with yet another name—"iLink."

By any name, the technology represents an easy way to connect high-speed devices to a PC. Although some machines come with FireWire ports, most don't. Luckily, it's relatively cheap and easy to add FireWire to a desktop, and even easier (but a bit more expensive) to add it to a laptop.

Connecting a FireWire device to a PC is identical to adding a device to the USB ports, and you can "hot swap" devices. In other words, you just plug a cord into a socket while the machine is still running, and you don't have to turn off the PC or the device to connect it.

The big difference between FireWire and USB is speed. FireWire operates at up to 400 Mbps, or about 50 MBps, whereas the current version of USB transfers at a slow 12 Mbps, or 1.5 MBps.

Expansion Slots: Room to Grow

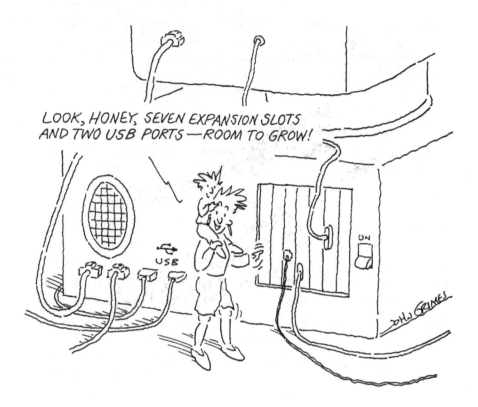

15

LOOK, HONEY, SEVEN EXPANSION SLOTS AND TWO USB PORTS — ROOM TO GROW!

If you think your hardware-buying spree is over once you get a computer, then you haven't heard about peripherals. Peripherals are all those wonderful things that increase the performance of your machine or add functions, from printers and modems, to scanners and video cameras. Until a couple of years ago, nearly all peripherals except printers and external modems required you to install an expansion card. Now all PCs have USB ports and some have FireWire ports, either of which can be used to add many external devices, without opening your computer's case.

Legacy-Free PC

Intel and some other companies are pushing the computer industry to develop what are being called "legacy-free PCs." These PCs would run the same software as regular machines but wouldn't have serial or parallel ports or any internal expansion slots. USB and possibly FireWire would be used to connect all of your peripherals. Such machines would be cheaper to build and more reliable. Microsoft and Intel say that expansion slots contribute to problems with PCs.

Some extras do still require an additional card: For example, if your PC doesn't have a FireWire (discussed in Chapter 14), you might want to add one by plugging in a card. Many machines don't come with Ethernet but you can add it to any desktop machine by—you guessed it—plugging in an Ethernet card. Also, as time goes by (isn't that the name of a song?), you may want to upgrade some of your components. To get a better video card, for example, or to add new technologies. Once USB 2.0 becomes standard, devices that use it will probably start appearing. If your PC doesn't have a USB 2.0 port, then you'll want to add one by plugging in an expansion card. (For more information, see the sidebar, "When a Floppy Isn't Big Enough," in Chapter 13.)

Some PCs come with as many as eight slots, and others have as few as three. More to the point, some computers use up most of their slots just adding basic items, like a video card or an internal monitor. The real question when you're buying a new computer, then, is how many slots the computer has free once it's set up with the basics. These days, most items you'll want to add can be plugged into a USB or FireWire port. Still, it's nice to have at least two or three empty slots so you have room to grow. So, practically speaking, the more slots you have, the better.

Most PCs these days have two or more **PCI** (personal component interconnect) slots and perhaps one or two **ISA** (industry standard architecture) slots. ISA used to be more common, but most cards now support PCI. These days many desktop PCs come with **AGP**s (accelerated graphics ports) that are designed to accommodate faster video cards. AGP is a special slot for special AGP adapters, which are faster than regular graphics adapters and designed primarily for the demanding video requirements of 3D graphics. With the right software, a 3D graphics adapter can display images that appear to have depth somewhat (though not quite) similar to what you would get if you were wearing 3D glasses. Applications for 3D graphics mostly include games and some advanced graphic-development applications that you probably won't be using unless you just got a job offer from Pixar, Silicon Graphics, NASA, or some other organization that does really way-out special effects. If your PC doesn't come with an AGP card, don't feel compelled to upgrade unless you're a gamer or a heavy graphics user.

16 Monitors and Display Adapters: The Face of the Computer

THE "DISPLAY ADAPTER"
(ALSO CALLED "VIDEO CARD")
WORKS IN TANDEM WITH
A COLOR MONITOR.

Computer monitors (sometimes called "displays" or "screens") come in color or monochrome, in many different resolutions, and in many sizes. A monitor is one product that I like to see in action before I buy. If you can, go to a computer store to look at some monitors before you buy yours.

A computer display is actually a two-part system:

- The monitor itself

- The **display adapter,** which generates the video information for the monitor

With most PCs, the display adapter is preinstalled. It plugs into one of your computer's expansion slots or, on some machines, is built into the motherboard. In the old days you had to be sure to match your monitor with your display adapter, but these days that's rarely an issue. Now most monitors are **multiscan monitors,** which means they're able to plug into different kinds of display adapters. That way, they don't become obsolete if you get a new display adapter.

Sometimes you'll hear display adapters referred to as "graphics adapters" (or "graphics boards") or even "video adapters" (or "video boards") or "graphics accelerators." Don't get confused: All these terms mean the same thing.

There are basically two types of video monitors.

CRT Monitors

CRT (cathode ray tube) monitors are the more common kind. They have a large picture tube similar to the one in a TV set. But when you're shopping around for a computer, remember: Not all CRT monitors are created equal. Even those that have the same "specs" don't necessarily look the same.

Some manufacturers are now offering "flat screen CRTs," which are thinner and easier on the eyes than the old curved monitors. They still take up a lot of desk space and use as much electricity as standard CRTs, but if you have trouble justifying the extra cost of an LCD monitor (and who can blame you?), then a flat screen CRT might be a good compromise.

LCD Monitors

There are some advantages and disadvantage to choosing an **LCD** (liquid crystal display) monitor over CRT.

Desktop LCD monitors use basically the same technology as laptop LCD screens. In both cases, most models use what is known as active-matrix thin-film transistor (TFT). Each dot or pixel on the monitor is actually made of three tiny transistors: one each for red, green, and blue. There's no gun scanning up and down or left and right, so you don't have the flicker effect you get with a CRT. (You can't usually detect that flicker but some experts say that it contributes to eye strain and fatigue.) Another advantage is that LCD screens give off fewer of the electromagnetic emissions that can interfere with other equipment or, according to some people, have an effect on health. (There's a lot of controversy on that last point.)

LCDs are also smaller—well, thinner at least. Since they don't have a big picture tube, they don't need to be as deep as a CRT, so they take up a lot less desk space. Also, LCDs use every inch of space. Some CRTs have a black area around the picture because of the curvature of the tube (though there are also "flat" CRT screens that don't waste space). So a 15-inch LCD gives you almost as much surface area for data as a 17-inch CRT.

One disadvantage to LCDs is that you don't have a choice of resolution. Every LCD screen has a "native resolution" that it's designed to display. Often it's 1024 by 768 but some screens— especially larger ones—have a higher reolution, such as 1,280 by 1,024. You can run the LCD at a resolution other than its native resolution, but it will be fuzzy, defeating the purpose of a high-resolution display. This can be a problem in some situations. I had a 15-inch display that was set for 1,280 by 1,024 and the type was just too small for my middle-aged eyes. I wound up sending it back and settling on one that displays at 1,024 by 768.

LCDs used to be a lot more expensive than CRTs but they've come way down in price, so shop around before you make a decision.

Color

There was a time when you actually had a choice between color and black-and-white. You still do, in theory, but monochrome (black-and-white) monitors are actually hard to find now. Virtually any monitor you see advertised will be color.

Resolution

"Display resolution" refers to the number of dots of light (called **pixels,** short for "picture elements") that your monitor can display. The higher the resolution, the easier the monitor will be on your eyes and the more detail you'll be able to see.

Today, the minimum standard for a Windows systems is **VGA** (for video graphics array), which displays 640 pixels horizontally and 480 pixels vertically. However, virtually all systems come with adapters that can display 800 by 600 pixels, 1,024 by 768, 1,280 by 1,040, or even higher.

Size

Monitors come in a variety of sizes, measured diagonally, like a television set. Most PCs that have a CRT come with 17-inch monitors, but you can also get a smaller one such as a 14- or 15-inch, or a bigger one such as a 21-inch or even larger.

Unless you plan to put your PC in the living room and use it as a TV set (which is not all that popular, by the way), you'll probably want to stick with a 17-inch monitor. If space is tight or if you want to save $100 or so, you can opt for a small monitor. It will do the job just fine.

Getting a 20- or 21-inch monitor for your desktop is only a good idea if you really need that extra screen space. They're quite useful for desktop publishers who need to see a full page of text, or even two pages side by side. They're also handy for people who work on very large spreadsheets.

But besides the obvious drawback in cost, large monitors take up a lot of desk space and can be too bright for many people. I just don't like staring at a very large monitor, but that's my personal preference.

Image Quality

A lot of different factors determine how good the image displayed by your monitor will look. The most important things to consider are **dot pitch, interlacing,** and, last but not least, your personal likes and dislikes.

Dot pitch applies only to color monitors, and it describes the resolution of each individual pixel on the screen. The lower the dot pitch, the better the image. For 14-inch monitors, look for a dot pitch of .28 or lower. Larger monitors may have a slightly higher dot pitch. Whatever you do, don't fall for any "bargain basement" monitor or system that has a higher dot pitch; it really makes a difference. If you are considering a machine with a monitor that isn't .28 or lower, tell the dealer to substitute a better monitor, and don't be impressed if he or she shows you a great-looking graphic on the screen. The real test of a monitor's resolution isn't its ability to display dazzling graphics or multimedia, but the clarity of its text. When comparing monitors, look at 10-point typefaces. That's where you'll see the difference, because viewing small, black type against a white background is an excellent way to judge overall resolution and quality. While you're at it, ask the dealer to show the monitor displaying both text and graphics in real-life applications such as a word processor, a spreadsheet, a graphics program, or a game that includes moving video.

Graphics adapters control the number of times per second the image on the monitor is repainted from top to bottom, called its vertical refresh rate. Interlaced monitors refresh every other line of the picture with each pass, and therefore require two complete vertical passes of the electron beam to refresh the display. (Televisions also use this method.) A noninterlaced monitor updates the entire display in a single pass and is less likely to flicker, so you're better off with this type of monitor.

Finally, and perhaps most important, is personal taste. It's hard to define, but you'll know it when you see it. I love the look of Sony and NEC monitors. But they also cost a bit more than other brands, and whether they're worth the extra dough is really just a matter of preference and priorities. My advice when buying monitors is to go with your gut feeling.

Are Two Monitors Better Than One?

It's possible to have two monitors on one PC. I know that seems strange, but it does have its uses. You can have one program running in one monitor and another in the other monitor. Mac users, especially those involved with desktop publishing, have been doing it for years. To make this work, however, you not only need two monitors, you need two display adapters (or one adapter designed to accommodate two monitors).

The Bottom Line

Confused yet? I'll make it simple: If you can afford it, seriously consider an LCD monitor. They're very cool. If you decide on a CRT, you can still get a quality display system—look for a non-interlaced Super VGA monitor and display adapter, with a dot pitch of .28 or below. If your PC comes with an AGP port (it probably does), so much the better. It might not do you any good, but there's no harm in it and, hey, maybe you'll discover a cool 3D game or two.

17 The Keyboard: Talking to Your Computer

I used to tell people that a computer keyboard is a lot like a typewriter keyboard, but these days, it's hard to find people who know how to use a typewriter.

The most important thing to remember is that in addition to all the letter and number keys, there are some special keys that actually perform functions in Windows.

Choosing a Keyboard

Keyboards vary in feel as well as layout. Some are virtually silent. Others click every time you press a key. Some keyboards are mushy; others provide a slight amount of resistance. You'll have to experiment to see which kind is best for you.

Preferences for keyboard layout are also subjective. The illustration on pages 70–71 shows just one possible configuration for a PC keyboard. Another keyboard might have the function keys on the left, or at both the left and the top. Some keyboards have no separate cursor keypad, since the numeric keypad doubles as a cursor keypad. I always look for a large Backspace key (the one I use to correct mistakes as I type).

You don't have to blindly accept whatever keyboard your system comes with (unless, of course, it's a laptop). Make sure you try out a keyboard before you buy it. After all, if you're a touch typist, you probably enter two or three thousand keystrokes per hour. A poorly designed keyboard can slow you down, increase your mistakes, and cause wrist strain. You should be fanatic about getting a keyboard that's right for you.

Most PC keyboards work with just about any PC, so a mismatch isn't likely. There are, however, three types of keyboard plugs. Keyboards used on PCs sold in the last few years usually have little round ones (sometimes called "PS/2 connectors," because they were originally designed for IBM PS/2 machines). Some keyboards now connect to the USB port. Older PCs may still use the larger round ones.

Ergonomic Keyboards

There are now several keyboards available from Microsoft, Key Tronic, and other companies that are specially designed to reduce some of the wrist and finger strain generally associated with typing for long periods on standard keyboards. Generally referred to as **ergonomic keyboards**, they're typically laid out in a wave design with a break in the middle so the two halves are at different angles, which lets you keep your wrists in a more natural position. There's also a movable type of ergonomic keyboard that's split in two so you can arrange the two halves in whatever position is most comfortable for you. I've tried a couple of ergonomic keyboards, and, frankly, I find them hard to get used to, but—as with so much about computers—it's really a matter of personal choice. Tests have shown that these keyboards can actually help reduce wrist injuries, but so can taking a few precautions like using a wristpad and setting up your workspace correctly. In Chapters 22 and 23 I talk about "safe" ways to use your PC. If you read no other part of this book, please check out these chapters so that you can continue to enjoy your PC—and the use of your hands—for many years to come.

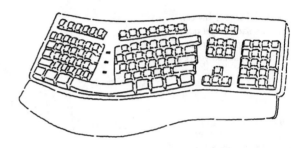

Resources

Microsoft
800-426-9400

Key Tronic
509-928-8000

The keys labeled F1 through F12 are called the function keys. These keys can be programmed, either by you with a macro program, or by a piece of application software, to carry out special, often-used functions. Usually, F1 means "give me some help." Most programs have preassigned functions for each key.

You might think that the Backspace key would move you back one character, but that's what the backward-pointing arrow on the cursor pad is for. The Backspace key deletes the character to the left of the cursor.

The Esc (Escape) key can often be used to get out of trouble. It backs you out of whatever situation you're in.

The Shift and Caps Lock keys change characters form lowercase to uppercase. Shift affects numbers, but Caps Lock doesn't.

You usually hold the Ctrl (Control) key down while you press some other key to perform a special command. With most word processing programs, for example, you press Ctrl-Home to go to the top of your document.

The key with the Windows logo on it pops up the Start menu, just as if you had clicked it with the mouse.

As with the Ctrl key, you hold the Alt (Alternate) key down while pressing some other key to perform a special command. In Windows, the Alt key activates the menu bar. To activate the File Menu, for example, you type Alt-F.

When you're typing, use the Enter (or Return) key to start a new paragraph. You don't have to press it each time you start a new line; word processing programs automatically do that for you.

The Print Screen key copies an image of the entire screen to the Windows clipboard. You can then paste that image into a word processing or graphics program. (Pressing Alt plus Print Screen copies the image of the active window.)

In most programs, Scroll Lock doesn't do anything.

When you're working in DOS, the Pause/Break key causes the screen to freeze until you press it again. Pressing Shift and Pause at the same time activates the Break key, which interrupts and discontinues some programs.

In many programs, when Ins (Insert) is on (that's usually the default), the cursor pushes characters to the right as you type. When it's off, you type over (erase) existing characters as you type.

Pressing the NumLock (Number Lock) key changes the numerical keypad so that the numbers are active. Pressing it again makes the numbers inactive and the arrow keys, Home, End, PgUp, and PgDn active.

C'MON UP HERE. IT'S TIME YOU LEARNED TO TYPE.

The numeric keypad has two uses, and you toggle between them with the NumLock key. When NumLock is on, you can use this keypad to enter numbers, as with a 10-key calculator. When NumLock is off, you can use this keypad to navigate around your document.

SORRY — OLD DOG, NEW TRICK

The arrow keys, also known as cursor keys, move the cursor around on the screen.

The Del (Delete) key generally deletes characters. Depending on the program, it may also delete entire words, lines, or even files.

Common Keyboard Functions

KEYBOARD COMMAND	FUNCTION
Ctrl C	Copy whatever is highlighted (you can paste it later)
Crl X	Cut whatever is highlighted (you can paste it later)
Ctrl V	Paste whatever you just cut or copied into another place in the document or in another document
Ctrl Z	Undo
Del or Delete	Delete whatever is highlighted
F2	Rename selected item
Ctrl Right Arrow	Move to the beginning of the next word
Ctrl Left Arrow	Move to the beginning of the previous word
Ctrl A	Select All
FI	Help
Ctrl Esc	Display Start menu
Esc or Escape	Cancel or "escape" from what you just did

Mice and Other Pointing Devices: Making Quick Moves   18

If you look closely at a mouse, you'll see how it got its name: It's about the size of a little rodent, and its cord resembles a tail. (Unless it's a cordless mouse, and then, I suppose, it looks like a tailless rodent.) Usually, a small ball in the bottom of the mouse tracks the mouse's movement on the desktop and communicates that information to the computer, which then moves the on-screen pointer in the same direction. But the new optical mice, such as the Microsoft IntelliEye, don't have a ball or any other moving parts—instead, they have a sensor that scans surfaces electronically to track movement.

Mice connect to the computer in one of two ports. Either they plug into the built-in socket, called a **mouse port** (sometimes called a "PS/2 Mouse Port"), or into the USB port.

All Windows machines require a mouse that has at least two buttons. If you have a mouse with only one button, it probably came with a Mac! Some mice have a third button (or even a fourth) that provides some extra features using the software that comes with the mouse.

Keeping Your Mouse Squeaky Clean

If you have an optical mouse such as the Microsoft IntelliEye, you don't have to worry about cleaning the moving parts because there aren't any. But if you have an ordinary mouse, you have to keep it clean.

After a while, your mouse will pick up lint, eraser shavings, and other common desktop detritus. When this happens you'll notice that the mouse just doesn't work as well as it should. Turn the mouse over and inspect the ball and rollers for debris. Remove what you see with a soft cloth, a brush, or clean fingers. Every few months you may need to remove the ball completely and clean the rollers inside with an alcohol-soaked Q-Tip. You can usually take the ball out by unscrewing the case.

Microsoft, IBM, and other companies are now offering mice that have a wheel or similar device that helps you scroll through a document or carry out other actions. Microsoft's IntelliMouse looks and acts like a regular two-button mouse, but the wheel in the middle lets you scroll up and down if your software supports it. (Both Internet Explorer and Netscape let you use the wheel to scroll through long Web pages, and Microsoft Office products and lots of other applications also support it for scolling documents.) Logitech and several other companies offer similar mice. IBM's innovative ScrollPoint Mouse scrolls both vertically and horizontally, thanks to a small stick (like the TrackPoint device on IBM and some other laptops) that lets you move the cursor in any direction. On some mice, including some from Logitech, the wheel is also a button that can be programmed to perform special tasks when you push it down.

Mice aren't the only way to move your pointer around the screen. Another device, called a **trackball,** does the same thing as a mouse, but in a slightly different way. It's sort of an upside-down mouse with the ball on top, and you move the on-screen cursor by rolling the ball with your hand. Some people find trackballs easier to use than mice, and because they stay in one place, trackballs work well where space is limited (including some notebook and laptop computers). You can get a trackball at any computer store, and they work with any program that works with a mouse.

DON'T TRY THIS AT HOME.

TRACKBALL

For games, you might want to use a **joystick.** Microsoft makes a really cool one called the "Sidewinder Force Feedback" which breaks new ground in game play by introducing a sense of touch, or force. Armchair pilots can now feel the "stick" shake as they enter a spin or fire a rocket at an enemy plane. Is this progress or what?

Notebook computers have a whole different set of pointing devices (covered in Chapter 8).

19 Printers: Putting Your Work on Paper

Almost everyone needs some kind of printer. Fortunately, there's a wide variety to choose from.

There are a number of different kinds of printers on the market, but most people opt for either an **inkjet printer** or a **laser printer.** These days most consumers choose a color inkjet because they're the most versatile and affordable.

An Inkjet Printer, Fax, and Copier in One!

Several companies, including Canon, Lexmark, Brother, and Hewlett-Packard, have multifunction devices that combine a color inkjet printer, a scanner, a copier, and sometimes a fax machine into a single device. I used to be down on these devices because they were barely adequate at each function, but that's changed. The most recent devices I've tested do a very good job at all their functions and they're a lot cheaper and take up less space than buying separate components.

Laser printers, which are popular in offices, are generally the fastest and produce very crisp black-and-white pages. A document printed on a laser printer almost looks as if it were professionally typeset. Until recently, color laser printers were out of the question, and though they're still pretty pricey, they've come down from the stratosphere. Inkjet printers have the advantage of being able to print in color and, thanks to new developments, are often almost as fast and almost as crisp as laser printers.

Inkjets

Inkjet printers are virtually silent, use almost no electricity when they're not in use, don't take up much space, and are lightweight, easy to move, highly reliable, and inexpensive. It works by spraying ink onto the page through tiny nozzles in the print head. The output from an inkjet printer isn't usually quite as sharp as that of a laser printer (the wet ink can blot a little when it hits the page), but the difference can be almost unnoticeable. Inkjet printers used to be a lot slower than laser printers, but that's not necessarily the case anymore. I've tested some inkjet printers that go as fast as 17 pages per minute in black-and-white. (They're always slower in color.) Less expensive inkjet printers tend to be slower, but that probably doesn't matter, since the total time for short jobs may be pretty close.

Some companies practically give away inkjet printers, but they aren't doing it just to be nice: They also sell ink and paper and they hope to make their money on consumables. My advice is to buy ink from the company that made your printer but don't bother buying their paper. I use cheap copy paper most of the time and it works fine for ordinary documents. When quality matters, I use more expensive, brighter paper, which does make for a better-looking document.

Most inkjet printers have three quality settings: Draft, Normal, and Best. Draft is often good enough for everyday printing and it's faster and uses less ink than Normal. Normal is better than Draft and Best is slowest and uses the most amount of ink. I always use Best when I print glossy photographs (I also use glossy paper, which is a lot more expensive than plain paper), but I never use it for regular text.

Laser Printers

A laser printer is almost mandatory if you print a lot of very long documents. It's usually faster and it's always more economical than inkjet. Laser printers are often categorized as "personal" or "office" models. The office models are built to handle printing for several computers linked over a network. They generally have faster print speeds, larger paper trays, and tougher components—and are a bit more expensive—than personal models.

Speed. Laser printers are rated in pages per minute, but it's a theoretical speed, kind of like miles per gallon. It's based on the printer's maximum operating speed, so your actual speed will be a bit slower. A lot of things affect how long it really takes to print a document, such as warming up the printer, and whether the document contains graphics or is all text. Also, it usually takes longer to generate the first page of a document than subsequent pages, especially if the printer hasn't been used in several minutes and has to warm up from its energy saving "sleep" mode. So if you print a lot of one- or two-page documents, an ink jet printer can actually be faster than a laser printer. Relatively inexpensive personal laser printers are typically rated between 12 and 15 pages a minute.

Resolution. The print quality of a laser printer is primarily a function of its resolution: The higher the resolution, the better the text and graphics will look. Most laser printers have a resolution of 1,200 dots per inch (dpi), which is very good.

Printing Fonts

Fonts are what determine how type looks on screen and printed out in documents. Before about 1990, the number, style, and size of the fonts you could print was determined by software in the printer. Now, however, all that (as well as the creation of graphics) is mostly handled by Windows. Windows has something called TrueType, which takes care of sizing (or scaling) and styling fonts. Windows comes with many fonts—probably enough for most people unless you're a graphic designer—but you can add more if you want.

Being able to print many fonts is nice, but you still need to have the fonts themselves—the actual alphabets in different styles. A lot of software programs come with extra fonts. If you install a greeting card program and publishing program, for example, you'll probably get extra fonts with it. Also, some "clip art" packages come with fonts as well as pictures.

If you want even more fonts, you can find many of them on the Internet. Search for "fonts" at www.download.com or www.google.com (my favorite Internet search engine) and you'll be overwhelmed with choices. My advice: Don't' bother adding a font unless you want to distinguish the stuff you print out from what everyone else does.

Paper handling. Printers vary in terms of how many sheets of paper they can hold at a time and how they handle envelopes, single sheets of paper, and special stock such as cardboard and transparencies. Office printers generally store 250 to 850 sheets of paper, and personal laser printers usually store about 100, though some handle up to 250. Some printers can handle two types of stock at once (for example, legal and letter size or letter size and envelopes) and many allow you to insert one envelope a time without having to remove the paper. Some printers offer extra paper-handling options for an extra cost; check with your dealer for your options.

Networking. Some printers are network capable: This is handy if you have more than one computer at home or at the office and want them all to share a printer. But even without a network-capable printer, you can share printers using the printer sharing feature built into Windows (see Chapter 37).

PostScript and PCL. These are the two most common types of laser printer, and the names actually refer to the languages built into printers. You can let your software worry about the languages, but there are some other differences between PostScript and PCL printers that you need to consider.

Look for a PCL printer, unless you plan to work with graphics professionally. PCL printers are cheaper than PostScript printers and generally a lot faster, too. PCL stands for "Printer Command Language," and it's built into most brands of laser printers. There are different levels of PCL. If you have a choice, it's a good idea to get the latest version of PCL, but for most users it doesn't matter all that much. There really isn't that much difference between them.

Color. Until a few years ago, you could only get monochrome laser printers, but that's no longer true. Several companies now offer color laser printers starting at under $1,000. I spent some time using a $999 Minolta QMS Magicolor 2200 and I was impressed. It was fast (once it started printing) and the per-page cost was pretty economical. My only complaints are that it's enormous—much larger than a monochrome laser printer or an inkjet—and that it takes a long time to warm up.

Brand Names. The LaserJet series of printers from Hewlett-Packard are the most popular and are of excellent quality. Other companies that make good laser printers include Lexmark, Xerox, Panasonic, Epson, Brother, and Canon.

Printing Color Photos

Today's top-of-the-line color printers not only do a good job with general printing, they can also print photos that look almost professional. Most color printers will do an OK job of printing photos on plain white paper, but if you want the best quality, you'll have to buy special glossy paper that costs as much as $1 per 8½-by-11-inch sheet. When you print at the highest quality (and slowest speed), the results can be pretty amazing. Epson's Stylus Color printers do a phenomenal job of printing color photos. Hewlett-Packard and Canon also produce some printers that do a great job with color photography.

Most of these companies also offer printers specially designed for color photos. These printers will do a better job at color photos than a general-purpose printer can, but that's all they can do. I recommend that you get a good, general-purpose color printer that is capable of high-quality photo printing and use it as your one-and-only printer.

The Bottom Line

Now that you've heard me describe all the options, you've probably guessed my recommendation: Most users should get a good color inkjet printer.

The main things to consider when buying your printer are speed, resolution (the higher the better), and the cost per page for both color and black-and-white printing (that includes the cost of the ink cartridges and the cost for any special paper you might need). Look for a model that can handle at least 100 sheets of paper at a time, and make sure it's easy to insert envelopes and other special kinds of paper.

It's especially important to get a printer that has a black ink cartridge you can replace separately from the color cartridges (which use red, green, and blue or cyan, magenta, and yellow ink to generate the full spectrum of colors). Some of the cheap, older color inkjets required you to either change your cartridges each time you switched between black-and-white and color printing or create black by mixing colored inks. Changing cartridges is inconvenient, and mixing inks produces lousy-looking black-and-white documents. And if you need to replace all the cartridges whenever your black runs out, you're going to spend a lot of extra money, since you're bound to use more black (for text) than any of the other colors.

Resources

Brother International
800-276-7746
www.brother.com

Canon
800-848-4123
www.ccsi.canon.com

Epson
800-463.7766
www.epson.com

Hewlett-Packard
800-752-0900
www.hp.com

Lexmark
800-358-5835
www.lexmark.com

20 Modems: Dial-Up, Broadband, and Fax

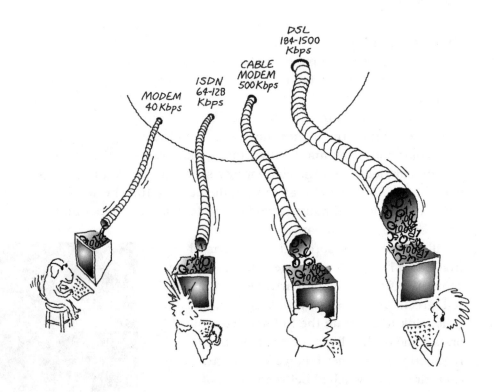

MODEM
40 Kbps

ISDN
64-128
Kbps

CABLE
MODEM
500Kbps

DSL
184-1500
Kbps

*Traditionally, a modem was a device that translated a
computer's data into sounds that could be transmitted over
phone lines. Today there are also other types of modems
that don't make sounds and don't use phone lines. You don't
need a modem to operate a PC, but having one gives you
access to a lot of information and services you can't get
without one.*

By far the most important use for a modem is that it lets you hook into the Internet and online services like America Online so that you can surf the Web, exchange email, meet new people in chat rooms, download free software, and get information at any time of day or night. I'll talk more about how these services in Part 4 of this book. Here, we'll just talk about the basic hardware you'll need to get online.

Dialing for Data

Chances are your PC came with an internal "dial-up" modem, so called because it requires phone lines to dial up Internet service. If you're not sure, check the back of your system and look for a telephone jack. If you find one, it's probably connected to a modem.

If you don't have a modem, now is as good a time as any to get one. Choosing a modem used to be complicated, but the modem industry is pretty standardized now so there really isn't a lot to think about. Modems are rated by speed, and these days virtually all dial-up modems operate at 56K, which means they transmit and receive data at 56,000 bits per second (abbreviated 56 Kbps). Some older or less expensive modems operate at 33,300 kilobits per second or even 28,800. (You may see these referred to as 33.3 or 28.8.)

Sharing Your Phone with a PC

Before you buy a modem, consider its effect on your phone service. If you're using your computer and modem a lot, you may need at least one extra line. This is especially true if you have a fax modem.

If you plan to use your modem only for short periods, you can probably get away with a single line. Remember, however, that when you're online, your phone is busy. If your phone line has a call-waiting feature and someone calls while you're receiving a fax, your fax transmission will be interrupted. (In most areas, you can turn off call waiting for the duration of outgoing calls or faxes.)

If you plan to use your modem often, or if you have a fax modem that you use for incoming fax messages, you are better off adding another phone line. Depending on where you live, a second line costs as little as $10 per month, after the initial installation charge. In most situations, you might not even need any toll-call service, since most online services can be accessed by a local call from most areas.

Broadband: Life in the Fast Lane

In addition to a standard dial-up modem, you may be able to connect to the Internet even faster using a broadband service, such as a cable modem (that connects to your cable TV system) or digital subscriber line (DSL, a high-speed service that uses standard phone lines).

In addition to speed, another advantage of a broadband connection is that it gives you a full-time connection to the Internet. This means that your PC is connected to the Internet whenever you turn it on, and you don't have to log on first to go to a Web site. Most dial-up services offer a flat-rate monthly (or longer) service.

Neither DSL nor cable Internet service is available in all communities. To find out if you can get a cable modem, contact your local cable TV company. DSL modems are offered by most local phone companies as well as by independent companies like Prodigy, Telocity, and Covad. Be sure to shop around to see what is available. Just before I wrote this edition of the book, one of the major DSL companies, Northpoint, went out of business, stranding all of its subscribers. Covad was in financial trouble but still above water. I don't understand how a cool service like DSL could lose money but apparently it can.

Cable modem. Cable companies send TV signals into your home over coaxial cables that can also carry computer data. A cable modem typically operates at anywhere from 500 Kbps all the way up to 5 megabits per second (Mbps). (Even 500 Kbps is nearly 10 times the speed of a 56K modem, and 5 Mbps is nearly 100 times the speed of a 56K modem.) In addition to the cable modem (which is generally supplied as part of the service), you will usually need a network interface card or an Ethernet card in your PC. Those cost about $50.

Caution: Internet Traffic Ahead

With all the types of modems discussed in this chapter, the maximum speeds are a bit theoretical. If you have a 56K modem, for instance, you'll never really get the full 56 Kbps from it. For one thing, the maximum actual speed is 53 Kbps due to government regulations in the United States and Canada. For another thing, maximum speed on any modem assumes that you have an extremely clean phone line. I've tested several 56K modems on a variety of different lines and generally experience downloads at between 40 Kbps and 45 Kbps. The "information highway," like the ones we drive on, can get pretty congested at times. When lots of people are trying to get to the same Web page at the same time, you can count on extra delays. Nevertheless, you're still better off with a faster modem. (To test the actual speed of your modem visit the Resources page of www.littlepcbook.com.)

DSL. Offered by phone companies and Internet service providers, DSL runs over standard telephone lines. It supports high-speed transmission at up to 9 Mbps (depending on your system). Like cable, DSL requires a special modem and, in some cases, a network interface card.

ISDN. The good thing about ISDN is that it uses the same twisted-pair wire found in regular phone lines, so the phone company may not have to run new wires into your house or business. A single physical ISDN line essentially offers two 64 Kbps phone lines (called channels) that can be used for both voice and data. Use both lines for data and you can get up to 128 Kbps—more than twice the speed of a 56K modem. And you don't have to worry about line noise: An ISDN line either works or it doesn't. ISDN is available in many areas of the United States, but most phone companies charge a per-minute usage rate, which makes it too expensive for most consumers.

Wireless. There are a few wireless solutions. For example, in some communities, Sprint Broadband (www.sprintbroadband.com) can install a microwave antenna on your roof to provide high-speed wireless Internet service.

Satellite. Though it tends to cost a bit more, a satellite system works in almost any part of the country, as long as you have access to the right part of the sky. The technology is similar to direct satellite TV, except that you need a two-way connection for the Internet to get data up to the service as well as down to your PC. Some satellite systems also require a modem and phone line but others, like Starband, are two-way.

Fax

The ability to send and receive faxes is practically a requirement for a home office. Fortunately, most modems are also able to transmit and receive faxes. Fax capability in a modem isn't exactly the same as having a stand-alone fax machine (I'll explain why later), but it's a great convenience.

When you have a fax modem and good fax software, sending a fax is as easy as printing; you give the Fax command, and voilà, your fax has gone to its destination. Faxing from the computer saves you the step of printing out the file and sticking the document into a separate fax machine. Computer-generated faxes are also generally more readable than those sent by a regular fax machine, because the fax machine's reader doesn't have to translate the image. When you receive a fax, it's stored on your disk, waiting for you to print it out or view it on screen. Since you print the faxes on plain paper from your regular printer, the pages won't fade and curl like normal fax paper. (In fact, that's a feature you would pay more for on a stand-alone fax machine.)

But if you're thinking of using your modem for faxes instead of getting a stand-alone fax machine, you should also consider some of the disadvantages. First, using a fax modem is more work than using a fax machine. You have to fool around with cables, software, and configuration files, and you can't receive a fax unless your PC is turned on and the fax software is running. If you want to send a copy of a brochure, newspaper article, or other document that's not in your computer, you'll have to get a scanner, which turns hard-copy information into graphics information for the computer. Add one more piece of equipment and one more step.

When I wrote the first edition of *The Little PC Book* back in 1994, the vast majority of people weren't using email, but that's

Faxing Without a Modem

As it turns out, you don't even need a special fax modem to send text messages from your PC. If you have a regular data modem, you can use the Internet or America Online to send a fax.

There are a variety of Internet fax services, including some that are free. eFax (ww.efax.com) and J2.com are Web-based services that will deliver your document over the Internet to countries all over the world, for a lot less than the cost of an international call. They're very convenient and will also let you receive faxes by email. The faxes are sent in the normal way, but instead of dialing a stand-alone fax machine, the sender dials a special J2 or eFax number that's been assigned to you and your fax either arrives in your email as a graphic file or is put on a special Web page where you can see it (and download it, if you wish).

starting to change. As more and more people get computers and Internet accounts, email is becoming a very popular means of exchanging information. Personally I much prefer email to fax. It's easier and cheaper and you can easily save your incoming and outgoing email on your hard disk so that you have a permanent record.

21 Getting the Picture: Scanners, Digital Cameras, Camcorders

In the last few years, the PC has undergone an amazing transformation. What used to be just a machine that crunches words and numbers is becoming a device that manipulates both still and moving images. An increasing number of ordinary people are using their PCs to edit their photographs and even make home movies.

If you want to edit photographs, there are three main ways to get your pictures into your PC: You can scan them in, you can transfer them from a digital camera, or you can download them from the

Internet. Scanners are useful if you already have photos, drawings, or text on paper, but don't have a computer file for them. Digital cameras are an easy way to get images into your computer, since they save photos as electronic files. Images from the Internet are also easy to use, since they're electronic files that go directly into your computer—but the quality of those images varies wildly. I'll discuss more about Internet images in Chapter 45, but first, let's concentrate on scanners and digital cameras.

Scanning

A **scanner** is like a copy machine, except that instead of producing a hard copy, it creates a computer file that you can view, edit, and print. Scanners are often rated by their color depth (for example, 42-bit color) and resolution in dots per inch (dpi). (Color depth, also called "bit depth," refers to the number of colors that can be captured or displayed. Any device you buy will seem to handle all the colors you can see, but the higher the depth the richer the color.) Although the quality of the image has something to do with these ratings, it's also a matter of how well the scanner is made, the software that comes with the scanner, and your subjective judgement of how the image looks. You don't have to pay a lot to get a decent scanner. You can now get decent ones for under $100—even under $60. The Hewlett-Packard 2200c, which cost about $79 when I wrote this chapter, does a very good job of scanning color photos.

Scanners can also be used for optical character recognition (OCR), which turns printed or typed text into documents your computer can read. OCR software usually comes with your scanner. OCR used to be an important scanner function, but it's not all that popular now that a lot of information is already in digital form. It's much easier to get a newspaper online and copy the article you want than to clip a newspaper and scan it in.

Before you invest in a scanner, though, read the rest of this chapter. You might discover that you don't need one. I have a scanner and I hardly ever use it.

Digital Camera

A **digital camera** looks and works pretty much like a film camera but images are saved to the camera's memory instead of on film. Digital photos don't have to be printed on special film paper, either: You can transfer them to your PC and print them on ordinary paper (or glossy paper, for better quality). You can also edit, enhance, and save digital images and put them on the Web or send them to your friends and family in email.

Just about all major camera companies and some PC companies make digital cameras. Prices start at as low as $99 and go all the way up into the thousands. You can now buy a pretty good camera for about $399. It's admittedly more expensive than a similar-quality film camera, but you'll appreciate the convenience of digital pictures.

For one thing, you no longer have to buy film or pay for developing, though you do have to pay for paper and ink when you print your pictures. When you're not using film, you'll find yourself less inhibited about taking pictures. It's only memory and the memory can be reused, so why not take as many pictures as you want?

Digital cameras tend to be rated by their resolution or number of **megapixels** (a million pixels or dots). You'll usually see it expressed as horizontal resolution multiplied by vertical resolution: A typical mid-range camera might have a resolution of 1600 by 1200, which comes out to 1,920,000, or 1.9 megapixels. The more megapixels, the higher the resolution—and, in theory, the better the quality. But, as usual, the numbers don't tell the whole story. What they don't tell you is the higher the resolution, the more memory a picture uses in the camera and the more space it takes on your hard disk. I have a camera that's rated at nearly 3 megapixels, but I usually set it for a lower resolution that takes less memory, and the image quality is fine for most of my purposes.

Personally, I think 2 megapixels is adequate for most photographers, but if plan to print your photos larger than 8 by 10, you may appreciate a camera that produces higher resolution pictures.

Camera Memory

In addition to image quality, pay attention to the amount and type of memory that comes with the camera. Don't get a camera that only has built-in memory. You're better off getting one that uses removable memory cards. For one thing, you can upgrade later if you want more memory. For another, it's pretty easy to transfer pictures from the camera to a PC by slipping the memory card into a special card reader for the PC. Finally, you can buy multiple memory cards and store even more pictures.

Memory cards are measured in megabytes. Low-cost cameras typically come with about 8 to 16 MB, but you can upgrade to 32 MB, 64 MB, and more. There are three types of memory cards in widespread use: CompactFlash, SmartMedia, and Memory Sticks. CompactFlash cards are square and tend to give you a good amount of storage for the buck. The SmartMedia cards are smaller but tend to have less memory. Then there's Sony's Memory Stick, which only works with Sony products.

Other considerations in buying a camera include the size of the camera, the quality of the lens, the camera's overall feel, and the type of battery. Personally, I like small cameras such as the Canon Sureshot 100 or the Kodak DC3800 because they're small enough to fit in a pocket. Of course, there will be lots of new models by the time you read this, so your best bet is to check out the latest reviews at www.cnet.com, www.pcmag.com, and other sites that review digital cameras. One thing I like about Kodak cameras (and some others) is that they use standard AA batteries. You can get rechargeable batteries, but if you find yourself out and about with a dead battery you can also use a standard disposable AA.

Web Cams

Don't confuse digital cameras with those small "Web cams" that fit on top of your PC. Although they're both digital cameras, a Web cam only works while it's attached to your PC. You can use it to take snapshots (the resolution is typically low) or you can use it to conduct a live video call with someone else. Video calls are one of those things that seem like a really cool idea but get old pretty quickly. The quality of a video call is usually pretty iffy, but some families get a kick out of being able to see each other long-distance. You can learn more about these cameras from the Web sites of vendors such as Intel, Logitech, and 3Com.

Digital Video Cameras

Now here's something really cool. If you have a **digital video camera** and your PC is equipped with a FireWire port, you can easily transfer video between the camera and the PC. That way, you can use the camera to take home movies and use the PC to edit them. When you're done editing you can transfer the movie back to the camera or save it to your hard disk or to a CD or DVD so you can share it with others. You can also transfer your videos to the Internet for others to see (but before you do that, you need to learn how to compress the images so the files are smaller and don't take too long to download).

Transferring from an Analog Video Camera to the PC

If you have an older-style analog video camera, you're not out of luck. There are a variety of ways to get your movies from an analog camera into your PC. An inexpensive—though limited—solution is the $70 Studio Online from Pinnacle Systems. It comes with a special cable that connects your camcorder's audio and video jacks to your PC's USB port. You don't need a FireWire card or any other hardware. The package also includes a simple but relatively powerful program that can capture, edit, and output videos. The program can output to three different file formats: AVI, Real, and MPEG. (Real and MPEG files are popular for use on the Web.)

Like all video-editing programs, the software lets you select clips from the tape and edit them together. You can put in titles, transitions, special effects, and music or voice narration in addition to the audio that's already on the tape. The only problem is that to get data through the USB port fast enough, you must compress it. And that means the image loses resolution and can look choppy. That's still OK if you plan to view your movie in a little window on your monitor, upload it to the Web, or send it by email, since you'll wind up compressing it anyway. You might, however, be disappointed if you view your production in full-screen mode or on a standard TV. Still, this is a pretty good way to get started with video editing at a very reasonable cost.

A more expensive—but far more elegant—solution is Hollywood DV Bridge from Dazzle. This $300 hardware-and-software combination works with Windows 98, Windows Me, Windows 2000, and Macintosh, but it requires a FireWire port in your PC. (You can add FireWire to a desktop machine for about $50.)

22 Accessories: Making Yourself Comfortable

Now that we've run through the parts of the computer itself, it's time to turn to the accessories—those small but important pieces of equipment that will keep you and your computer in working order. Accessories such as mouse pads and surge protectors are just as important to your work as a good keyboard. Luckily, they're also very inexpensive.

Wrist Rests

If you type 50 words per minute, you'll enter 18,000 keystrokes in an hour. Keep that up for a full work day and that's a lot of pounding at the keyboard. It's no wonder that tens of thousands of computer users have complained about hand and wrist pain.

The repetitive motion of typing and clicking the mouse can lead to stiffness and minor pain in the hands and wrists. But beware: Those symptoms, if ignored, can turn into major, disabling injuries. Since computers have come into widespread use, doctors have seen a burgeoning number of hand and wrist problems, including Carpal Tunnel Syndrome, a sometimes crippling disease caused by inflammation of the wrist tendons.

The best way to avoid the trouble is to make sure your wrists are in the proper relation to your keyboard. The keyboard needs to be lower than your elbows, and your wrists should be higher than your fingers. In addition to making sure your desk is the proper

Carpal Tunnel Syndrome

Carpal tunnel syndrome is a serious kind of wrist injury linked to computer use. It results from inflammation of the tendons or the synovial sheaths that surround and protect the tendons.

The symptoms of carpal tunnel syndrome vary, but they often include numbness, tingling, or a burning sensation in the palms, fingers, or wrists. Over time, the condition can lead to a weakening of the muscles. You could also experience loss of sensation, pain, or weakness in the arm or other parts of your body.

If you're experiencing pain or weakness in your wrist, hand, or arm, see a doctor or a chiropractor. It may not be a full-fledged case of carpal tunnel syndrome, but it's a good idea to give any pain early attention. It's also a good idea to look for a doctor who is familiar with the diagnosis and treatment of carpal tunnel and other stress-related injuries.

height, a good way to ensure the best posture is with a **wrist rest,** a simple device that elevates your hands so that your wrists remain straight while typing.

You can get a foam wrist rest at any computer store or business supply store for around $10. Fancier ones go up from there. One person I know uses a rolled up towel to serve the same purpose.

Mouse Pads

A mouse pad is a small pad of soft material that sits under your mouse to give it better traction. You don't need one with an optical mouse, but if you have a regular mouse with a ball in it, you do need one. In fact, one may have come

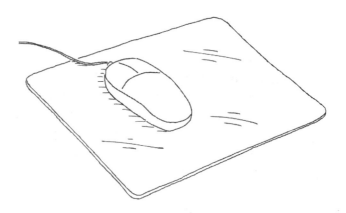

with your PC. If you don't have one, they're cheap ($3 to $10 at office supply and computer stores) and they make a big difference.

Surge Protectors

Surge protectors are designed to insulate your computer from electrical surges that can happen during lightning storms, when your refrigerator's motor kicks in, or for no reason at all. Some electrical engineers I've spoken with claim that surge protectors are not necessary because circuits inside your PC's power supply will automatically protect your system in case of an electrical surge; others claim that they're very important. I think they're a good idea, especially if the power in your area is unsteady (I live in

California where we have "rolling blackouts"). You can get surge protectors for about $20, but the more expensive ones offer better protection. Surge protectors are rated in joules, and the higher the number the better. You'll get basic protection at 200 joules, but there are products that go much higher (over 600 joules) and give much better protection.

Uninterruptible Power Supply

So what happens when the power suddenly goes out while you're using your computer? Well, your computer shuts down instantly and everything you're working on is lost unless it's been saved to disk. One way to avoid that is to get an **uninterruptible power supply** (UPS) that will keep your PC going for a few minutes, giving you time to save your work and shut down your machine. Low-cost UPS devices such as the $79 Back-UPS Office 350 from APC (www.apc.com) will keep a standard computer and monitor running for about 11 minutes. That's not enough time to finish your novel, but it is sufficient to save your file and shut down your computer. Make sure you plug your monitor as well as your PC into the UPS, but don't bother connecting the printer.

Backup Power, Just in Case

If you live in an area where the power goes off a lot you may want to consider a battery backup system. Unlike a UPS, it can keep your computer running for at least 2 hours.

A battery backup system is not a generator. It doesn't require gasoline or other fuels, and the only noise is the hum of a small fan. Also, a generator must be outdoors, but this unit can be used inside an office or home, as well as outdoors.

Store4Power (www.store4power.com) offers a reasonably-priced device (it was $279 last time I checked) consisting of a 12-volt dry-cell battery and an inverter that converts the DC power from the battery to standard AC household current. The battery is similar to the deep-charge "marine" batteries used on pleasure boats and recreational vehicles. But unlike most of those, this battery is dry-cell, so there is no chance of a chemical spill, if you happen to be concerned about that kind of thing. I have one that's smaller than a carry-on suitcase, and though it weighs 47 pounds, it has wheels and a handle, so it's easy to move around.

When you aren't running it, the device remains plugged into the wall, so it's constantly recharging. A "smart" charger keeps the battery from being overcharged. When the power goes off, you turn on the device and plug in whatever equipment you wish to keep running. The xPower also has an adapter for your car cigarette lighter so you can recharge it from the car. You can buy extra batteries to extend the running time.

23 Putting It All Together

OK, you've brought your PC home. Now it's time to put it all together. That's not as difficult as it may seem. If you have a desktop PC, you just plug your various components into the matching sockets on the back of the PC. If you have a laptop, you don't even have to put it together—just install and charge up the battery.

Here's how to set up a desktop PC, step by step.

1. The first thing you should do is plug the keyboard into the system unit. The keyboard usually has a circular plug that goes into a round socket at the back of the system unit. Some machines use other arrangements, such as a USB port (described in Chapter 14).

2. Next, plug in the monitor. There are two cords coming from the monitor. One provides power; the other—the funny-looking one with nine little pins—handles the video signals.

Be careful with the video plug. They sometimes have fairly wimpy pins. It's easy to try to plug them in upside down, and if you exert too much pressure, you'll bend the pins. Since most monitor cords are hard-wired to the monitor, you'll encounter a hefty service charge if you have to have the plug replaced.

TURN YOUR SYSTEM'S POWER OFF BEFORE YOU START MESSING AROUND BACK HERE.

PLUG YOUR PC INTO THE WALL OR POWER STRIP JUST BEFORE TURNING IT ON.

THE KEYBOARD AND MOUSE PORTS ARE ROUND. THEY LOOK IDENTICAL, BUT ONE'S FOR THE KEYBOARD AND THE OTHER'S FOR THE MOUSE.

So before you start, look very closely at the plug and at the socket in the back of the machine. Don't exert pressure until you have aligned the plug, right-side up, with the socket. Now, insert the plug slowly.

Some computers have an outlet on the back of the system unit where you can plug in your monitor's power cord. If yours doesn't have one, you can just plug the monitor directly into a wall socket or power strip.

3. Next comes the printer, if you have one. Some printers use a cable with a large connector that goes into the parallel port of your PC. One end of the cable plugs into the printer and the other into the PC. The end of the cable that plugs into the PC is the "male" connector (the one with the pins), which plugs into the "female" connector (the one with the holes) on the back of the PC.

SOME MACHINES HAVE AN ETHERNET PORT FOR A NETWORK, OR CABLE, OR DSL.

THE MONITOR PLUG HAS 15 PINS IN 3 ROWS AND GOES HERE.

SOME MACHINES HAVE A 1394 ("FIREWIRE") PORT FOR VIDEO CAMERAS, EXTERNAL HARD DRIVES, AND OTHER ADD-ONS.

THE INTERNAL MODEM PHONE JACK IS HERE.

THE PRINTER USUALLY PLUGS INTO THE PORT WITH 25 HOLES.

SERIAL PORTS HAVE 9 PINS.

THERE ARE USUALLY 2 USB PORTS. SOMETIMES YOU PLUG THE PRINTER INTO ONE OF THEM AND THE MOUSE INTO THE USB PORT ON THE PRINTER.

Some printers connect through the USB port. If you have that type of connection, you can plug the printer either directly into the USB port on your PC or into a USB hub (like a power strip for USB devices) that you can purchase from a computer store.

4. If you have anything else, like a scanner or digital camera, you can plug those in now or you can wait and plug them in later. My advice is to wait. You'll have plenty to do just getting used to the basics. It might be best to leave those extra devices in the box, just for a little while, until you're comfortable with the PC itself.

5. The final step, after you have everything else connected, is to plug your PC, monitor, and printer into a wall outlet or power strip. You may want to use a surge protector and possibly even an uninterruptible power supply. (See Chapter 22 for more about these.) If you use a power strip, you can leave the switches of your computer and monitor on and then just turn on the whole system using the power strip's on/off switch.

That should do it. You now have a working system.

Use the Proper Plugs

You should plug your PC, printer, and other peripherals into a three-prong, grounded electrical outlet only. Connecting one of those three-prong cheater plugs to a two-prong outlet is not a good idea unless you also run a ground wire to a furnace, pipe, or other grounded device. Radio Shack and hardware stores sell an inexpensive device that determines whether an outlet is properly grounded.

Drivers: The Software That Goes With the Hardware

In order to run devices like a printer or a scanner, Windows needs to know how to talk to that hardware. Providing those instructions is the job of the driver: a piece of software that comes with the hardware, usually on the accompanying CD-ROM. Any hardware that came bundled with your PC (such as a keyboard, mouse, and monitor) probably has the necessary drivers already installed. But if you bought the pieces separately, or if you add a new peripheral to your original setup, you'll need to install the hardware driver.

The Windows XP installation wizard will, in almost all cases, recognize what type of new hardware you have installed and what software it needs. That means that if all goes well, Windows will prompt you with instructions to insert the disk with the necessary driver, then it will automatically run the installation software for you.

It's very common for hardware companies to revise their drivers to fix bugs, improve performance and add features. In theory, the Windows XP Update (see Chapter 31) will scan for new drivers and let you know. But this is a new service for Microsoft and I'm not yet sure how good it's going to be. For that reason, I suggest you periodically check your hardware vendor's Web site to see if there are any new drivers available for your hardware. If you don't know the location (URL) of their Web site, you can look it up with the Search the Web feature on www.littlepcbook.com.

The Dreaded Case Removal

OK, so you broke down and bought a new sound card, TV tuner, or other device that requires the installation of an expansion card. That means you're going to have to take apart your system unit to install it. Don't panic. Less technically inclined people than you have taken apart their PCs and installed hardware.

Before you break out the screwdriver, remember that, for an expert, this is an extremely easy procedure. Most computer stores will do it for under $50, so if you're really squeamish, you could always go that route. Also, see if any of your friends has ever installed hardware in a PC and can help you.

The first thing you need to do is unplug everything. Then you remove the PC's case. Sometimes that's relatively easy but at other times it's a royal pain, depending on the way the case was designed. It's probably covered in your manual or you can call your PC company's tech support department (or check its Web site) for instructions. Generally there are Philips head screws in the back of the case that you remove, and once they are all removed, you lift the case off of its chassis. This isn't always true, though. Today's cases come in all shapes and sizes and some have plastic thingies that you have to pry off. I've built several computers and know my way around inside them, but there have been times when I've had to call tech support to figure out how to remove the case.

Once the case is off the machine, you should touch the PC's power supply (the big metal box inside) before you touch any electronic components. This isn't a religious ritual; it is a way to discharge any static electricity in your body. If you've been walking around on a carpet or just sitting in a padded chair, there is a possibility that you have built up some static electricity. You know how it feels when you touch someone who has built-up static electricity. You get a mild shock. You can survive a shock like that, but some electronic components can't. Touching the PC's power supply discharges any static. Don't worry. You won't get electrocuted. (You did unplug the PC first, right?)

At the rear of the system unit there are slots. Some will have cards in them and others might be empty. Remember, too, that (as I described in Chapter 15) a PC may have several different kinds of slots: ISA, PCI, and AGP. The documentation that came with your board will tell you what kind it fits in, and the documentation that came with your PC will tell you which slot is which in the system unit. (It should also be clear just by looking at the slots; your board will only fit in the type of slot it's designed for.)

There is probably a piece of aluminum screwed down over the empty hole in the back of the unit. Your first step is to remove the aluminum cover and put it aside. (You won't need it anymore unless you remove the device.) When you unscrew the aluminum cover, be careful not to drop the screw into the PC case. If you do, you'll have to remove it very carefully; loose screws inside your case can cause a short. Besides, you'll need the screw again, as I'll explain in a minute.

Being sure you've discharged the static electricity, take the plug-in card and insert it firmly into the appropriate slot. Press down firmly until it's completely seated. Don't force anything. The slot should offer some resistance but if it's hard to insert, you may have a mismatch between the slot and the board. The connector from the card (assuming there is one) should be accessible from the rear of the unit. Now screw the board in place with the Philips-head screw.

Most manuals now tell you to put the case back together but I don't do that until I've tested the device. With the case cover off but with the new card firmly screwed into place, connect the device you're installing and turn on the PC to make sure everything works OK. (A PC can run just fine with the case off as long as you don't spill anything into it.) If everything is working right, then unplug the device and put the case back together again. If it's not, it's time to check your manual or call the tech support line of the company that made the board.

24 Setting Up Your Workplace

One of the most important things to think about before you sit down at your computer is just how you're going to sit down at your computer.

You can get away with plopping a PC on a table or desk, plugging it into the wall, and sitting down any which way to type. But making things pleasant and comfortable takes some thought. And it's more important than you might think. You can actually hurt yourself if you don't have your computer set up correctly. Typing for hours in an uncomfortable hunch over the keyboard can cause neck and back pain, eyestrain, and painful injury to your wrists. In this chapter, I'll tell you how to set up a workspace that's safe and comfortable for both you and your computer.

Choosing an Area

Plan your work area from the floor up. A carpeted area will be quieter than wood or linoleum floors, but if you can, stay away from plush carpets. They generate too much static electricity, which can be dangerous for your equipment.

A Comfortable Chair

Don't skimp on your chair. A dining room chair is designed for the length of a meal, not a workday; you need something that will allow you to work comfortably at a desk for several hours at a time. The chair should let you adjust the seat height and the position of the backrest. It should be comfortable and offer you plenty of lower-back support. Check with an office supply dealer for a chair designed to be used with a computer, and test it out before you buy.

The Desk

You don't have to spend a lot of money for a custom-made computer desk. The main thing is to be sure that your keyboard is at the right height. The keyboard should be about 26 inches from the floor—or low enough that your elbows are higher than your wrists while you type. A desk that is too high can result in repetitive stress injuries to your arms and wrists. (Chapter 22 has more on Carpal Tunnel Syndrome and other injuries that can result from typing all day at a badly positioned keyboard.) Most office desks and dining room tables are too high. The computer desks that you see at KMart and most other discount stores don't look great and may fall apart after a few years, but if they're the right height and depth, they'll do the job just as well as the fancy ones you get from office supply stores. It's better to sit at a cheap computer desk than at an expensive office desk that's too high for your keyboard.

If you don't want to invest in a new desk, there's another option. Most office supply stores will sell special keyboard holders that attach to the underside of a desk and let you adjust the keyboard to a comfortable height. Providing a shelf for the keyboard also adds some extra desk space.

Lighting

Don't forget the lighting. Your workspace should have plenty of light, but the light should be diffused so that it doesn't create glare on your screen and strain your eyes. Adjustable lamps and lamps that let the light bounce off the ceiling work well for that purpose. If you have a window nearby, use drapes or shades, or install antiglare film on your windows, to block the excess light.

Give Yourself a Break

Even once you have set up your workspace correctly, you still need to do some thinking about how your work habits at the computer can affect your health. Computer health experts point out that even if you've got all the right equipment in just the right position, working at the computer for extended periods can cause aches and pains. The National Institute of Occupational Safety and Health recommends that you take a 15-minute stretch break for every hour you sit at the computer in order to uncramp your muscles and give your eyes and wrists a break.

The problem seems to be that working at a computer is too easy. Unlike at a typewriter, you don't need to feed in new sheets of paper, raise your hands to apply white-out to a mistake, or do the other varied tasks that more traditional work requires. Constant, uninterrupted work can cause repetitive stress injuries. So take a break. It's good for you.

The Monitor

OK, you have a low desk so that your keyboard is below your elbow level, and now your monitor is so low that you have to bend over to see what's on the screen. That can't be good.

You're right, it's not. Your monitor should be up around eye level—when you're sitting up straight. Most monitors these days come on tilt-and-swivel bases, but in many cases they don't offer a wide enough choice of adjustments. You can buy many different kinds of gadgets to take care of this problem, ranging from simple monitor platforms to elaborate adjustable arms that enable you to set your monitor in almost any position and height. If you don't want to spring for one of those solutions, however, try propping last year's Yellow Pages under the screen.

LOOKS LIKE
A FAST ONE,
HONEY.

Your computer is all set up and ready to go. Now what are you going to do?

Well, you could just turn it on and see what happens, but as with any powerful gadget, you'll get a lot more out of it if you learn a few basic rules that will give you the lay of the land and help you to maneuver around roadblocks.

In Part 2 I'll take you through the basics of using Windows XP. This is the "meat and potatoes" of using PCs (with all due apologies to vegetarians). Whether you're new to computers or just new to XP (and who isn't?), I think you'll find it pretty easy to follow.

You've installed Windows XP on your PC and you're ready to go. Now what? In this section, I'll walk you through the new desktop, Start menu, and Control Panel, teach you how to work with files, folders, and accessories, explain the ins and outs of networking, backing up, and shutting down, and of course, tell you how to get help when you need it. Let's get started!

Working with Windows **XP**

two

25 Starting Your Computer

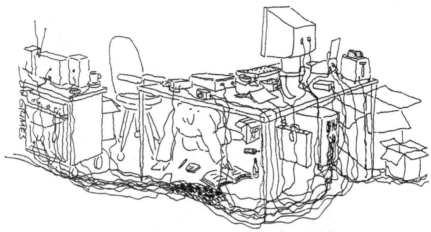

"NOW, IF YOU CAN FIND THE POWER SWITCH, FLIP IT ON."

Turning on a PC is often called "booting" it. The term comes from the expression "pulling oneself up by one's bootstraps." That's because the machine gives itself all the instructions it needs to go through its startup process, using information that's built into its chips and stored on its disk.

Let's start with the absolute basics: The first thing I want you to do is turn on your PC.

- If you have all your equipment plugged into a power strip, just flip the power strip switch and your whole system will spring to life.

- If everything is plugged in separately, you'll have to find the switches on your system unit, monitor, and printer. They're at a different place on each brand, so you're on your own here.

While you're waiting for the Windows opening screen, the computer may be flashing all sorts of messages on the screen and flashing some lights on the system unit. For the most part, you can ignore all that. If your system beeps at you, though, it might want something from you. If you hear a beep, look on the screen to see if there is a message that tells you what to do.

At the end of the startup process, you'll see the Windows desktop, which I describe in the next two chapters.

Congratulations! Your computer has successfully started.

How to Fix Things That Go Wrong During Startup

Sometimes during startup, your computer may beep at you and display the message

```
A:>

Non-System disk or disk error.
Replace and strike any key when ready
```

Don't worry—there's probably nothing wrong with the computer. Chances are you have a floppy disk in the floppy drive—the drive that your computer looks in first for its system files. Just remove the floppy disk and press any key on the keyboard. Your computer will continue its startup process.

Things seem to be happening, but nothing shows up on screen.

If you turn your monitor on and the screen stays dark, don't panic until you've checked the brightness control. (You should find brightness and contrast controls at the front, side, rear, or bottom of the monitor.) A lot of monitor service calls to fix "broken" monitors turn out to be false alarms—they just have the brightness turned all the way down.

The machine starts up but Windows XP doesn't load successfully.

Although things don't go wrong all that often, there are a lot of things that could go wrong. It could be, for example, that your video driver (the software required to display video on your screen) isn't loading correctly. Or perhaps some software that you recently installed is failing to work properly.

If Windows fails to start, you can try to start it in Safe Mode by holding down the Ctrl key or F8 as you start the machine. In that mode, Windows uses the minimum amount of drivers and software just to get going. Once in Safe Mode you can try to fix any problems, remove software, or use System Restore (see Chapter 38) to roll back the system to an earlier state when you know it was working properly.

If you can't solve the problem with Safe Mode, trying pressing F8 as you start the machine and, when the menu comes up, select Last Known Good Configuration followed by Enter.

If all else fails, call your PC manufacturer's tech support. It could be something easy to fix, or you might need a repair.

26 The Windows XP Desktop

An operating system's desktop is what you see once your computer finishes starting up and is ready to use. In the past, the Windows desktop was filled with all sorts of icons and shortcuts to various programs and services, many of them essentially advertisements for Microsoft and its partners. That's no longer necessarily the case.

Originally, Microsoft planned for a clean Windows XP desktop that held only the Recycle Bin, with all the program icons and short-cuts living in the Start menu. However, as a result of the antitrust case against Microsoft, the company agreed to let PC makers put their own icons on the desktop. So if you buy a new PC, you might find icons on your desktop that were put there by the PC maker. It's also possible that Microsoft will wind up promoting its Microsoft Network (MSN) on the XP desktop. Also, when you install software, some programs automatically put an icon on the desktop, so yours may look different than the one pictured here.

Here's the standard XP desktop.

Just because there isn't much on your desktop doesn't mean it has to stay that way. Just like your desktop at home—which was clean when you first got it, remember?— you have the option of adding things to it. You can copy files, folders, or even a shortcut to My Computer from the Start menu directly to the desktop. Simply click on whatever you want to copy or move and drag it onto the desktop. Or, if you can't see the desktop from the file or a folder you want to copy, you can right-click the folder once, select Copy from the context menu that pops up, and then go to the desktop and select Paste Shortcut. That will put a shortcut to the item on your desktop. (If you don't know how to use your mouse yet, see Chapter 28. For more on shortcuts, see Chapter 34.)

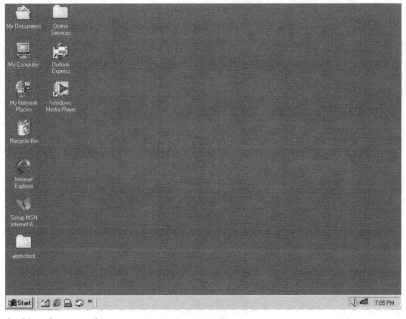

And here's one with some program icons on it.

Cleaning Your Desktop

Windows XP also provides a feature that automatically "cleans" your desktop by moving icons to a folder. (I wish I had someone to do that for my actual desktop.) To access this feature, click the Start menu, select Control Panel, and click on Appearance and Themes. Now click Change the Desktop Background, then Customize Desktop, and finally Clean Desktop Now. Any icons on the desktop will be tidied into the Unused Desktop Shortcut folder on your desktop.

You can also remove shortcuts and icons on your own, if you like, by dragging them onto the Recycle Bin icon. Removing an icon is not the same thing as deleting a program or file. Icons, in most cases, are just shortcuts that point to a file. The file is still there, even after you "throw away" the icon.

Select Control Panel from the Start menu to clean your desktop or change the way it looks.

The Start Menu: Gateway to Windows XP

27

In Windows XP, the Start menu takes on extra importance because it truly is the place where you start everything. You'll no longer access everything from the desktop; now you'll use the Start menu instead.

In XP, the Start menu holds all your programs.

The Start menu is divided into two sections. On the left, you'll find programs that you've installed. Some may be listed directly on the menu, but they're all available by clicking on the large green All Programs arrow. Click the arrow (or the words) and you'll see a menu that contains all of your programs. Some of the programs are listed directly, but sometimes you may find them within a submenu. (See Chapter 28 for more about submenus.)

Upgrader's Tip

While in the Start menu you only need to click a file folder once. No need to double-click. This only applies in the Start menu.

On the right side of the Start menu you'll see special programs that control windows and icons for your computer files. These include the folders My Documents, My Pictures, and My Music, as well as a shortcut to My Computer and, if you're on a network, to My Network Places. Lower down, you'll find shortcuts that take you to the Control Panel, Network Connections, Help and Support, the Search tool, and other programs. It may not look like much, but these few icons are all you need to take complete control over your computer. The right side of the Start menu takes you to your files, your network (if you have one), and the Windows Control Panel, where you can customize Windows XP to meet your needs.

My Documents

The My Documents icon is a shortcut to the folder where Windows XP keeps all of your files. If you've used Windows 95, 98, or Me, you may already be familiar with the My Documents folder, but this one is a bit different. For one thing, Windows XP is a multi-user operating system that allows more than one person to share a computer. So everyone who shares your computer has his or her own individual My Documents folder. The My Documents folder that you see here is for you only.

Many programs, including Microsoft Office, will automatically store files in My Documents. What's more, if you click My Documents, you'll find two other folders inside: My Music and My Pictures. You might find it confusing that there are icons in the Start menu for My Music and My Pictures, as well, but there's a simple explanation: They're all shortcuts to the My Music and

So Where Is My "My Documents" Folder?

Although you can easily open your My Documents folder from the Start menu, it may not be as easy as it used to be to find it using the Windows Explorer (see Chapter 32). As I mentioned before, there is a separate My Documents folder for each user. So the My Documents folder is stored within that user's Documents and Settings folder. To find it, you can use either Windows Explorer or My Computer to go to your C drive and click the folder called Documents and Settings. Within that folder is a separate folder for each user, even if there is only one user. And inside each user's folder is a My Documents folder that contains folders called My Music and My Pictures (and possibly others, depending upon what software you have installed).

Microsoft sort of hides all this from users on the theory that you don't really need to know where the files and folders are in order to use them. That's like hiding the battery on a car: It's fine until something goes wrong and you need a jump start. In a perfect world you'd never need to know where your files and folders are located, but life—especially life with computers—is far from perfect.

My Pictures folders and it's possible to have more than one shortcut to the same folder. In fact, it's very helpful.

My Music and My Pictures

The My Music and My Pictures folders, like all Windows XP folders, are used to store files. But these folders have special attributes and are used for special files.

My Music

If you open the My Music folder, you'll notice some special options on the left side of the window, including Play all and Shop for music online. If you select Play all, it will queue all of your music files to play in the Windows Media Player—the audio player software that comes with Windows XP. If you click Shop for music online, it will take you to one or more Web sites where you can purchase downloadable music. I'm sure you won't be shocked to learn that these sites are either operated by Microsoft's MSN (Microsoft Network) or have a business arrangement with Microsoft.

Click Play all to queue all of your music files to be played in the Windows Media Player.

My Pictures

The My Pictures folder also has some interesting special features. To begin with, the icon for any folders inside My Pictures will, by default, show small thumbnail images of the first four files in the folder. So instead of just seeing a blank folder, perhaps with words on it, you'll actually see some of what is in the folder.

My favorite is the option View as a slide show. If you single-click any folder within My Pictures, then single-click View as a slide show, Windows will start playing a slide show of all the pictures inside the folder. In the upper right, you'll see what looks like a set of VCR controls. Press the Play button and your show will begin. It can be quite entertaining. (Before you can take full advantage of the My Pictures features, you have to get some pictures into your PC. That's covered in Chapter 45.)

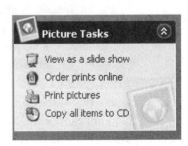

The tasks options in the My Pictures folder. This only pops up if the folder contains picture files.

Another neat feature lets you order glossy prints over the Internet from one of Microsoft's photo partners. Microsoft sure knows how to encourage e-commerce.

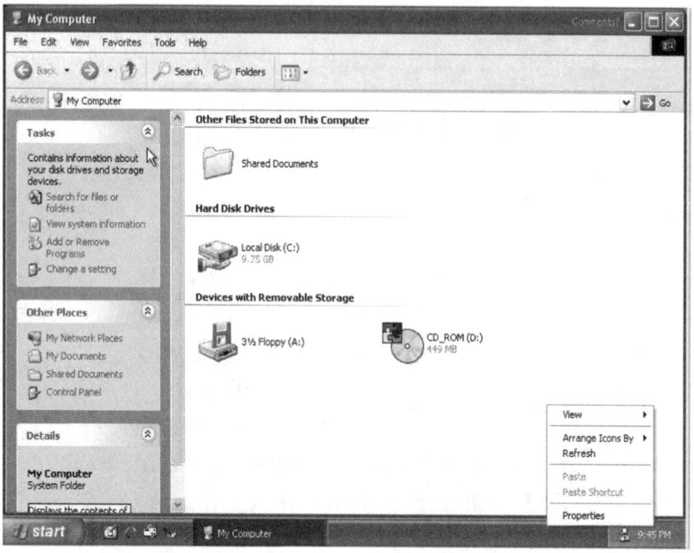
My Computer
File Edit View Favorites Tools Help
Back
Search
Folders
Address
My Computer
Go
Tasks
Contains information about your disk drives and storage devices.
Search for files or folders
View system information
Add or Remove Programs
Change a setting
Other Places
My Network Places
My Documents
Shared Documents
Control Panel
Details
My Computer
System Folder
Other Files Stored on This Computer
Shared Documents
Hard Disk Drives
Local Disk (C:)
9.75 GB
Devices with Removable Storage
3½ Floppy (A:)
CD_ROM (D:)
449 MB
View
Arrange Icons By
Refresh
Paste
Paste Shortcut
Properties
start
9:45 PM

The My Computer folder shows some of your folders, your hard disk, and any other drives.

My Computer

If you've used an earlier version of Windows, you may remember the My Computer icon on the desktop, usually in the upper-left corner. Don't worry, it didn't go away, it just moved into the Start menu.

Click once on My Computer and it opens into its own window. But it may look quite a bit different than it did in your previous version of Windows. Now it will probably show you some of your folders (but not necessarily all) as well as your hard disk and any other drives. Your hard disk will look like an external disk drive being held by a hand.

Local Disk (C:)
9.75 GB

Your hard disk will look like an external disk drive being held by a hand.

A lot of experienced Windows users will be shocked the first time they click the C drive. Instead of seeing all your files and folders as you did in previous versions of Windows, you see a screen that reads "These files are hidden," with a warning not to modify its contents. Microsoft says that this makes the interface easier to use. I've been using Windows since it was first released so I'm used to the old way. To be fair, I can certainly understand why Microsoft made these design changes. The company wants its operating system to appeal to a very wide variety of people, and hiding some of

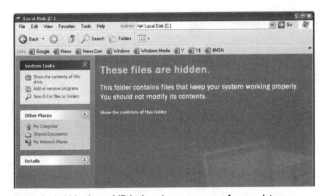

the intricacies of the system makes the software a bit more user friendly. At least that's the theory.

When you first click the C drive, you'll see this screen (left) informing you that your files are hidden. Fortunately,

By default, Windows XP hides the contents of your drives. Click Show contents of this drive...

if you like being able to see all of your folders and files, you can easily modify this screen simply by clicking Show the contents of this folder. That changes the view to show you all the folders on your C drive. It doesn't look exactly the same as in previous versions of Windows, but it does give you an opportunity to explore the contents of your folders. Opening folders works just the same as in previous versions: Double-click a folder and it opens, revealing its files and any subfolders.

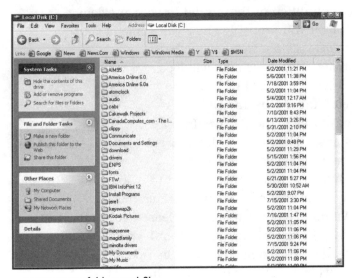

...to view your folders and files.

Windows XP allows you to have several user accounts. This is the welcome screen for my family.

Where Windows XP Actually Stores Your Documents

Windows XP is designed to be shared easily by several people. You don't have to share it (no one else gets their mitts on my PC) but it's set up so that you can (see Chapter 30 for more on this). Each person who has an "account" on your PC will have his or her own folder within the main Documents and Settings folder. If you haven't set up any accounts, Windows will create a default account called Administrator (they're so creative in Redmond, Washington). Once you set up an account, XP will create additional folders within the main Documents and Settings folder—one for each account name.

The ABCs of Disk Drive Names

In the My Computer window, you'll notice that each disk drive has a letter as well as a name associated with it. A: refers to your floppy drive; C: is your computer's internal hard disk; and your CD-ROM or DVD drive is probably D. If you have other drives installed they are named, E:, F:, and so on. This is just a way to keep the different drives straight.

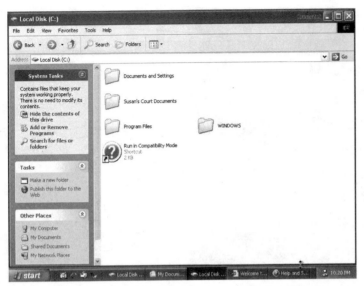

Each person who uses your machine has a personalized working area.

XP also keeps a separate Documents and Settings folder for each user, where it stores that person's documents and folders. This is how each person who uses the same machine can have a personalized working area as well as different settings.

Upgrader's Tip

You can set up accounts when you install Windows XP or add accounts any time from the Control Panel. For more details, see Chapter 30.

Giving Commands in Windows

28

Windows XP is now yours to command, and in this chapter, I'll teach you how to tell it what to do.

The first thing you need to know is that there are usually several ways to do anything in Windows, and that goes for giving commands, too. But once you learn the tricks, you can apply them almost anywhere—to just about any icon, window, or menu you find, in Windows or in most application programs you use. I'll teach you the basic ways of giving commands in this chapter, and you'll apply them as you learn to do all the other basic tasks I talk about in the rest of the book.

Mouse Commands

Windows is designed to be used with a mouse. As you move the mouse around on your mouse pad or desk (an optical mouse doesn't need a mouse pad), a pointer on screen moves along with it, allowing you to point at the object that you want to use. (For more on mice, see Chapter 18.)

You can double click on a word to Select it.

When an item is selected, it is usually highlighted (changed to a different color).

Clicking the mouse buttons tells Windows what you want to do with the item you're pointing at. One click means one thing, two clicks means another, and clicking with the right button means something else again. The vocabulary is pretty simple, and it's the same in Windows or in any Windows application. Here's a description of the basic mouse commands and some of the situations you'll use them in.

"CLICK" (PUSH) AND RELEASE THE LEFT BUTTON TO "SELECT" SOMETHING.

Clicking. To **click** something, you point to it and press, then release, the left mouse button.

Clicking is most often used to select something you want to act on—an icon or a button, for example. Clicking in text places an insertion point, which tells the program where you want to insert text you're about to type or move from another place.

In Windows XP there are some exceptions. In the Start menu and in the Taskbar, a single click with the left mouse button takes action. There is no need to double-click.

TO "DOUBLE-CLICK," SIMPLY PUSH AND RELEASE THE LEFT BUTTON TWICE."

Double-clicking. To **double-click,** you point to an item and press, then release, the left mouse button twice in quick succession.

Double-clicking an object—a program or folder icon for example—usually opens it. Double-clicking in text usually selects the word you double-

Some Programs Don't Follow the Rules

Not every program obeys the "rules" of the Windows interface. You are likely to come across programs whose developers want to do it "their way." I'm not happy about it because it actually makes life a little more difficult, but that's the way it is.

clicked. Again, in the Start menu and Taskbar, you would single-click, not double-click.

If double-clicking doesn't work, you may be waiting too long between clicks or clicking too quickly. Try speeding up or slowing down the process until you get it right or modifying the mouse's behavior. You'll find the Mouse control icon in the Control Panel under Printers and Other Hardware.

TO "DRAG" SOMETHING, "SELECT" THE ITEM, THEN HOLD THE LEFT BUTTON DOWN AS YOU MOVE THE MOUSE.

Dragging. Dragging means pressing the mouse button and moving the mouse while keeping the button held down. Usually, you drag with the left mouse button down, but in special cases (you'll be told when), you drag with the right mouse button down.

Dragging a selected object usually moves it from one place to another. Dragging over text or a set of icons on the screen selects everything you drag the pointer over.

Right-clicking. Right-clicking means clicking the right mouse button.

Right-clicking calls up a menu that lets you do something with whatever you're pointing at. For example, if you right-click an item on in the Start menu, you'll see a menu (sometimes called a context menu) that lets you open it, remove it, copy it, or perform other tasks on it. In some programs, right-clicking a word calls up a menu that lets you change the font, size, or some other attribute.

IN WINDOWS, RIGHT-CLICKING BRINGS UP A MENU OF CHOICES FOR THE OBJECT YOU CLICKED ON.

Menu Commands

You can carry out a few common tasks using just the mouse, but most of the time, you'll use the mouse to select the item you want to act on and then tell the PC what to do with that item by choosing a command from a **menu.** When an item is selected it is usually highlighted (changed to a different color).

A menu bar appears across the top of most windows you have open on screen.

Clicking the name of a menu in the menu bar reveals all the commands in that menu. Clicking a command name executes the command.

The **menu bar** lists the names of all the menus available in that window. Clicking any of the menu names shows the commands available in that menu. Then, clicking on a command name executes the command.

In many cases, you'll see a right-pointing arrow next to a command within a menu. When you point to one of those commands, a **submenu** will roll out, offering a whole new set of subcommands, and some of those subcommands might lead to submenus of their own. These are called **cascading menus** or pull-down menus. When you find the command you want, you click it to execute it, just as you would in any other menu.

Menus also appear when you right-click an object. (Right-clicking, you remember, means clicking the right button on your mouse.) The pop-up menus that appear when you right-click let you carry out common tasks on those items.

Most windows include a special menu called the **system menu,** which you can see by clicking the icon at the window's top-left corner. The system menu items let you close and resize the window.

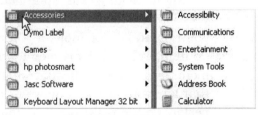

If a menu command has a right-pointing arrow next to it, selecting that command will display a submenu.

Reading a Menu

Menus have more information than just the name of the various commands you can perform. Other symbols and signs in a menu give you information about how the commands can be used. The callouts below describe that vocabulary.

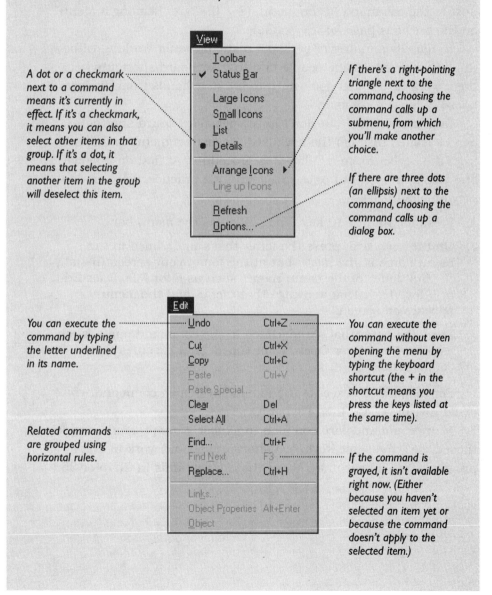

A dot or a checkmark next to a command means it's currently in effect. If it's a checkmark, it means you can also select other items in that group. If it's a dot, it means that selecting another item in the group will deselect this item.

If there's a right-pointing triangle next to the command, choosing the command calls up a submenu, from which you'll make another choice.

If there are three dots (an ellipsis) next to the command, choosing the command calls up a dialog box.

You can execute the command by typing the letter underlined in its name.

You can execute the command without even opening the menu by typing the keyboard shortcut (the + in the shortcut means you press the keys listed at the same time).

Related commands are grouped using horizontal rules.

If the command is grayed, it isn't available right now. (Either because you haven't selected an item yet or because the command doesn't apply to the selected item.)

Keyboard Shortcuts

Menus tell you what commands are available for the items you selected. Many menu commands have special **keyboard shortcuts,** which let you issue commands without using your mouse to select items from a menu. For the ones that do, the shortcut is listed next to the command in the menu. (See the box "Reading a Menu" on the previous page for an example.)

It's largely a matter of personal taste, but after working with the PC for awhile, some people find that keyboard shortcuts help them work faster; you don't need to lift your hands from the keyboard to issue a command.

Even commands that don't have special keyboard shortcuts can be issued through the keyboard. To issue a menu command from the keyboard, just follow this procedure. At first do it slowly, one step at a time, but once you get a little practice, you can do it very quickly.

1. Press the Alt or F10 key. That activates the menu bar.

2. On the keyboard, press the letter that's underlined in the menu name in the menu bar at the top of your screen (usually the first letter of the menu name, such as F for File, E for Edit, or V for View). That activates that menu, and the menu appears on screen.

3. Press the letter that's underlined in the command name, such as N for New, O for Open, C for Close. That executes the command.

For instance, to execute the File menu's Open command, you could just press Alt, then F, then O.

Many commands are common to almost every program, and in those cases, the same keyboard shortcuts should work in every program. (You'll hear more about those commands in Chapter 35.)

Working with Dialog Boxes

Sometimes Windows or an application program will need more information from you before it executes a command. In that case, a **dialog box** will appear after you issue the command, supplying a place where you can provide that information. When a menu command has three dots following its name, that means it has a dialog box associated with it.

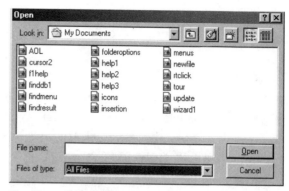

The Open dialog box.

For example, when you choose the Open command from the File menu, you will see a dialog box that looks something like the one above.

Dialog boxes have several different kinds of controls in them, which you will also find in application windows and other places throughout Windows and Windows programs. The illustrations below describe how to use them.

Command buttons are generally rectangular, tinted, and look sort of three-dimensional. To activate the command written on the button, you click it.

Check boxes list options that you can either turn on or off. When the box has an X in it, the option is chosen. You can check a box (put an X in it), or uncheck it, if it is already chosen, by clicking it.

When you can choose only one option of a set, the options are provided with **option buttons.** Clicking one button will select it and deselect the others in the set.

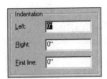

Text boxes provide a space where you can type your choice.

Sometimes a text box or other field will have a **pull-down list** associated with it. The list gives possible options for the field. To see the list, click the text box or the down arrow at its right. You can select an item in the list by clicking it.

Tabs mark the different "pages" of a dialog box. Clicking a tab opens the set of options it labels.

The **question mark** in the upper-right corner of a dialog box offers help with that dialog box. Click it for instructions. The X (the close button) closes the dialog box without executing the command.

When a dialog box is open, you generally have to close it before you can do anything else. (If you click elsewhere on your desktop, you'll probably just hear a beep, and nothing will happen.) If you close a dialog box with the **close box,** the dialog box will close without executing the command. To execute the command and close the dialog box, you need to either click an action button or just press Enter.

Using Toolbars

Windows and many Windows programs feature a row of buttons across the top of their windows called a **toolbar.** Toolbars let you carry out commonly used commands by simply clicking once on the button.

The commands that the buttons represent change from window to window (they generally let you carry out the most common tasks for that window), but you'll see many of the same buttons in

The toolbar (the one shown here is from Microsoft Excel) lets you execute commands with a single click.

many different windows. Sometimes, you can find out what a button does by just pointing at it (without clicking) for a second. A tiny box, called a **ToolTip,** will pop up, naming the command that the button executes. But sometimes this doesn't happen.

A window may have several toolbars or none at all. Just because you don't see a toolbar in a window, though, doesn't mean that one isn't available. Click the View menu and look for a toolbar command or the names of toolbars. Clicking a toolbar name (and putting a checkmark next to it) displays the toolbar. Clicking again (to remove the checkmark) removes the toolbar from the screen.

Pick the Method That Works Best for You

You've now learned four ways to give a command. Look at the Copy command in the Edit menu, illustrated on page 127. You now know four ways to execute that command. After selecting the item you want copied, you could

- Use the mouse to click the menu and then the command name.

- Press the Ctrl and C keys (at the same time) on the keyboard.

- Press the Alt, E, and C keys (one after another).

- Click the Copy button in the toolbar.

All those commands have the same effect, so you can use whichever one works best for you at the time.

29 Using the Taskbar

The Windows taskbar is a handy tool for switching from one program to another and for launching programs. You'll find it at the bottom of your screen, below the desktop and to the right of the Start menu.

The **taskbar**'s main purpose is to allow you to switch from one task to another (hence the name). To see what I mean, launch a program and look down at the taskbar. You'll see the name of that program. Now launch another program and you'll see both names. To quickly switch from one program to another, just click on the one you want. If you're running a program like Word that lets you open multiple windows, each window will have its own place on the taskbar. However, if the taskbar starts to get crowded with too many open windows, XP cleverly groups tasks according to the programs they're in. So, if you have multiple windows open in Word, or multiple Internet Explorer windows open, they will be grouped together and numbered as in the two images below.

The "6" to the left of Internet E... indicates that there are six Internet Explorer pages open and they're all hidden on that tab.

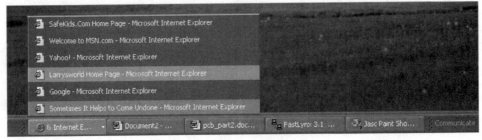

Click on the tab to see which pages are hidden on the tab.

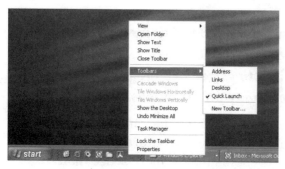

Left-click Quick Launch
to add this toolbar.

The Quick Launch Toolbar

As you know, the Start menu is your main portal for launching applications. But there's an optional toolbar, called Quick Launch, that you can install on your taskbar so you can launch programs (or open folders) from there. The Quick Launch Toolbar stores icons (shortcuts, actually) for any programs, folders, or files you tell it to. Then when you want to launch them, you don't have to go through even the minor inconvenience of opening the Start menu.

To add the Quick Launch Toolbar, right-click any portion of the taskbar where there's no icon showing (usually the "blank" blue area). That brings up a menu. Left-click the word Toolbars and then left-click Quick Launch.

As soon as you do that, you'll notice a new area on the taskbar, just to the right of the Start menu. You can now drag icons, files, and folders directly into this area and simply single-click to open them.

Show Desktop Icon

Once you add the Quick Launch Toolbar to the taskbar, you'll notice a new icon that can be very handy. It's the Show Desktop icon and it immediately minimizes all your open windows and shows your desktop whenever you click it. If you like to keep folders and files and icons on your desktop, you'll probably also like Show Desktop since it allows you to get to them immediately. It's also handy if you have too many windows open at once. Just click Show Desktop to minimize all of them and then click whichever ones you really want to see.

30 Windows Control Panel

Like the cockpit of an airplane, the Windows Control Panel is your PC's control center. It's the place where you add new users for your PC, adjust your settings, remove programs, and change your time zone, among many other options.

Like most everything else in Windows XP, you'll find the **Control Panel** in the Start menu. By default, Windows XP shows the Control Panel organized by category. This makes more sense than in previous versions of Windows when it was organized by specific function, but if you're an old Windows hand, then you may want to click Switch to Classic View in the upper left-hand corner.

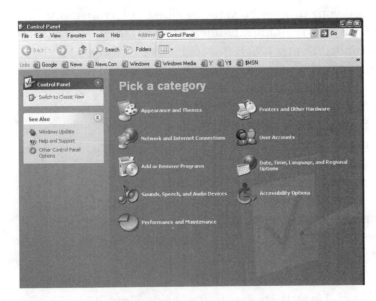

This is the new look and feel of the Control Panel in Windows XP. If you prefer the old version, click Switch to Classic view.

Appearance and Themes

Generally speaking, the items in this menu control how things look on your screen. Some of them, like the desktop theme or screen saver, are simple aesthetic choices, subject only to your tastes and whims. Others, like screen resolution, are more complicated and can even affect the overall performance of your PC.

The theme is the overall look and feel of the Windows XP desktop. Although it comes with a desktop theme already installed (the default theme), Microsoft provides a number of other options you can change it to. You can even switch to the Windows Classic look if you're nostalgic for your old version of Windows. You can also get other themes from various Web sites, including Microsoft's.

Here's the classic version of the Control Panel. To go back to the new look, click Switch to Category View.

Screen Saver

You can also set up a screen saver in the Appearances menu of the Control Panel. **Screen savers** got their name because there was a time when screens would be ruined if they displayed a static image for too long. Those days are long gone, but screen savers are still around (thanks in part to the popularity of the funny and wacky designs concocted by a company called Berkeley Systems—you may remember its Flying Toasters screen saver).

Today, screen savers do nothing to save energy. In fact, they waste energy if you use them instead of the power-saving options discussed later in this chapter. You can set your power options from the Screen Saver area just by clicking on Power near the bottom of the Screen Saver tab.

Here are just a few of your choices for desktop themes.

Click on the Screen Saver tab under Display Properties to choose a new screen saver like My Picture Slide Show.

XP comes with several screen savers, including some that display ads for Microsoft. Click the Screen Saver tab to choose one. The Screen Saver tab is also where you specify how many minutes your computer must be idle before the screen saver shows up.

My favorite included screen saver is My Picture Slide Show. After you select it, use the Browse tools to select the folder that contains your pictures. Then every time your computer has been idle for a while, you'll see a personal slide show of your own digital pictures.

Network and Internet Connections

In this menu, you can set up or change your Internet connection or configure Windows to connect to another computer in your home or office. For details, see Chapter 37.

Add or Remove Programs

The **Add/Remove Programs** icon does just what its name implies. It's critically important for deleting programs, but you probably won't use it very often to add programs. Most of the time, when you add a new program, you'll use the installer that came with the program (it usually runs automatically when you insert the program's CD-ROM into your drive, but you may need to click the program's setup icon).

The Remove function is usually the best way to get rid of programs you no longer need. Although it's possible just to drag a program's files from your hard drive into the Recycle Bin and delete them, that's really not a good idea. Programs don't just occupy space on your drive. They also put code into a special file called the **Windows Registry** and they sometimes put files or code in other places as well. If you don't use Remove Programs, you can't be sure that all vestiges of the program are gone. And the leftover bits could slow down your PC or make it work erratically.

Fortunately, removing a program with this Control Panel item is pretty straightforward. Click the Add/Remove Program icon, select the program you want to remove and click the Remove button. Windows will ask if you're sure and if you click Yes the program will be gone for good. Unlike deleting files there is no undelete feature. The only way to get the program back is either to reinstall it or to do a System Restore (see Chapter 39).

Sounds, Speech, and Audio Devices

We've come a long way since the days when the only sounds you could hear on a PC were beeps from the tiny little speaker inside the case. Now, PCs can talk to you and play music and movies. Your PC's CD drive isn't just for reading data: It can also play audio CDs (though you need to add better speakers to hear them properly). If you have a DVD drive you can watch—and listen to—full-length movies.

In the Sounds, Speech, and Audio Devices area of the control panel, you can control many aspects of your PC's sound, from the volume to the default playback and recording devices. (You shouldn't have to mess with this last one, unless there is a problem with your sound system. If that's the case, seek help from an experienced user.)

Most PC speakers have a control that lets you adjust the volume, but you can also check or change volume and other sound attributes by clicking Adjust the System Volume in this area of the Control Panel. The actual controls depend, to some extent, on your specific audio card.

The Sound Scheme, which you can also control here, determines which sounds are tied to specific events such as starting Windows, shutting down Windows, and closing a program. Each sound is associated with a "wave" file (.wav). If you want to change the sound associated with an action, browse for the new wave file. If you have a microphone attached to your PC, you can even record your own wave file.

You can also click on this icon to access audio controls.

On some machines, you can also access audio controls by clicking the little icon in the taskbar that looks like a speaker.

One thing to watch out for: an increasing number of audio cards and speaker systems support digital sound. If you choose to use the digital sound option be sure to set your audio controls for digital output. You can generally do that either in the Advanced area of the Control Panel settings or by clicking the audio icon in the lower-left corner of your screen in the taskbar.

Performance and Maintenance

This section provides information about your computer, as well as some tools that will keep your PC in tip-top shape.

See Basic Information About Your Computer

The first thing you'll see when you click this option is the General tab, which provides basic information about which version of the operating system you're using, the type and speed of your PC's CPU, and how much memory (RAM) your PC has installed.

In the Computer Name tab you can name or rename your PC. This may not be important if you only have one PC, but if you have more than one, especially if they are networked, it can be a handy way to tell them apart. The information you type here will help your network keep track of what data goes on what PC.

You use the Hardware tab to help install new hardware, but in most instances it's not necessary. Typically, when you plug in a piece of hardware, Windows XP's Plug and Play feature will recognize the hardware and prompt you to insert a CD-ROM or floppy disk that contains the necessary software (called drivers) for that device. If this doesn't happen and Windows doesn't recognize your hardware, you can click the Add Hardware Wizard button.

The Automatic Update tab controls how often you want to be notified about your software, operating system, and other program updates. This is a service that Microsoft has added to Windows so you can download updates over the Internet. If you go with the default configuration, whenever you're connected to the Internet Windows XP will automatically check to see if there are updates available. This way you'll always have the latest "fixes" to Windows XP as well as the latest drivers for your printer and other hardware. Although Microsoft should always be up-to-date when it comes to its own software, you should periodically check the Web site of your hardware vendors to see if there are any updates. Some vendors let you sign up for an email list that will automatically notify you of any new updates.

The Advanced tab controls visual effects, memory, advanced desktop settings, and other things that, frankly, most people will never have to deal with.

Adjust Visual Effects

This relatively advanced option allows you to control such things as whether XP animates windows when minimizing and maximizing and how it fades or slides menus. You can make whatever changes you want, but on my machine I just leave the default option checked and let Windows choose what's best for my computer.

Free Up Space on Your Hard Disk

This area of the Performance and Maintenance Control Panel is your link to a very useful service. You can use it to get rid of all sorts of unnecessary files that can clutter up your hard disk.

When you click this item you usually get a dialog box asking you what drive you want to clean up. Typically, this is the C drive.

Once you select the drive, you'll see a menu of items that can be checked or unchecked. For the most part, you can go with the default selections. Most are temporary files that you probably don't need. If you have any doubt, you can select View Files for any checked item to see exactly what files the program is about to delete. Obviously, if there is a file you think you might need, don't let this feature delete it. Once you've finished checking and unchecking items, click OK and Windows will delete the checked files.

Rearrange Items on Your Hard Disk

This option really does improve your PC's performance. Let me explain.

Over time files on a computer disk become **fragmented,** which means that bits and pieces of each file are scattered throughout the disk. This doesn't prevent Windows from accessing the data (Windows is smart enough to put the little pieces back together), but it can slow down access as your disk drive's read-write heads have to jump all over the disk to find the data. When you select this rearrange option, Windows defragments your hard drive by putting all the data back in order so that files are contiguous. This is a great program to run once a month or so, but it takes a while to defragment a disk so it's best to use it when you're about to take a break.

Power Options

One last option to talk about under Performance and Maintenance: I live in California where saving energy isn't just a matter of saving money, it's also a way to help prevent "rolling blackouts." Although PCs aren't the biggest energy hogs in the world, considering the number of them, they collectively put a lot of strain on our power system. You can do your part to save energy (and money) by taking advantage of Windows XP's energy-saving features.

The Power Options in Windows XP tell your PC to go into **sleep mode** after whatever period of inactivity you specify. You can have Windows turn off your monitor or hard disk (or both) and put your system into **standby mode,** which requires only a fraction of the power that normal operation uses. Don't worry, your computer won't shut down while you're using it. The times that you set determine how long Windows will wait before it takes action, but the clock stops whenever you press a key or move the mouse. So, if you set the monitor to turn off after 30 minutes, that's 30 minutes from the last time you touched the mouse or keyboard.

You'll notice that there are several optional "power schemes," depending on the type of machine you're using and how you use it. If you have a laptop you might want to use a more aggressive power-saving scheme when the machine is running on batteries than when it's plugged into the wall. Windows knows whether your machine is plugged in and will switch power schemes accordingly.

Printers and Other Hardware

As I've mentioned, in most cases, the Plug and Play feature of the most recent versions of Windows will automatically recognize any hardware you install and prompt you to insert a CD-ROM or other necessary software. It's a great option, but Plug and Play only works if the hardware maker has embedded a little information about the hardware on a chip in the hardware itself.

If Plug and Play doesn't work, or if you want to remove hardware you have already installed, you might have to use the Printers and Other Hardware section of

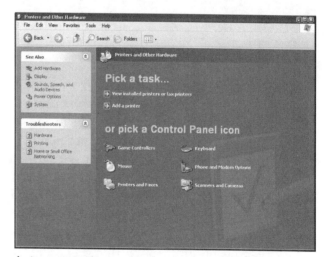

As its name implies, you can use this section of the Control Panel to install and uninstall printers and other hardware.

the Control Panel. This area can also change the way your printer operates. For example, you can use this to tell your printer to use draft mode (which is usually the fastest) instead of normal mode. (For more on printers, see Chapter 19.)

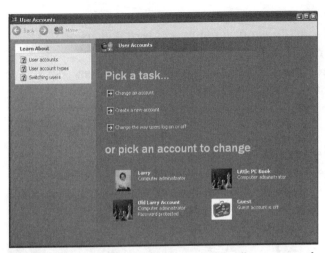

XP allows you to create separate accounts for different users of the same machine.

User Accounts

Let's say you have programs that you use to keep track of your personal finances, but you don't want your kids or other members of your household to access those programs. You can set it up so that those programs show up in your Start menu, but not in the Start menu of other users.

You can also create your own environment—your own screen saver, your own desktop, even your own customized version of many programs. You might, for example, want to install a program that keeps your kids away from inappropriate content on the Internet (see Chapter 51) but not put such restrictions on the accounts used by adults. And you might also want to assign a password to each member of your family so that other people (your kids' friends, for example) can't mess with your files or programs. All of this customization is done by creating separate user accounts through this section of the Control Panel.

Adding and Changing User Accounts

The process of adding, changing, and deleting user accounts is pretty straightforward. To create a user account you have to have "computer administrator" privileges. This means that you need to be signed on in an account that's set up for an administrator. If you were the one who set up your PC, then you probably do have administrator privileges.

User Accounts Are Not All That Secure

Before you set up you user account, you should realize that even with a password they provide only a low level of security. Anyone with a little advanced skill can work around them. The Windows user accounts and passwords are not meant to provide fool-proof security.

Windows does allow you to make certain folders private so that other users can't see them. Create a folder inside My Documents and right-click on it. A pull-down menu will appear. Select Sharing and Security and another menu will appear. Check "Make this folder private." No one else will be able to access the contents of that folder.

Also don't confuse XP user accounts with Internet accounts. A user account is simply designed to divide the machine up so that different people have different experiences with that particular machine. It has nothing to do with the Internet. (For information about Internet accounts, see Chapter 51.)

To set up an additional account, click Create a New Account and fill in the name you wish to give the account. It can be one or more words like "Susan Smith" or "Jimmy's PC Account."

Click Next and you're asked whether that account's privileges should be administrator or limited. An administrator account has all privileges, so that the person can do anything with the PC, including wiping out other people's accounts and files. A person with a limited account can still do some damage, but not as much or as easily as with an administrator account.

Once you've established the account, you can click on Change an Account and make modifications, such as adding a password or changing the default graphic that goes with the account. (You can even use a digital photograph for this.)

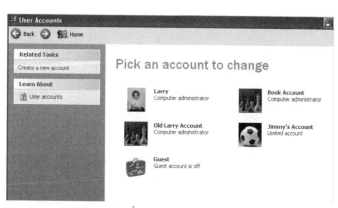

Here are some of the different accounts on my computer. See the little black-and-white picture next to my name? That's me when I was a baby.

Date, Time, and Language and Regional Options

For reasons I've never understood, the clock on that expensive computer of yours isn't as accurate as most cheap watches. Fortunately, Windows lets you change the time on the clock and in Windows XP you can now automatically set it to one of the **atomic clocks** (accurate to within a fraction of a second) over the Internet. You can even have Windows synchronize the clock weekly, so it's never far off.

You can also use this area to change the date and the language that XP displays and set certain regional options, such as the way numbers, dates, and currency are displayed. If you are using your PC primarily to write to people in another country, you might consider making that country's regional options the default.

Accessibility Options

This section can be very helpful to people whose vision is impaired or who have other conditions that make it difficult to use a computer. For example, you can make the type larger by changing the default font size or set the **StickyKeys** options so that you don't have to use two hands to issue certain commands. The best way to adjust your PC is to use the **Accessibility Options** wizard by clicking Configure Windows to work for vision, hearing and mobility needs. Like most wizards, this one is self-guiding so there's really no need for me to document it. (See Chapter 31 for more about using wizards.)

The Help and Support Menu 31

Select Help and Support (in the second column) from the Start menu...

The Help and Support menu provides lots of information about Windows XP, including a section on "What's New in Windows XP" and information about printing, faxing, networking, and troubleshooting. The help system may not answer all of your questions (that's why you need this book), but it will take you a long way. And, unlike a book, the help menu is interactive. If you don't see a topic that meets your needs, you can search for just about anything.

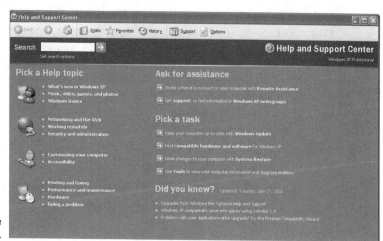

...to access the Windows help system.

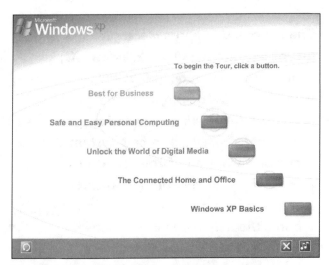

To begin the Tour, click a button.

Best for Business

Safe and Easy Personal Computing

Unlock the World of Digital Media

The Connected Home and Office

Windows XP Basics

Choose the type of help that best suits your needs.

Windows Tour

To get the most out of Windows, you really should take the **Windows Tour.** If you haven't already come across an invitation to take the tour (or if you want to take it again) you can find the tour by typing tour into the Search box in the upper left-hand corner the help system and clicking the arrow. That will show you a list of search results that includes the Windows Tour. Or you can select Help and Support from the Start menu, then choose What's new in Windows XP, and finally, Taking the Tour. When you click the Tour entry, first you'll get an animated and audio tour beginning with what amounts to an advertisement from our friends at Microsoft.

Windows Update

One new feature of Windows XP is that you can tell it to update itself and some of the hardware drivers over the Internet. (Of course, to use this feature you have to be online.) You access it from the Help and Support section of the Start menu by selecting Keep your computer up-to-date with Windows Update. That will

Getting Additional Help

For additional help, consult the Knowledge Base on Microsoft's Web site (http://search.support.microsoft.com). It's the same tool that Microsoft tech support people use when they're baffled.

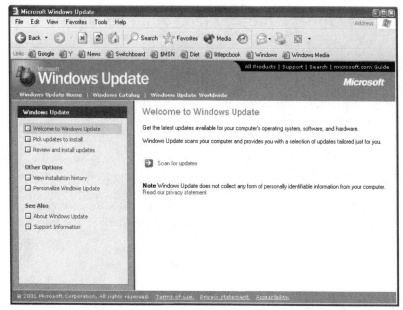

Click Scan for updates to see whether your hardware or software has been modified since your machine was last updated.

take you to the Windows Update screen, where you can click Scan for updates. Windows will then check your hardware and software and then go to a special Microsoft Web site to see whether anything has been modified since your machine was last updated. If there are updates, Windows will automatically download the new software for you to install.

The first time you go through this process, Windows may ask you to check a box to confirm that you "trust" software from Microsoft. This is a way to allow people to block automatic downloads to protect them from hackers or viruses. Regardless of your personal feelings about Microsoft, I think it's safe to assume that you can trust the company not to deliberately plant a virus on your computer.

Does Windows Update Jeopardize Your Privacy?

You certainly have a right to ask whether Windows Update in anyway violates your privacy. After all, you are sending data from your PC to Microsoft. Microsoft has a privacy policy for Windows Update posted online that assures users that the company "does not collect your name, address, e-mail address, or any other form of personally identifiable information." Microsoft has also gone to great lengths to reassure people that they are not uploading any personal data files.

Now, maybe you're a conspiracy theorist and suspect that the company's lying about this, but I honestly think that Microsoft has other things on its plate besides collecting trillions of bytes of personal information from millions of users. (Now, if you happen to work for the Justice Department or one of Microsoft's competitors, all bets are off. Just kidding!) There are plenty of reasons to be concerned about privacy, but I wouldn't lose sleep over this one. (For more on protecting your privacy, see Chapters 38 and 51.)

Wizards

One last thing about getting help: As you use Windows XP and many Windows applications, you'll probably come across some wizards, like the Maintenance Wizard and the Accessibility Wizard. These are not magical people in strange hats, but tools that help you accomplish certain tasks.

A wizard, in most cases, is an automated guide that gets you through a task step by step. Some wizards are almost fully automated: Just tell them what to do and sit back while they carry out the task. Other wizards act more as advisors that help you along the way. Almost all wizards, however, do at least part of the work for you, while most help systems simply tell you how to fix the problem yourself.

The key to using a Wizard is to pay close attention to the onscreen instructions. Generally you move on to the next step in the wizard by clicking the Next button but, sometimes you can skip several steps and cut right to the chase by clicking a Finish button.

Working with Files 32

The My Computer icon in the Start menu is your gateway to much of what is on your computer, including all of your disk drives which, in turn, store your files.

If you click My Computer and then double-click your C drive, you'll probably see a screen telling you that your files are hidden. But if you click Show the contents of this folder, you'll see all of the folders on your hard drive. You might also see some file names, if there are any files in the main directory of your hard drive. Then you can click any file folder and open any folders within those folders to locate your files. (I'll discuss more about folders in Chapter 34.)

A word of warning: Whenever you access files, you can get yourself into trouble. If you delete or rename the wrong file, you could lose data, find yourself unable to run a program, or even cause Windows to crash. (That last one isn't very likely, but it is possible.) That's one reason that Microsoft wanted to hide all of your files on the desktop. If Bill Gates had his way, you would only access your files through My Documents, My Pictures, and My Music. That route is fine for many users, but there are also a lot of things you can do within the operating system if you know how to get around.

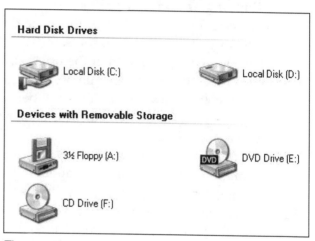

There are the various disk drives on my computer.

Loading a File and Program By Clicking

No matter how you choose to display your list of files, double-clicking a file in the list will open that file, usually with the program that created it. XP knows what program should open the file based on the file's extension. You may not see it but every file has a three-digit extension at the end (such as .doc) that tells Windows what type of file it is. So Windows can load that program along with the file you double-clicked. This link between the file extension and the program is established by the Setup program when you install any new program. (See Chapter 33 for more on extensions.)

Copying and Moving Files

You can copy a file either in the same directory or a different directory. If the copy is in the same directory, the new file must have a different name than the original. If it's in a different directory, it can have the same name, though that's not a good idea because it can lead to confusion. When you move a file, you are removing it from the directory (or disk) where it was and moving it to a different one.

There are two basic ways to copy or move files in the My Computer area, as well as an optional (and I think easier) way using Windows Explorer, which I'll discuss later in this chapter.

The first way only works if you can display both the window your file is now in (the source folder) and the window you want to move or copy your file into (the destination folder). To move your file, click it once with the left mouse button and, while holding the button, drag it to the destination folder. If you want to copy it using this method you need to right-click the file, drag it to the new location, and when you let go select Copy from the list that pops up. If you select Move, your file will be moved and if you select Create Shortcut Windows will place a Shortcut to that file in the destination folder.

The second method works even if you can't see both windows. Just right-click the file or folder and in the menu that pops up, select Cut if you wish to move it and Copy if you wish to copy it. (Cut may sound like you're deleting your file, nothing actually happens to it until you Paste it in its new location.)

Caution: Moving Files Can Cause Problems

Moving files can sometimes cause a program to stop working. While it's generally OK to move data files, it's not OK to move program files—those that end in .exe, .dll, .dat, and certain other extensions. The Setup program that you used to install your program placed files in certain locations for a reason and the program expects them to be there. If they're not where the program expects them, the program will likely either not run properly or not run at all.

Then, find the folder where you wish to place the object, right-click the new folder, and select Paste from the menu that pops up. If you initially selected Cut, your file or folder will be moved to the new location. If you selected Copy, a copy will be placed in the new location.

Windows Explorer

As an alternative to clicking on My Computer and navigating through your folders, you can also access any folder or file using a program called **Windows Explorer.** Not to be confused with Microsoft Internet Explorer, Windows Explorer has nothing to do with surfing the Internet; it's only for browsing your own PC or files on your network, if you have one.

The advantage of Windows Explorer is that it makes it a lot easier to copy or move files and folders by dragging and dropping from the main window on the right to another folder.

To run Windows Explorer, click the Start menu and select All Programs (the green arrow near the bottom). Now select Accessories, followed by Windows Explorer. When you're in Windows Explorer, you'll see your folders on the left. If you click a folder, you'll see all of its files in the large area to the right. You can view the contents of Windows Explorer using Thumbnails, Tiles, Icons, List, and Detail, just as you do when you view folders from My Computer. The process is exactly the same.

Click on the magnifying glass to access the Search tool.

Searching for Files

XP has a very powerful tool for finding files. It's called Search and you can access it directly from the Start menu by clicking on the magnifying glass. The search tool can search all the disks on your machine as well as any other computers on your network. It can also search the Internet.

When you open the search system, you'll see a menu that lets you choose what type of file to search for. If you know you're looking for a picture, music, or video file, go ahead and use that option. If it's a type of file not listed or you're not sure, use the All files and folders option. That searches everything.

Once you select the type of file, the Search system asks you some additional questions. For example, if you're searching All files and folders, you will be asked to enter all or part of the name of the document you want, or alternatively, a word or phrase within that document. Seach will then ask you to fill in the Look in box so that it knows where to search for the file.

Finding a File or Folder

When you're looking in a folder with lots of files or subfolders, you can sometimes save a bit of time by typing the first letter of the folder or file. The cursor will jump to the object so you can select it immediately. If there is more than one folder or file the starts with that letter, just press the same letter to jump to the next one.

Searching can take a while, but the more information you can provide the faster it will go. For the fastest results, enter at least part of the file's name. If you enter some text from the file instead, the search will take considerably longer. Similarly, if you don't know the file's location, you can speed things up by clicking "When was it modified" or "What size is it" to provide more information.

Once you find a file or folder using Search, you can open it, copy it, delete it, or use any other commands, just as you would within any other window.

Copying Files to a CD

If you have a CD-R or CD-RW drive, you can write your own CDs. Although there are commercial programs that help you create CDs, Windows XP lets you copy files from your hard disk to a CDR without any special software.

To copy files to a CD, just insert a blank CD into your CD-R drive. If the drive window doesn't open automatically, go to My Computer from the Start menu and double-click the drive.

This should open a CD Writing Tasks window that you can use to copy any type of file from your hard drive to the CD. At this point, go back to My Computer, find the files you want to copy to the CD, and drag them into the CD's Window. When you click Write These Files to a CD, Windows will pop up a CD Writing wizard that will walk you through the rest of the process.

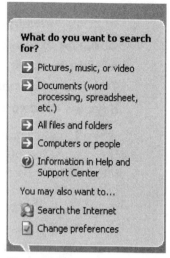

Choose the type of file you want to search for.

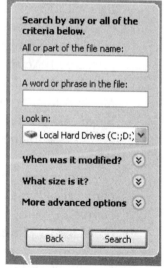

The more information you provide, the faster your search will go.

33 File Naming Conventions

Windows files have two names—a first name and an exten-sion. The extension is usually three letters added at the end of the file name that tell Windows what kind of file this is. The two names are separated by a "dot" (what in the old days we used to call a period).

If you look at your file names in My Documents you may not see the extensions but they're always there. For example, if you have Microsoft Word on your PC, all of your Word documents will end in .doc. If you have Excel, all of your spreadsheets will end in .xls. You've heard of MP3 files, the music files that people like to download—well, guess what, they all end in .mp3.

There are literally hundreds of different file extensions, but the good news is that you usually don't have to worry about them. When you install a software application, the setup program auto-matically associates that software with the extensions that it opens. For example, when you install Microsoft Office, the Office setup program automatically associates .doc files with Word, .xls files with Excel, and so on.

Also, Windows automatically associates certain extensions with certain programs. Files ending in .txt, for example, are asso-ciated with Notepad, the basic text-editing program that comes with Windows. Likewise, files ending in .mp3 or .wma (Windows Media Audio) are automatically associated with Windows Media Player. So if you double-click a file with one of these extensions, Windows launches Windows Media Player and plays the song in that file.

Sometimes, though, there is more than one program that can access the same file type (often these programs are from competing companies). For example, there are a number of other media players besides Windows Media Player. If you install the RealPlayer from Real Networks (www.real.com) or WinAmp from NullSoft (www.winamp.com), these programs will attempt to change the default association for .mp3 files from Windows Media

Player to themselves. They usually give you a chance not to accept the change, but if you just click OK to each question the setup program asks, you can bet that program will "steal" the association from Windows Media Player. The same is true with other file types. Some programs don't even ask your permission. If that ever happens to you, I suggest you write an email to the company expressing how you feel about that practice. Personally, I think it's a dirty trick.

Unhiding File Extensions

By default, Windows XP hides the extensions for file types it knows about. I hate this feature. Sure, the screen is a little less cluttered without them, but it can be really useful to see the extensions, so you know at a glance what type of file you're dealing with. Fortunately, it's easy to change this.

First select My Documents from the Start menu. Click the Tools menu and select Folder Options, then the View tab. Scroll down to Hide extensions for known file types and click

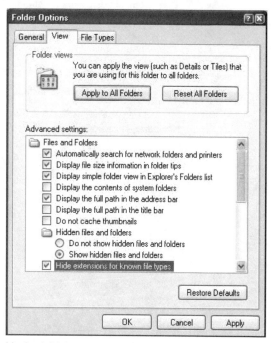

Uncheck Hide extensions for known file types.

the box to uncheck it. Finally, click Apply and then OK. But be sure not to check or uncheck anything else unless you're sure you know what you're doing. If you make a mistake, you can always click Restore Defaults to put everything back to the Windows XP defaults.

Common File Extensions

Extensions Associated with Programs

.AAIF	Audio file mostly used on Macs
.AU	Audio file mostly used in Unix
.AVI	Video for Windows
.BMP	Bitmap graphic
.CDA	Compact disc audio (a standard audio file for commercial audio CDs)
.CLP	Windows clipboard
.CSV	Comma-delimited format used to exchange files between spreadsheet programs
.DBF	Database
.DOC	Word processor text, including Microsoft Word
.EPS	Encapsulated PostScript file (used in Adobe PhotoShop and other high-end graphics programs)
.GIF	Bitmap graphic
.HTM	A Web page
.JPG	Bitmap graphic
.MID	MIDI music file
.MOV	QuickTime movie
.MP3	MP3 music file
.MPG	MPEG video file
.PDF	Adobe Acrobat file
.PNG	Type of graphic file
.RAM	RealAudio file
.TIF	Bitmap graphic
.TXT	Plain text
.WAV	"Wave" audio file
.WKS	Microsoft Works or Lotus 1-2-3 spreadsheet
.WMA	Windows Music Audio file
.WPS	Microsoft Works word processing file
.XLS	Microsoft Excel spreadsheet

Common File Extensions *(continued)*

Program Files

.COM   A type of "executable" program (not to be confused with the "dot com" Web site designation)

.DAT   Special data that the program itself uses

.DLL   Stands for "Dynamic Link Library," but all you need to know is that it's put there by a program and that you mustn't delete it. The same is true of .DAT, .IFN, and .SYS files. Don't mess with them unless you really know what you're doing.

.EXE   The main program file for an application

.INF   "Information" that the program uses to store certain default settings

.SYS   System files created by Windows

Naming Files

You can call a file anything you want as long as it doesn't contain more than 256 characters and doesn't contain any of the following forbidden characters:

Forbidden Characters:

\\   backslash

/   forward slash

:   colon

*   asterisk

?   question mark

<>   angle brackets

| bar

If you try to name a file with invalid characters, you'll get an error message, warning you of your mistake.

Changing the Program that Opens a File Type

You can always change file associations if you want to, regardless of what program created the files.

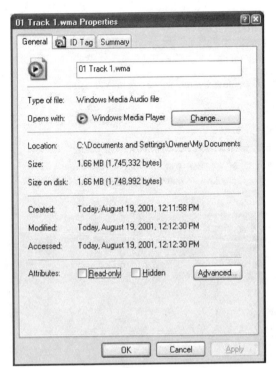

To change the program that opens the file click Change.

First, locate the file whose association you want to change (either by clicking the directory where it is stored in My Computer or by using the Search command in the Start menu). Then right-click the file name and select Properties from the context menu. Near the top of the Properties dialog box, find the Type of File section and click Change to change the program that opens the file. Next use the pull-down list to select the program you wish to associate with that file type. If you can't find the program on the list, click the Browse button and browse through your folders until you find it. (It will probably be in a subdirectory of your Programs directory.) Caution: If you associate a program with a file type, the change will affect all files of that type, not just the file you started with. Make sure the program really is compatible with that file type: Microsoft Word, for example, can't play a media file.

Working with Folders   34

In the last two chapters, you learned all about working with files. Soon you'll have so many, you'll wish you had a place to put them. That's where folders come in.

Remember, in XP, all your files are hidden by default until you click Show the contents of this folder. When you reveal the contents of your C drive you'll see a number of folders, including one or more with whatever user names you created when you set up Windows XP. That's where Windows, by default, stores your documents. Shared Documents is where you can store documents that can be accessed by anyone using your computer. The folder cannot be made private. The rest of the folders belong to individual users.

Creating a New Folder

Windows comes with several folders for your files but you can add as many folders as you want. You can put folders anywhere: on the desktop, on the C drive, or within other folders. You can, for example, create subfolders within My Documents,

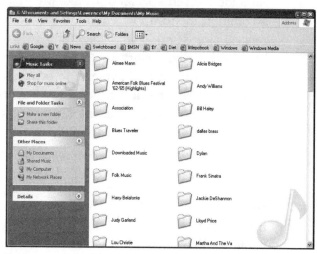

Folders inside My Music help organize my music collection.

My Pictures, and My Music to organize your documents in ways that will make sense to you. You can even have sub-sub folders or folders within folders. For example, inside My Music you could have a folder for Folk Music and another for Rock and Roll. Inside Rock and Roll you could have one for The Rolling Stones and another for Janice Joplin. (OK, I'm dating myself by my taste in music, but you get the point.)

To create a new folder, navigate your way into a folder and right-click anywhere inside the folder. That brings up the context menu for folders. Select New, followed by Folder. Windows will create a new folder and name it New Folder but you can immediately rename it just by typing, as long as you haven't clicked the mouse button again. If you've already clicked the mouse button you can still rename it, it just takes more work.

You can rename any folder or file by right-clicking it once and selecting Rename from the context menu. This is the same menu you use to delete, open, copy, or create a shortcut to any folder or file.

Common Attributes of All Folders

All folders (even special ones like My Pictures and My Music) have a common menu and a common way of behaving in Windows. Just like most programs, folders have a set of menus that include File, Edit, View, Favorites, Tools, and Help.

You can use the File menu to create a new file or a shortcut or to delete or rename a file. For anything other than creating a new file, you first need to click the file you want to affect and then make your selection from the File menu.

You can use the Edit menu to copy, cut, or paste a file just as you do in programs, or to copy or move a file to a particular folder. Highlight the file or folder you wish to copy, cut, or paste, and select the command from the Edit menu. If you're copying or cutting it, go to the folder where you wish to paste it and select the paste command. The cut command doesn't remove the file from where it is until you have successfully pasted it somewhere else.

The View menu affects how your folders will look. You can show or hide toolbars or the status bar (at the bottom of the screen), and you can view your files and folders in a variety of alternative ways, such as thumbnails, tiles, icons, list, and detail. (We'll talk more about all of these options in a moment.)

The Favorites menu is based on the same menu in Internet Explorer. It lets you add your favorite Web pages, folders, or files to the menu so you can get to them quickly. For example, if you're in My Documents and you click Favorites then select Add to Favorites, your My Documents folder will be accessible from any other folder (or even from Internet Explorer) using the Favorites menu.

The Tools menu can help you map a network drive so that it looks as if it were a local drive on your PC (see Chapter 37). You can also use the Tools menu to change folder options and synchronize local files and folders to their counterparts on other computers on your network.

Help brings up the Windows help system.

Folder Controls

Title bar
Displays the name of the object (file or icon) you're looking at. Drag the title bar to move the window on screen.

System icon
Click here to view the System menu.

Menus
Choose commands to act on the contents of the window.

Toolbar
Click on a tool to quickly execute a command.

Status bar
Lists information about the contents of the window. The Status bar is optional. You can turn it on and off on the View menu.

Minimize button
Click here to remove the window from the desktop without closing the file.

Maximize button
Click here to make the window fill the screen. If the window is already full size, click here to shrink it.

Close button
Click here to close the window. If the window holds a file, closing the window also closes the file.

Scroll bars
Click in a scroll bar or drag the scroll box to view more of the window's contents. (Scroll bars appear only if the window is too small to show all of its contents).

Border
Drag the border to resize the window. (The pointer turns into a double-pointed arrow when it is positioned correctly over the border.) Drag a corner of the window to resize the window in two directions.

Every window has a standard set of controls.

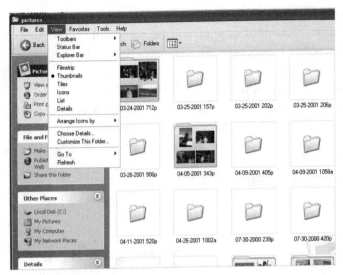

The View menu lets you change the way you see files and folders.

Using the View Menu

Now comes the fun part. You can use the View menu to change how you see the files in your folders or even the folders within the folders.

Most of the options—Thumbnails, Tiles, Icons, List, and Details—apply to any type of folder. The Filmstrip option applies only to folders that contain digital images (pictures).

Choosing Thumbnails gives you a look into the document, whenever possible. With some types of files, such as photos and Web pages, you'll see a tiny preview of what the document will actually look like. That's very handy, because you pretty much know what you're going to get before you open the file.

The Tiles option is similar to ordinary icons but the tiled icons are larger and offer more information, such as the size of the file and the name of the program used to create it.

The Icons option shows a picture representing the file and the name of the file.

Choosing List provides a listing of the files and folders.

Details is by far the most useful way to display files. It not only provides the most information, but it lets you quickly sort your files by the criterion you choose and even in the order you

Tiles are basically the same as icons only larger.

choose. When you first click Details you'll see, by default, an alphabetical list of your files with columns headed Name, Size, Type, and Date Modified. If you click on the top of the column, the files and folders in the list will be sorted by that criterion. If you click the column heading again, you'll see a little arrow flip to the right of the word, and the list is re-sorted in the opposite order (if your list was A to Z, it will now be Z to A). For me, the most useful way to display files is by Date Modified, with the arrow pointing down; that sorts the files by date with the most recent first. If I'm working on a document, chances are pretty good that the one on top will be the one I want.

In addition to giving you control over the presentation of files and folders, XP also lets you arrange or sort them in a variety of different ways. If you click Arrange Icons by in the View menu, you'll see that the options are name (sorted alphabetically), size (sorted by the size of the file), type (arranged by the type of file such as a .doc file or a .exe file), and modified (which sorts files by the date and time they were modified or created).

Creating and Using Shortcuts

If you see an icon with a little arrow at its bottom, that's a short-cut icon. Shortcuts in the Start menu don't have an arrow, but they're essentially the same. Shortcuts are pointers to programs or files that exist somewhere else on your computer. They give you easy access to that icon from the shortcut's location.

One popular use for shortcuts is to place icons for often-used programs, folders, or files on the desktop, where you can get to them easily. By putting a shortcut of the object (instead of the object itself) on the desktop or in the Start menu, you keep the original object safe in its folder with the other files it needs in order to work correctly. You also avoid the confusion of having multiple versions of a file scattered throughout your hard disk. You could make a copy of the object instead, but shortcuts take up very little storage space. Another important difference between a shortcut and its original program icon is that if you delete the shortcut you don't delete the program, but if you delete the program's original icon, you're actually getting rid of the program itself.

Adding Shortcuts

You can make shortcuts to any icon: a disk, folder, file, program, or anything else you want quick access to. One way to make a shortcut is to right-click on the original object's icon and choose Create Shortcut from the context menu. That will immediately create a file called Shortcut to whatever in the same directory. If Windows can't put the short-cut there, it will offer to place it on your desktop. Either way, you can move (drag or Cut and then Paste) that shortcut to wherever you want it.

Outlook Express
Shortcut
1 KB

Shortcut icons usually have an upward-pointing arrow at their bottom-left corner.

If you're making a shortcut of a program icon to place on the desktop or in the Start menu, there's an even easier way. Just drag the program icon to the desktop or Start menu, and Windows automatically creates a shortcut there.

Yet another way to make a shortcut is to right-click any icon and drag it to a new location. When you let go of the right mouse button, Windows will ask you if you wish to Move, Copy, Create Shortcut, or Cancel. Select Create Shortcut and you'll have a shortcut to the item. Be careful not to select Move, as moving a program icon to the wrong location could cause the program not to work.

You can have several shortcuts to the same thing; for example, you can put shortcuts to the Calculator in any folder where you might need it. You can also rename a shortcut anything you like. (Right-click the icon, choose Rename from the context menu, and type a new name.) When the shortcut is no longer useful, you can just delete it and the original program stays safe. (Just be sure that the icon you're deleting has a little arrow pointing to it, showing that it's really a shortcut and not the program itself.) In the case of the Start menu, don't worry about the little arrow because the Start menu only holds shortcuts, not programs.

If you wish to place a shortcut to a program or file in the Start menu, simply left-click and drag it into the menu. Normally that procedure moves the file, but the Start menu is special. Any time you drag something to the Start menu, Windows creates a shortcut to the program or file and leaves the original where it was.

35 Working with Programs

Obviously, the steps you take to alter a digital photograph in an image-editing program are different from those you take to write a letter in a word-processing program. Likewise, two competing word-processing programs may have subtle differences in the way they work. But most Windows programs have some similarities. That's good, because once you've learned to use one, the rest are a lot easier to master. It also makes transferring data between programs a much simpler task.

No matter what program you're using, there are a few basic tasks—things like creating, opening, saving, printing, and closing files; moving, copying, and deleting parts of files; and exiting the program—that you'll always need to do. The steps covered in this chapter are likely to be the same or nearly the same with almost all of the programs you use. In some cases, you may click an icon instead of selecting a command from a menu, but most programs offer both and let you choose.

Expanding Menus

Microsoft Office and some other programs have short menus and long menus. Short menus are a bit more user friendly because they don't present you with too much information. But, as you might expect, they're also limited in what they can do.

Microsoft Office has an interesting trick: The menus expand as they are used. So, you may see a Short menu, but at the bottom of each menu are a pair of downward facing arrows. If you click on them you'll see more options. If you select an option, it magically appears on the menu for future use on the assumption that you are likely to use it again. If you don't use it, it will eventually disappear, but it can always be found by clicking on those down arrows.

Explore Your Options

Whenever I try out a new program, I check out the various menus, just to see what they offer. Call me lazy (I prefer "adventuresome"), but sometimes I do that instead of reading the documentation

because it lets me learn by doing. I also recommend exploring any icons that are displayed on
the screen. Sometimes the functions of those icons
are less than obvious, but often if you hold the
cursor over one for a few seconds, a text box will
pop up with an brief explanation. Also, see if there
are some hidden toolbars with even more options
for you to explore.

The Open command
in the File menu of a
Windows program
opens a new, blank file.

The File Menu

Virtually all programs have a File menu which is
used to create a new file, save existing files, and
issue print commands. Sometimes the File menu
has other options as well.

Creating a New File

Creating new files is easy. In most cases, you'll find a New command in your program's File menu that does the job, creating a
blank file in a new window. Often, a program will create an empty
file automatically when you start the application.

Some programs also have icons that you can use to create a new
file. Typically they look like a blank sheet of paper.

The Edit Menu

The edit menu can house lots of commands, but it almost always
features Cut, Copy, and Paste, the three commands you'll use
most often when you're editing a document. They let you move a
part (or all) of your document from one place to another—either
within the same document or to another document altogether.
Copy leaves the information where it is and lets you Paste a copy
of it somewhere else, whereas Cut deletes it from its original location before letting you Paste it somewhere else. Cut is the first
part of moving something, and copy is the first part of copying it.
Paste is the second part of both.

Using Cut and Paste to Move Data
Between Documents

Remember this little trick the next time you need to get a graphic, for example, into a word-processing program. Instead of trying to open the file in your word processor, just open the original file, select the part you want to copy, and paste it into a word processing file. You can practice this now:

1. Use the Start menu to open the Paint Application (it's in the Accessories area).

2. Paint something and then select it using the selection tool in the upper right corner.

3. Copy part or all of your painting into the Clipboard. (Use the Copy command in the Edit menu or the Copy button on the toolbar.)

4. Open WordPad (also in the Accessories area).

5. Click in the WordPad window and choose the Paste command (from the Edit menu or the toolbar) to paste the picture into your WordPad document.

To use these functions, first highlight the section (usually by dragging over it with the mouse). Then choose Cut or Copy from the Edit menu and that data goes onto something called the Windows Clipboard, an area of memory that stores images, text, spreadsheet data, or anything else until you put it somewhere else. To place it in its new position, you just move the pointer to the new position and choose Paste.

Undoing What You Just Did

Another common editing command you'll learn to love is the Edit menu's Undo command. It does just what it says: It undoes your last action, whether that's typing, deleting part of your document, adding a new color to a picture, or any other operation.

Usually it just works on the last action you took, though there are some programs with multiple levels of undo. That means you can undo an Undo command (in effect, redoing whatever you just undid) by giving the Undo command again. (In such programs, the command usually changes to Redo in the Edit menu.) In other programs, gving the Undo command again and again lets you undo several editing steps, which enables you to return to an earlier state of the file if you decide you've taken a wrong turn in the editing process.

Select All

Some Edit menus offer the Select All command, which selects all of the data in a document, making it easy to copy it into another document or change a font. Be very careful how you use it, though. Once all the data is highlighted, you can erase it just by pressing any key. Once I left a document open with the all the data highlighted and my cat walked across the keyboard, wiping it all off the screen. Fortunately, she didn't step on the Save command so I was able to recover the data by closing the file without saving (see "Closing a File" later in this chapter).

Find and Find and Replace

The Find command is sometimes (but not always) located in the Edit menu. You'll find it in all word processing programs, spreadsheets, Web-editing programs, and even Internet browsers. When you select Find (or Search, as it's sometimes called), a dialog box pops up with a text box. You simply type in a string of characters you want to find and the program locates them for you. Usually the Find command is not case sensitive by default, but if it is, there is usually a way to adjust that.

Some programs also have a Find and Replace command, which allows you to automatically modify text by replacing one word or phrase with another word or phrase. This can be a great time-saver, but it should also be used cautiously. Rather than using the automatic Find and Replace option, you can usually choose to approve each change individually, just to make sure the search command doesn't make a mistake. For example, if you want to replace "man" with "person" throughout your document, you would type "man" in the Find text box and "person" in the Replace text box. But if you let the search command automatically replace every "man" it finds, what happens when it comes across words like "manual" or "mandate"? "Persondate" isn't in my dictionary, although it does seem somewhat politically correct.

Spell Checkers

As long as we're on the subject of mistakes, be careful with spelling checkers, too. (They're often found in the Tools menu in word-processing programs.) My kids' school papers never have spelling mistakes, but they have all sorts of incorrect words that come from letting the spell checker make a correction without looking at it carefully. I'll admit, once I misspelled "warehouse" by typing "wherehouse." The spell checker changed it to a word that's spelled almost the same by simply replacing the first e with an o. Now that's an embarrassing mistake.

Format Menu

Not all programs have a Format menu, but many do. This is usually used to set the fonts, line spacing, and other formatting issues. Often there are different levels of formatting such as Font and Paragraph. Font usually refers to specific information about the style and size of type. Paragraph settings refer to the overall look and feel of the document such as line spacing, margins, etc. It's also common for programs to have rulers and other ways to adjust margins and page settings.

Ironically, the Format menu is rarely used to adjust the format of the printed page. That is usually done with a menu item called Page Setup, which is typically in the File menu. Go figure.

Saving Your Work

When you open a file, whether you're creating a new one or opening one that already exists, the program creates a space in your computer's memory where it keeps the information while you work with it. Remember what I told you about memory, though: Anything in memory exists only as long as the computer is on. To keep the file safe when you turn off the computer, you must give it a name and save

The Edit menu displays short-cut keys to the right of each command.

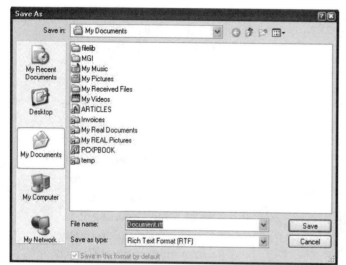

The first time you save a document, the Save As dialog box (this one is from Windows WordPad) will appear asking you to give the file a name and choose the directory you want to save it in.

it to disk. You can save a file by selecting Save from the File menu. The keyboard shortcut—the gesture that should become automatic—is usually Ctrl+S (pressing the Ctrl and S keys at the same time). The first time you save a document, Windows will display the Save As dialog box, where you can name the document and select the folder you want to save it in. Every time you save after that, the program will save your changes in the same document and in the same directory.

Many programs help you out with an automatic save feature, which saves the file every few minutes. (You can usually set the interval or turn the feature off in the program's Preferences dialog box.) This can be a lifesaver if you're absent-minded.

Programs often have a Save icon which typically looks like a floppy disk.

Keyboard Shortcuts

Windows XP has lots of keyboard shortcuts, which are handy ways for experienced users to save time. Here are the most commonly used shortcuts for programs:

Commands from the File menu

Save	Ctrl+S
New	Ctrl+N
Open	Ctrl+O

Commands from the Edit menu

Undo	Ctrl+Z
Copy	Ctrl+C
Cut	Ctrl+X
Paste	Ctrl+V
Select All	Ctrl+A
Find	Ctrl+F

To learn these shortcuts, remember that you usually type the Ctrl key plus the first letter of the command. If you forget, they are displayed next to their commands in most menus.

Just under the Save command in the File menu you'll notice another command, Save As. You can use this command to save a file under a new name, in a different format, or in a new location. This lets you use one file as a template for several others. If you want a new document to be patterned on an older one, you just open the old file, select Save As, give the file a new name in the Save dialog box that appears, and click OK. This results in two files: the old one, still saved under the old name, and a new one, under the new name, that you can edit to create a new version.

Auto Save

Some programs give you extra protection with Auto Save, which periodically preserves both the last version and the current version of any open file. This is a lifesaver on those occasions when you do something bad to your file (like delete most of it) and then absentmindedly save the messed-up version. You can often check the configurations of Auto Save in the program's Preference menu.

Why You Should Save All the Time

I'm not naive or egotistical enough to believe that you're going to pay attention to everything I say, but in this case, please do—it's very important.

Common sense might suggest that you should save your file to disk once you've finished working on it. Wrong. *You need to save your file every chance you get:* when you get up to stretch, when you stop work for a minute to think about what you're going to do next, when you switch between programs, and especially when you answer the phone. It should become an automatic gesture. When you create a new file, it's a good idea to give it a name and save it right away, before you even start to work on it. Once it's saved the first time, you can save it easily at short intervals.

YOU WILL SAVE YOUR WORK FREQUENTLY. YOU WILL SAVE...

Why? Because more often than you might expect, something goes wrong. If your cat trips over the power cord, if a three-car pileup a mile away takes out a power line, or if your computer just freezes up (which it sometimes will, believe me) and you need to restart it, you will lose everything that isn't saved to disk. Perhaps the most important time to save is just before you print a document, since printer problems are probably the most frequent reasons computers freeze up. Another time to save is if you want to start using another application program. If that program "crashes," it could bring your whole system down with it. That's not supposed to happen, but life doesn't always work out the way we plan.

Invariably, thanks to Murphy's law, foul-ups become almost inevitable just before a deadline, or when you've just created something that will win you international fame—and you haven't saved. Don't worry about saving too often. That's impossible.

Changing File Extensions in the Save As Dialog Box

As I discussed in Chapter 33, Windows uses a file extension to identify which program each file belongs to. That's how Windows knows which program to use to open the file. Programs can only work with files that are in a file format they recognize. Almost every program has its own proprietary format in which it saves the files it creates. Application programs can usually open files in a few different formats—their own proprietary format and some others as well.

Some programs let you use the Save As command to assign a different extension to a file. In most word-processing programs, for example, you can save a file as ".rtf" (Rich Text Format), which is a good thing to do if you plan to send the file to someone who uses a different word processor. Most photo-editing programs have their own file format but they also let you save files as ".jpg" (JPEG) or other commonly used formats. (For more on JPEGs, see Chapter 45.)

Just typing in the new file extension doesn't usually create a new format. Usually you have to select it from a drop down menu in the Save As dialog box.

Printing a File

The Print command is almost always in the File menu, and the keyboard shortcut is usually Ctrl+P. Many programs also provide a print option on the toolbar—just press the icon that looks like a printer.

Giving the Print command will bring up a Print dialog box, from which you can select options such as print quality and the range of pages you want to print. There is often a Properties button which gives you even more options such as quality (draft, normal, or "best" mode), whether or not to use color and so on, depending on the options supported by your printer. The printing dialog box is controlled, to a certain extent, by the driver software that came with your printer. (For more on printers, see Chapter 19.)

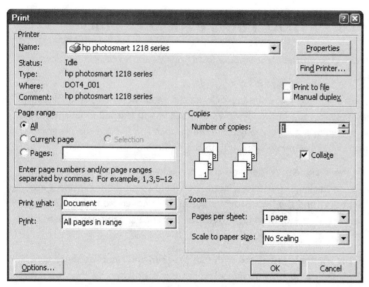

You can select from many options in the Print dialog box.

Closing a File

When you're done working on a file, you close its window. You can do this by clicking the window's close button, or you can use the application's Close command (Ctrl+W), which you'll find in the File menu.

When you close a file, the computer just removes the file from its memory. Closing is different from saving, and if you don't save your work before you close the file, any work you've done since the last save will be lost. If you haven't saved all your changes when you give the Close command, the program will usually notify you of that and ask you if you would like to save your changes before closing. If you don't get the "Save changes?" dialog box when you close a file without saving first, that's probably because your program has an automatic save feature that has already done the job for you.

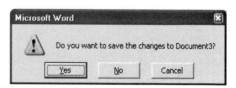

If you try to close a program without saving your work, most programs will ask you if you want to save changes before you leave the program.

Minimize, Close, or Exit? They're All Different

All three of these functions remove the file's window from your desktop, but each command has a very different effect.

Minimizing a window doesn't actually close the file, or even the window. When you minimize a window (by clicking the minimize icon in the window's title bar, as you learned in Chapter 34), the window remains on screen as a program button in the taskbar. The file and the program stay open in memory, just as if the window were still on the desktop.

Closing a window is a bit more extreme. When you close a window (by choosing Close from the window's File menu or by clicking on its close icon), the window and the file inside it are closed (removed from memory), and the file's program button is removed from the taskbar. But closing a window—even if it's the only window open for a particular program—doesn't exit the program.

Exiting a program closes any windows associated with that program and removes those files, and the program itself, from the computer's memory. You can exit a program by choosing the Exit or Quit command from the File menu (Ctrl+Q) or by shutting down your computer.

Windows Accessories 36

Windows comes with a number of programs, called accessories, that perform a wide variety of functions from entertainment to helping with critical system tasks. The accessories are stored in their own portion of the All Programs area of the Start menu.

If some of them look familiar it's because other areas of Windows commands (such as the Control Panel) have their own accessories, which you can access from either place. If I've already covered an accessory, I'll let you know where, so you won't waste time reading about it again here.

Accessibility

Accessibility Wizard. Covered in Chapter 31.

Magnifier. This is a cool accessory that makes Windows look as if you're viewing it through a magnifying glass. Try it even if your vision is not impaired. It doesn't make any changes to your system, just gives you a really close look at a portion of your screen.

Narrator. This accessory reads aloud to you. The voice isn't exactly natural—it sounds like a drunken Scandinavian. But if your vision is impaired, it can make your life a lot easier.

Here is a list of all the categories of accessories.

Use your mouse to type with the onscreen keyboard.

Onscreen Keyboard. The onscreen keyboard is designed for users whose mobility is impaired. You can type by selecting the key from the keyboard that pops up on the screen.

Utility Manager. This tells you what utilities are running and allows you to set which Accessibility features will start automatically.

Communications

HyperTerminal. This program lets you log on to a computer as if you were using a "dumb terminal" (a type of terminal program used extensively until the early '90s to log on to computer bulletin boards and online services). If you need further information, search for Hyperterminal in the Windows Help system. The rest of the Communications accessories are covered in Chapter 37.

The Communications section of accessories features HyperTerminal and several networking options.

Entertainment

Volume Control.
Covered in Chapter 30.

Sound Recorder.
Sound Recorder is a
fairly basic utility that
allows you to record
audio from a micro-
phone or other audio
device that is plugged
into the your sound
card. There are several

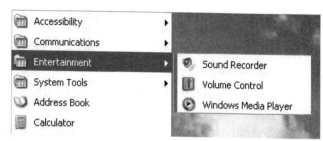

The Entertainment accessories menu by default contains short-
cuts to Sound Recorder, Volume Control, and Windows Media
Player. It might also include other installed software such as the
RealPlayer from Real Networks.

more sophisticated sound-editing programs, but Sound Recorder
is a good place to start. Actually, there are some neat things you
can do with this program. First, be sure you have a microphone
plugged into your sound board or the sound input socket on your
laptop. There may be multiple inputs and sometimes the icons
they use to label these sockets are confusing. Assuming you figure
out where to plug it, try running the program, clicking the red
Record button, and talking. If the levels are too loud or too soft
you can change them using the Volume Control accessory.

The Sound Recorder inter-
face should look familiar to anyone who's used a tape recorder.
You can use the arrows to
rewind and fast forward or you
can drag the bar just above the
arrows to get to the right position. Once you've created a
recording you can save it. Then
you can include it in any document, even in Microsoft Word or
WordPad. Just load the record-

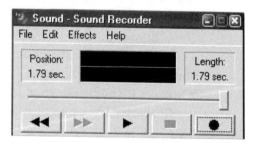

Sound Recorder looks like a tape recorder. Use
your mouse to click on the arrows for rewind,
fast forward, play, stop, and record (left to right).

ing you wish to copy, select Copy from the Edit menu, and use the
Paste command in the Edit menu of whatever program your document is in.

When you paste a sound recording into a document, you see a little speaker. If you click on that speaker, you'll hear the recording.

Windows Media Player. Covered in Chapter 27.

System Tools

Activate Windows. In order to prevent piracy, Microsoft is requiring everyone who purchases XP to "activate" it over the phone or Internet. Then, if you try to install the same copy on another computer, it won't work. (Microsoft says that you won't have any problems if you upgrade your machine or even replace the hard disk.) The activation process is pretty easy and doesn't send any personal information to Microsoft (unlike registration; see Chapter 42). If you don't want to Activate Windows when you install XP, you'll be reminded to do so later. However, if you don't Activate Windows within 60 days of installation, XP will stop running.

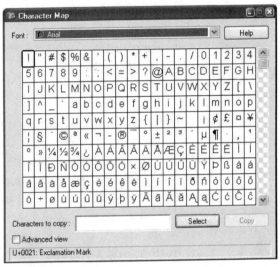

Click on the down arrow to the right of the font name to select another font.

Character Map. Ever wonder how to get special characters like a copyright symbol (©) into a document? One way is with the Character Map accessory. You can insert any of these characters into most Windows documents simply by clicking it, then clicking Copy, returning to your document, and issuing the Paste command from the Edit menu.

File Transfer Wizard. This program lets you save and transfer settings from Internet Explorer, Outlook Express, other programs, and even your desktop from one PC to another. The wizard works by creating a folder with files that contain your settings. When you run it, you need to tell it what settings or documents to transfer and where to put the files. If you have the two machines connected (with a cable or over a network), you can place the files directly on the new machine. But you can also place the files on your old machine or on a removable drive that is connected to your old machine but movable to your new one. Having your settings on a removable drive is also helpful if you ever have to restore your machine after reinstalling Windows (for example, if you install a new hard drive or experience a really bad system crash).

Scheduled Tasks. If you have a program that you need to run regularly, you can do it automatically using the Scheduled Tasks program. Some anti-virus and personal finance programs will schedule tasks for you automatically so you don't have to think about them. But, if you want to schedule something on your own, unschedule something, or just check what's scheduled, you can run this program.

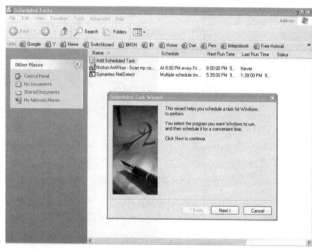

As soon as you open Scheduled Tasks, you'll see a list of programs that are currently scheduled. Double-click a task to

The Scheduled Tasks program helps you set up other programs to run automatically.

see when the program will run and get other information. You can then change or delete the task, the schedule, or the settings. If you want to add new tasks, select New from the File menu, give the task a name, and double-click the name to enter the settings. If you want the task to run a program, you'll need to use the Browse feature to locate the program's icon.

The Calculator is simple and easy to use.

System Restore. Covered in Chapter 38.

Calculator. This accessory is pretty straightforward. You use it as you would use just about any four-function calculator. It's not very fancy but, unlike that pocket calculator I bought for $5, I can always find this one when I need it. Note that you can transfer data or results between the calculator and other programs using the Calculator's Edit menu.

Command Prompt. If you've been using computers for a long time, you may remember the MS-DOS command prompt (the old PC interface before Windows). It's still there, you just don't usually see it. Believe it or not, there are still some things you can do with the command prompt.

NotePad and WordPad. Windows comes with two text editors, Notepad and

The MS-DOS command prompt lets you type in commands.

WordPad. The difference between the two is that Notepad is a bit more rudimentary and it can only be used to open and edit standard text files.

WordPad, which is just shy of a full-featured word processing program, is actually pretty good. It has word wrap (which automatically formats the lines as you type), lets you use multiple fonts, and does lots more. About the only major thing missing is a spell checker. WordPad can be used to open and create most of the same files as Microsoft Word. So if someone sends you a Word file (ending in .doc), you can try opening it in WordPad.

Tour Windows XP. Covered in Chapter 31.

Windows Explorer. Covered in Chapter 32.

Windows Movie Maker. Covered in Chapter 44.

Networking

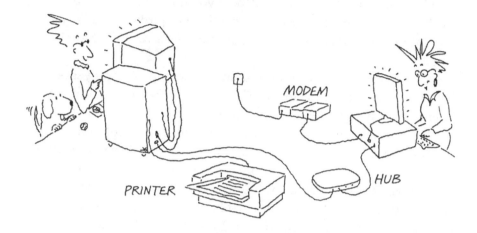

Computers are no longer isolated islands of information. You can connect two or more computers using wires or radio waves, locally or over the Internet. Connected computers can exchange information and share printers other resources.

For years, it's been common for businesses, government agencies, and universities to tie all of their computers together in a local-area network, or **LAN.** But now, an increasing number of households have two or more PCs, so LANs are showing up at home as well.

Whenever you have more than one PC, it's quite handy to be able to share resources and data between them. A LAN is one of the easiest ways for all the PCs in the house to share the same Internet connection as well as a single printer. You also can use a LAN to access files on other machines. (In fact, even if you only have one computer, you may need to set up a rudimentary LAN if you get a high-speed Internet connection such as a cable modem or DSL.)

Network Wires

Windows XP comes with the software you'll need to set up a network, but of course it doesn't come with the hardware. So before I go into the software part of the equation, let's review what else you'll need.

Until recently, a LAN required special wiring. Several years ago, I hired a contractor to run Ethernet cables (more about this later) between a couple of rooms in my house. But we didn't wire the entire house, so the LAN only existed in those two rooms.

But the wiring hardly matters any more. Now there are LAN kits that use standard phone wires or no wires at all. In fact, I wrote part of this chapter from my bedroom with the laptop connected to my bedroom phone jack, and I've worked on other parts of this book from my backyard using a wireless LAN adapter.

To set up a network you'll need some type of **hub,** or central controller, and you'll need a **network adapter** in each PC that you want to connect. (Don't be intimidated by the word hub: It's a simple and inexpensive device. For as little as $25, you can get a four-port hub that will support up to four PCs.) Unless you opt for a wireless LAN, you'll also need wires to connect your PCs, though you may be able to use the phone wires that you already have in your house.

The type of equipment and wiring you'll need depends on the type of network you wish to set up. The good news is that you can mix and match network types and equipment from different vendors, because there are industry-wide standards when it comes to networking.

Ethernet

Let's start with the Ethernet network commonly used in businesses, universities, and many homes.

An **Ethernet** network uses special wires to connect several computers and a central hub. The wires look sort of like phone wires, but the cable has several strands of wire instead of just two strands. These wires are called 10BaseT or Category 5 (insiders call it "Cat 5"). You don't need to know much about the wires themselves other than that they end in a connector, called an RJ-47 connector, that looks like a bigger version of the connector used for phone wires. You just plug one end into the Ethernet connector on each PC and the other into a hub, which is like a power strip for data.

Some PCs now come with Ethernet adapters. If yours doesn't have one, you can buy one for as little as $20. They typically plug into a PC expansion slot inside the machine, but you can also buy Ethernet adapters that plug into the USB port so you don't have to take your machine apart. For laptops, you can buy an Ethernet adapter that plugs into the laptop's PC card slot.

Alternatives to Ethernet

Of course, Ethernet isn't the only thing out there. You can also set up a wireless home network or one that operates through regular phone lines.

A wireless LAN uses short-range radio waves to transmit signals throughout your home or office. Don't confuse this with "wireless Internet," which you can use anywhere. A wireless LAN only extends for the range of its "base station" (basically a transmitter/receiver). You put the base station somewhere in your home and install wireless network cards or devices in each machine on your network, so they can talk to it. An increasing number of companies (and some universities) are using wireless because it allows employees (or students) to access the LAN and the Internet from any location in the building or the campus.

The technology used for a wireless LAN is called *802.11b* or "WiFi"; it transmits data at 11 Mbps, which is faster than any cable modem or DSL service. (The older 802.11 technology operated slower and isn't compatible with the faster 802.11b products out today, so be sure to look for the "b." That said, the 802.11A technology now being developed will be about 10 times faster.) Companies that make 802.11b adapters and base stations include 3Com, SohoWare, SMC Networks, Nortel, D-Link, NDC Communications, and Cisco Systems. Both 2Wire and 3Com offer home gateway products that offer multiple services, including standard wired Internet and wireless and phone wire networking.

There are basically two uses for this technology. The first is simply as an alternative to Ethernet LANs. The second, more exciting, use is in public locations such as airports, hotels, and coffee shops to allow visitors to access the Net from their laptops. That's how I'm able to access the Internet from my local coffee shop. In fact, many Starbucks now have 802.11b adapters which you can access for a fee. I hang out at the Palo Alto Cafe, which offers them for free.

Piggybacking on Phone Wires

Another method of home networking uses standard phone wiring. The best thing about this technology, called home phone line alliance (HPNA), is that you don't have to run any new wires. HPNA "piggybacks" data on your phone line, so you use the existing wires in your home to connect your computers and still use the computers, the network, and your phone all at the same time. You simply plug your hub into a phone jack and, using a special adapter, plug each PC into a phone jack connected to the same line. I've tested it in my home and it works.

You can get a listing of companies that make HPNA equipment at www.homepna.org. Most of these same companies also make wireless and Ethernet equipment.

Do You Need a Router?

If you're setting up a network just to share data between your home PCs, you probably won't need a "residential gateway," or router. But if you want the machines on your network to share a single Internet connection, you may need one. However, there are a couple of ways to get around using a router. One is to use multiple IP addresses, and another is to use one of the PCs on your network as a server that connects all of the other machines.

By now you're probably either frantically searching the glossary or questioning the claims that this book is user friendly, but before you demand a refund, let me explain a little about IP addresses and servers so that you can decide on the best setup for your network.

IP Address and DHCP

Without going into too much detail, I'll just tell you that "IP" stand for "Internet protocol," and every machine that's connected to the Internet needs to have its own IP address. It's a unique code that identifies that machine to the world—a little like the license plate on a car. When you get a cable modem or DLS, you usually get only one IP address, which means, in theory, you can use it to connect only one computer.

Although some cable modem or DSL services provide you with extra addresses, there is a way to "fool" the system so you can connect more than one computer, using only one IP address. This is known as a DHCP server (short for dynamic host configuration protocol). Basically, your entire network uses the "real" IP address, and each individual computer on the network is automatically assigned an internal address. The rest of the Internet doesn't even know that they're there and just sends all messages (email, Web pages, whatever) to the network, where DHCP sorts it all out.

Some cable modem and DSL services automatically support DHCP, but most don't. Most give you a single IP address or have some other way to "limit" you to only one computer. But there are two ways you can get around that.

One method is to connect only one computer on your network to the Internet and then let all the others connect through it. That "master" computer, then is acting as a kind of server.

The method I prefer is to install a Residential Gateway, or **router,** on your network. The router uses DHCP to create as many IP addresses as you need. You don't need to do anything special with your PC. In fact, Windows is designed to use DHCP by default, so if you plug your computer into that router or into a hub that's connected to it, Windows will automatically assign itself an IP address that will let you access the Internet.

Is this legal? In most cases, yes, it is. Some cable modem and DSL services do specifically prohibit routers in their Terms of Service agreement, but a lot of companies have no such restrictions. It's a little like hooking up several phones to a single phone line or several TVs to a single cable TV outlet.

Routers Are Easier Than You Think

I realize that all this sounds complicated, but it doesn't have to be. Residential Gateways start at about $125 and are pretty easy to set up. About the only complication is that you might need some fancy information from your Internet service provider such as your IP address and "gateway." You usually access the router by entering a number or a set of words in your Web browser and you enter the data in a form that pops up on your screen. Once you configure your router, you're done because XP is preset to address any router you attach.

There are also products called home gateways, that simplify things even more. A home gateway is basically a combination router and hub, and they're usually easy to set up.

Configuring XP for Networking

Setting up a Windows network used to be a daunting task and it can still be troublesome. Although, Windows XP has a Network Setup wizard that makes the process a lot easier, I have to admit that I've had Windows networks fail to work, even under Windows XP. The technology is great when it works but there are times when it mysteriously fails to work. So if you have problems, don't feel stupid.

Before you run the networking wizard make sure you have all your hardware installed and working.

1. Click the Start menu, and select All Programs followed by Accessories. Click on Communications followed by Network Setup Wizard.

The Network Setup Wizard walks you through the process of configuring XP for networking.

2. When the wizard comes up, click Next, heed the warnings on the screen, and click Next again.

3. If you have more than one device in your machine that can act as a network card, Windows may highlight one of those devices and say that it's disconnected. But it gives you the option to "ignore disconnected hardware." Check that and click Next.

4. You will then be asked to make your first decision. The wizard will ask you to check one of the following:

This computer connects directly to the Internet. The other computers on my network connect to the Internet through this computer.

OR

This computer connects to the Internet through another computer on my network or through a residential gateway.

There are other options, including connecting directly to the Internet through a hub.

I'm going to assume that you've taken the easy way out and are connecting your machine through a residential gateway. (It really is the easiest and safest way to connect.) If you bought a router it is for all practical purposes the same as a gateway, so click on the residential gateway option.

5. Check the option that lets Windows "Determine the appropriate connections."

6. Click Next and enter a description of your computer, such as "The one in the den."

7. Give the computer a name. Each computer on your network must have a unique name.

8. Microsoft will assign your network the name MSHOME. Either accept by clicking Next or enter a different name.

9. Wait while Windows configures your network. This can take a few minutes.

At this point you have the option to "create a network setup disk." If you select that option you'll be asked to insert a floppy disk. Windows will then write a floppy disk that you can use to configure other machines on your network so you won't have to enter all of this information again. When you want to configure another machine on the network, just insert that disk into the new machine's floppy drive, select My Computer from the Start menu, double-click the A drive, and double-click the Netsetup icon. That will bring up the same network wizard but some of the questions will be answered by the information on the floppy disk. (You'll still need to name the computer.)

It's Not Foolproof

I wish I could tell you that everything will work from now on, but I'm not 100 percent confident when it comes to Windows networking. I'm not saying that you shouldn't try but just be aware that networking isn't exactly a walk in the park. Things can go wrong and if they do don't blame yourself. Just get help from someone with a bit more experience. And watch what that person does, so next time *you'll* be the person with a bit more experience.

Preventing and Recovering from Disasters   38

GRANDMA, READ A REALLY SCARY STORY.

HERE'S ONE ABOUT A YOUNG ASTRONAUT WHO TRIES TO SAVE TIME BY NOT BACKING UP MISSION-CRITICAL FILES.

~ NO WAY.

Computers are pretty reliable these days, but they're far from perfect. There are a number of things that can go wrong, ranging from software glitches to human error. There are also non-computer-related disasters that can affect your data, like earthquakes, fires, floods, and theft. Although you can't predict what will happen and when, you can at least be prepared for the worst.

Backing Up

The one thing I can say for sure about backing up is that it's important. It may not even be a disaster that undoes all your hard work. I can think of several times when I've wiped out a file or two by mistake, just dragging the wrong thing into the Recycle Bin. And laptop computers are especially vulnerable to being lost, stolen, or damaged.

I think you get the picture. The point is: Back up early and back up often. You can never be too careful when it comes to your precious data.

Built-In Backup Program in XP Professional Edition

Windows XP Professional edition does have built-in backup software. You can access it from the Performance and Maintenance section of the Control Panel by clicking Back Up Your Data.

The Backup Your Data section features a Backup or Restore wizard that walks you through the process of backing up and restoring your files. It's pretty straightforward and self explanatory, but the trick to making it easy is to have some type of storage device—other than a floppy disk—that allows you to store large amounts of data on a single disk. An external hard drive is a good candidate, as is a Zip drive. Although a CD-RW drive is a good choice, it doesn't work with this software.

Once you've backed up, you can use the same Control Panel feature to restore the data to your hard disk. Run the wizard again, select Restore files and settings, click Next, and click on the + sign to the left of the File icon in the left side of the What to restore box that pops up. Finally, click on the drive you want to restore to followed by Next.

Now the good news: Backing up isn't nearly as difficult as it used to be. And you don't necessarily need to back up up everything on your computer. Don't worry about backing up your software as long as you have your original installation CDs or copies of those CDs. You can always reinstall the software, but you can't recreate the data.

While the Home edition of Windows XP doesn't come with a built-in backup program, there are still several ways to back up your data just in case

Backing Up to CD

One option is to get a CD-RW drive (discussed in Chapter 13) that lets you write to CDs. A CD is a great way to back up data because you can store up to 700 MB on a single disk that costs as little as 30 cents. All CD-RW drives come with software that lets you copy files. Although some people like to use the rewritable CD-RW discs for their backups, I prefer the single-use CD-R discs. First, they're cheaper, and second, they're easier and faster to write. Finally, the whole idea of a backup is to have a permanent copy of important data. If you update your data, just burn a new CD.

Your CD-RW drive will come with software, as well as instructions on how to copy files, but you may wish to check out some

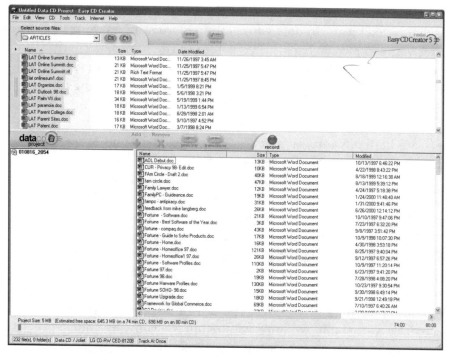

I use CD Creator to back up all the articles I write for the *Los Angeles Times*.

other CD-RW programs. By far the most popular software is Easy CD Creator from Roxio. To back up files you run the software and simply drag the files or folders to the appropriate spot on the screen. You can also use the CD copier feature built into Windows XP.

Backup Hardware and Software

There are lots of other backup devices besides a CD-RW drive that you can purchase, including Zip Disks from Iomega (www.iomega.com) and various tape backup systems. You can also get an external hard drive such as the Que QPS FireWire drive. Yet another method is to use a commercial backup program such as Retrospect from Dantz Development Corp (www.dantz.com). Any of those products will come with step-by-step instructions to walk you through the process of backing up your files.

Backing Up Over the Internet

Finally, if you don't want to deal with getting more stuff for your computer, you can always back up your files to the Internet. There are several services such as @Backup (www.@backup.com) that allow you to back up your files to a Web server for a fee starting at about $50 a year. Last time I checked, @Backup was offering a 30-day free trial.

There are both advantages and disadvantages to online backup systems. The biggest drawback is that it can be slow if you're using a standard dial-up modem. If you have a DSL or cable modem (see Chapter 20) it will still be somewhat slow but it's a lot faster than a dial-up. And you can schedule your backup in the middle of the night so speed might not be an issue. The main advantage to an Internet backup is that your files are being stored on a secure and well-maintained server that's outside your home or office. If something should happen to your PC, or even your building, your data is safe. Another advantage is that the process can be automated, so once you install the software that comes with the service, you don't have to think about it.

Starting Over

Restart is a command on the Start menu that simply restarts your computer. You'll find it comes in pretty handy if your machine suddenly slows down for no apparent reason or if some of your programs stop responding properly. Sometimes you'll use it after you install or uninstall software, too, unless the installation process restarts your computer automatically.

In theory, Windows XP doesn't need to be restarted very often because, unlike previous versions, the code is fairly stable and fairly forgiving of problems caused by software. However, there is always a difference between theory and practice. As good as XP is, it does hiccup now and then and the best cure is a good restart.

To restart your computer, go to the Start menu and select Turn Off Computer, which you'll find near the bottom right. A screen will pop up listing three options: Stand By, Turn Off, and

Restart. Click the last one and your machine will appear to power down before springing back to life.

Escaping from Trouble

If you've been using PCs for awhile, you are probably already familiar with Ctrl-Alt-Delete. By pressing these three keys at the same time, you can restart your computer.

Now, with Windows XP, you're supposed to choose Restart from the Start menu (see Chapter 39), but Ctrl-Alt-Delete still has its place. It brings up the Task Manager, which can be used to shut down individual programs that aren't behaving properly. If a program crashes, runs improperly, or simply isn't responding, you can close it by pressing Ctrl-Alt-Delete to bring up the Task Manager, clicking the Applications Tab, and pressing End Task. If you don't find the program you want to shut down on the Applications Tab, try clicking on the Processes tab. And if your computer is frozen and you can't access the Start menu, Ctrl-Alt-Delete is still a handy way to restart your computer.

The Task Manager can also be used to see how your machine is performing. The Performance tab shows you how much memory you're using and how your CPU is holding up to the demand. Likewise, you can check how your network is doing and what resources, if any, are being used by other people who are logged on to your PC.

Click End Task on the Task Manager to shut down a program that's not responding.

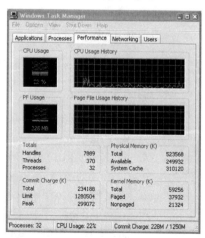

Check the Performance tab of the Task Manager to see how your PC handles its workload.

Turning Back the Clock to Recover from a Problem

Sometimes it's not what you do that's important. It's what you undo.

Say you install a program that not only doesn't work correctly but it also causes the machine to become unstable. Or you make a change to a document only to find out that you were better off before you messed with it. Or what if, perish the thought, you get hit by a virus?

I once had a PC act as if it were completely brain-dead because—as I found out about four hours later—it didn't like the mouse I had plugged into its USB port. The symptoms can vary: The machine runs a little slower than usual, programs function improperly, or the PC won't even start.

If something does suddenly go wrong, your first line of attack should be to think about what you did just before you noticed the problem. If you installed a new piece of software or hardware, there's a reasonably good chance that's the culprit. Consequently, my strategy is to try to undo whatever I just did. If I just installed software, I try to uninstall it. If I just plugged in a new board or a USB device, I unplug it and restart the computer. If all is well, then I contact the manufacturer or publisher of the offending product to see if there's an explanation.

System Restore: Your Built-in Life Saver

Windows XP comes with a program called System Restore, which can be a real life saver if something goes wrong. It can restore your computer's software configuration to its previously happy state.

You can access System Restore from the Help and Support Menu by clicking Undo changes to your computer with System Restore, or you can access it from the System Tools menu by clicking Start and selecting the green All Programs icon, followed by Accessories, then System Tools.

System Restore doesn't affect your data. If you delete a data file or write over it, this won't bring it back. But System Restore will undo any changes to your Windows XP operating system— including installing software.

For System Restore to work properly, it has to have what are called restore points. These are points where you have taken a snap shot of your XP configuration. Once you've done that, you can return to that particular configuration. You can do it manually, but XP also does it automatically for you at certain intervals.

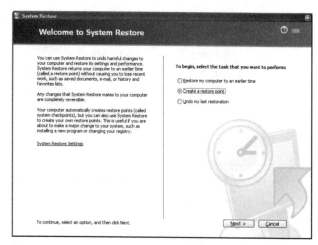

First click Create a restore point and then, if something goes wrong, you can select Restore my computer to an earlier time.

Still, I like to manually set a restore point if I know I'm going to do something potentially dangerous, such as installing a piece of software I downloaded from the Internet.

To manually set a restore point, run System Restore and click Create a restore point. When you click Next, the program will ask you to give the restore point a name. You might type in "Just before installing XXX" or maybe the date. Either way, it will also assign a time and date to the restore point. Then, if something goes wrong, you can run System Restore again and select Restore my computer to an earlier time. At that point, you'll see a calendar. Pick a time and date that precedes your problem. Don't go back too far, though, because if you've done

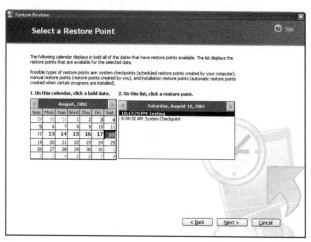

Pick a time and date that precedes your problem.

any good stuff since the restore point you pick, such as installing software you want to keep or making configuration changes that are OK, you'll loose that, too.

Windows will then ask you to restart and when it reloads it will be just like it was at the date and time of the restore point. I think that's pretty cool.

Recycle Bin

If you accidentally delete a file, you can bring it back to life by double-clicking the Windows **Recycle Bin,** single-clicking the file you want to restore, and selecting Restore. That puts it right back where it was. Once you choose Empty Recycle Bin, though, you can't restore anything unless you use a utility program such as Norton Utilities that includes an "unerase" feature. Even Unerase doesn't work 100 percent of the time, but it's more reliable than the restore feature built into Windows.

Viruses, Worms, and Trojan Horses

By now you've undoubtedly heard about viruses. The "I Love You" virus was all over the news back in 2000 after it infected millions of computers. The "Code Red" worm also made the news, because it wormed its way into hundreds of thousands of Internet servers. Neither of these famous viruses wiped out data—they just clogged up the Internet and annoyed people. But viruses can and often do destroy files on people's PCs.

In fact, viruses can do an entire range of damage, from minor annoyances to major catastrophes.

Viruses, worms, and Trojan horses are all malicious and potentially destructive computer programs, but they are somewhat different. A **virus** is a program that you have to run before it will do any damage. It can be an executable program (which typically ends in .*exe*) or it can be a script or macro that is run from within Windows or a Windows program. Word files (generally ending in .doc), for example, can contain a virus because Word has a macro language that can execute mini-programs from within Word. Still, even if a virus is on your machine, as long as you don't click it (open it) it can't do any damage.

A **worm** executes all by itself. Once it gets onto a machine, it runs itself and does the damage. Worms usually affect servers and other machines attached to a network, but they can also infect PCs.

A **Trojan horse** (like the one in Homer's *Iliad*) appears to be a benign program but it's actually destructive. Like viruses, Trojan horses can't do any damage unless you open them; but since they look like something else, people do click on them all too often. So, to put a modern spin on the old moral of the story, beware of geeks bearing gifts.

You'll often hear the term *virus* used to include worms and Trojan horses. All of them can be spread by floppy disks, Web sites or downloaded programs, and even instant messages. But the most common means of transmission is by email. Someone sends you a message with an attached file and, if that file contains a virus, it does its dastardly deed as soon as you open it. Of course, you can set your email program not to automatically open attachments. That way, if you don't recognize the sender, you can delete the email without opening the attachment.

Unfortunately, that's no longer a foolproof way to avoid viruses. It's common these days for viruses to send themselves automatically (replicate) to people in your email address book, especially if you're using Microsoft Outlook or Outlook Express. Consequently, you might get a virus from someone you know because your name and email address is in your friend's address book. So if you get a file, even from a friend, don't open it unless you know that person intended to send it to you. If you're in doubt, write that person a note or make a phone call to be sure it's a clean file.

As a general rule, I think people should avoid sending attached files with email whenever possible. Then we'd all be a bit more circumspect whenever we received one. Many times, you can just write a regular email text message or copy and paste the text from the word processing program into the email program. Besides, attached files are much bigger than regular email messages which mean they take longer to send and receive and put unnecessary traffic on the Internet which slows things down for us all.

The best way to protect yourself from viruses is to avoid them and, as it turns out, there are a number of software programs that help you both avoid viruses and get rid of them should you become infected. The two leading anti-virus companies are Symantec and McAfee. You can find out more about Symantec's program, Norton Anti-Virus, at the Symantec Anti Virus Research Center (www.sarc.com). That Web site also provides a great deal of information about viruses. McAfee's Web site (www.McAfee.com) has software you can purchase or download as a free trial, as well as plenty of information.

McAfee also offers Internet-based anti-virus protection. When you sign up at the Web site (and pay the annual fee), the site automatically installs a small program on your machine that prompts the McAfee Web site to scan your machine and rid you of any viruses it finds. Because it works over the Internet, it's always up to date.

Whether you use software or an Internet-based anti-virus service, it's important that you keep it up to date. Norton Anti-Virus, for example, has a "live update" feature that checks Symantec's Web site for any updates. The people who write viruses are constantly coming up with new ones, but the anti-virus professionals are hot on their heels with free updates to the software. Be sure to update yours often.

Fending off Internet Hackers

If you have a broadband Internet connection such as DSL or a cable modem, the good news is that you probably enjoy full-time high-speed access to the Internet. The bad news is that someone else could be enjoying access to your computer.

Being constantly connected to the Internet increases your risk of being hacked—anything from a harmless prank to the destruction of data on your hard disk. But there are safeguards that can protect your machine from invasion—including some that are free.

People who log access the Internet with a standard dial-up modem are not totally immune from someone peering into or damaging their machines, but the odds of an incursion are much lower. Windows users who have a broadband connection and share their files with others on a network are more vulnerable because current versions of Windows make it possible for even unsophisticated hackers to gain access to your hard drive.

I found that out when I gave Steve Gibson, president of Gibson Research, permission to break into my PC. I told him my Internet protocol, or IP, address—something he could have figured out on his own—and five minutes later, he had complete access to my machine. He told me the names of several files on my hard drive, then he planted a file on my Windows desktop. It was an innocuous text file, but it could just as easily have been a virus designed to destroy files or invade my privacy.

Gibson's Web site (www.grc.com) includes several free utilities to test whether your machine is vulnerable. One utility, Shields Up, probes your PC to see just how open you are and reports that to you. After running that program, I closed the holes it exposed.

The best way to protect yourself against hackers is to put up a "firewall" between your computer and the Internet. This doesn't prevent you from accessing the Net, but it does prevent unauthorized people from accessing your PC.

A **firewall** can be hardware or software. If you have a network, you may already have a piece of hardware called a router, which can prevent hackers from breaking in. This isn't the same as a network hub or a cable or DSL modem, so don't assume you're protected unless you know you have a router with a built-in firewall.

But even if you have a router, you're not safe from a Trojan horse that sends data from your PC to someone else. For that, you need software that blocks both unauthorized incoming and outgoing traffic between your PC and the Internet.

One of the best firewall programs happens to be free. Zone Labs (www.zonelabs.com) offers a free version of its ZoneAlarm firewall software to individuals and nonprofit organizations. The company sells a more sophisticated version, ZoneAlarm Pro, for $39.95 to businesses and individuals who want to be able to customize their level of security.

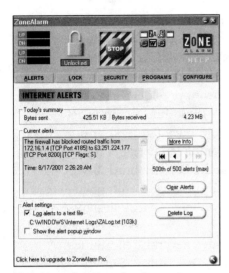

ZoneAlarm free firewall software detects an online intruder.

ZoneAlarm blocks all programs that try to access the Internet, but you can tell it to let certain ones through. Of course you'll authorize your Web browser and email program to access the Net. But if a program you're not sure about tries to access the Net, you can click No and block that program from sending or receiving data.

ZoneAlarm also blocks access to your PC by others and provides a log showing you whether anyone has tried to probe or invade your machine. It's free insurance and well worth the few minutes it takes to download and install the program.

Shutting Down, Standing By, 39
and Logging Off

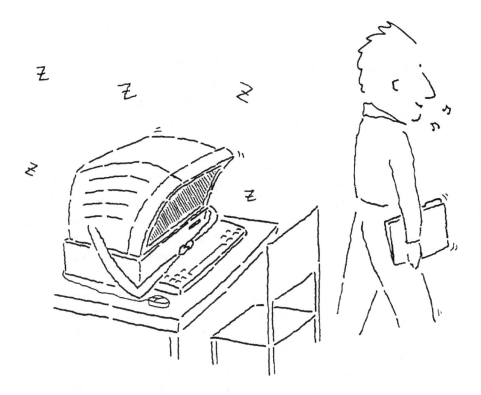

PCs are great but there are times when you want to—or must—do something else, like eat a meal, walk the dog, go to sleep, or spend time with a loved one. When that time comes, don't just walk away—think for a moment about whether you need to shut down your PC or put it to "sleep."

First, make sure you save and close any files that are open. As I've said in earlier chapters, I save all the time. But when I leave the PC—even just for a moment or two—I like to close the files as well. That way, I don't have to worry about something happening to them. (Remember, I have that cat who likes to walk across the keyboard, deleting data as she goes. Maybe you have a cat or a kid or some other accident waiting to happen, too.) The easiest way to make sure that all files are closed is to exit from your programs or just click the little red X in the upper right corner of each open window.

Your next decision is whether to shut down your PC, let it go into sleep mode, or log off as a user. These are all different concepts that more or less accomplish the same thing but by very different routes.

Shut Down

Shutting down involves turning off the power. But you can't just flip a switch or pull the plug. Instead, go to the Start menu and select Turn Off Computer, which you'll find near the bottom right. (Doesn't it seem odd that you select Start when what you really want to do is *stop* your PC? Just another illogical thing about computers.)

Once you select Turn Off Computer you get a screen with three options: Stand By, Turn Off, and Restart. (For more on restarting your computer, see Chapter 38.) To turn off the power, select Turn Off. If you're on a network or if you have multiple accounts, you may see a screen that says "Other people are logged on to this computer. Shutting down Windows might cause them to loose data. Do you want to continue shutting down?" If you're sure that it's not going to cause a problem for someone else, select Yes. Windows will then shut down. On most newer machines, the power will go off automatically. You may see a screen telling you it's OK to shut off your computer, in which case, turn off the power.

Choose Standy By, Turn Off, or Restart.

What Happens After an Improper Shutdown

What if your computer suddenly crashes or loses power and you don't have a chance to shut down properly using the Turn Off command? If that happens, turn your computer back on and you'll get a message telling you that your computer was shut down improperly and that Windows is checking for errors. That's just a safeguard to make sure everything is still in order with your filing system. Just let it run, and then use your computer as usual. If Windows doesn't check for errors automatically, it's a good idea to run it yourself. You'll find it in the Start menu under Programs, Accessories, and System Tools.

Stand By

Stand By doesn't actually turn off the PC, it just puts it into a low power "sleep" mode. The monitor will go dark, the disk drive will stop spinning, and the machine's CPU will go into a very low power state. About the only thing that keeps working is the memory that stores information. If your machine is in Stand By you can get it going again very quickly when it's time to resume using it. (With most PCs, you just move the mouse to wake it up from sleep mode. Others, including most laptops, require you to push a button.)

You can also configure your machine to go into Stand By automatically. Go to the Control Panel, select Performance and Maintenance and then Power Options.

Log Off

Logging Off isn't the same as shutting down, but it does close all of your programs and files. If other people use your computer and you don't want them messing with your stuff, it's a good idea to Log Off when you leave the machine. If you use a password, others can't get access to your programs or files (well, not easily anyway) without your permission. (For more on multiple user accounts, see Chapter 30.)

You can log off (or switch users without actually logging off) by selecting Log Off from the Start menu.

Even if you're not an expert yet, you now have a pretty good understanding of how Windows XP works and how to perform basic tasks. You can turn on your computer and shut it down. You're familiar with commands, files, folders, programs, and accessories. You're even ready to tackle tough subjects like networking and backing up your data. And remember, whenever you get stuck, XP's Help and Support menu can answer many of your questions.

Now that we've covered all the hard stuff, you've earned the right to have fun. So, on to part 3, "Cool Things You Can Do with Your PC."

In this section, I'll talk about all the cool things you can do with your PC. Many, like creating your own CDs, are fun. Some, like managing your finances, aren't all that much fun, but they're useful.

You'll find that you already have everything you need to do some cool stuff, just using the software that comes with Windows. And of course I'll tell you about some additional software you may want to buy so you can do even more cool things.

three

40 Stocking Up on Software

Whatever you want to use your PC for—business correspon-dence, working out a budget, touching up photographs, writing music, finding information on the Internet—you can be pretty sure there's a program to help you do it. And once you start hunting through magazines, catalogs, and Web sites, you'll find all sorts of games, utilities, and accessory software that you won't want to do without.

Software Categories

Category	What It's For
Word processing and desktop publishing	Writing and formatting documents
Spreadsheet	Working with numbers
Financial management	Managing budgets, investments, and taxes
Presentation software	Creating visual aids to accompany presentations
Graphics and image-editing	Working with illustrations, photographs, and video
Database management	Tracking lots of information
Utilities	Managing the computer itself
Entertainment	Stuff to do in your spare time
Children's software	Having fun and learning skills
Internet	Web browser, download manager, ftp
Communications	Communicating, on the Internet or off, including by email, chat, and videoconferencing

Although there are an enormous number of programs to choose from, most of them fall into just a few categories that cover most of the work you'll do on the computer. There are lots of applications that don't fall into these basic categories, too—for example, specialized programs for tasks like accounting, type design, or music composition. There are also really broad software packages that help people run all aspects of their businesses. But the software I'll be covering here fall into these "general-interest" categories:

One type of program I didn't include in this edition is personal information managers, or PIMs. These days, PIMs are often built into email programs or come with handheld devices like Palm organizers. Microsoft Outlook, which is included with the Microsoft Office suite of programs, is a very sophisticated PIM, as is the Windows Address Book that comes with Windows XP (you'll find it in the Accessories menu).

Software You Already Have

There are some simple application programs preinstalled with Windows XP, including a rudimentary word processor (WordPad), a painting program (Paint), some games, and some utilities. You'll find these programs in the Accessories menu by clicking Start, selecting All Programs, and clicking Accessories. You might find that these programs are sufficient for your needs, and you don't need to buy anything else in that category.

But you probably will want to get your hands on additional software. Notice, I didn't say "buy." Well, believe it or not, you don't always have to pay for software. No, I'm not suggesting that you steal it: There are actually programs you can get for free—with no strings attached—and some that you're allowed to try out for free and only pay for if you decide to keep them.

Choosing Software

If you do decide that you need more software in a particular category, you'll most likely find lots of different programs that do pretty much the same thing. Here are some general things to consider before you choose a software package.

What Will XP Run?

One of the nice things about XP is that it runs most of the programs designed for Windows 98, Windows Me, and Windows 2000. It won't run all of them, though, especially older games and programs that were designed specifically for earlier versions of Windows. Most software boxes and Web site download areas (and many software reviews) will list the program's minimum system requirements—the hardware and software you'll need to run the program. If you have a program that you absolutely must run and it doesn't say it works with Windows XP, check with the software developer before you upgrade to XP to make sure your program will still work. Some manufacturers made modifications to make sure their products would support XP, but they might not have updated the information yet.

Windows XP Compatibility Wizard

The Compatibility Wizard prompts you to try out the software with various Windows settings, going all the way back to Windows 95.

Let's say you have a program that doesn't work right in Windows XP, but you know it worked fine in Windows 98 or Windows Me. Run the Compatibility Wizard and select that program from a list of software that pops up. Then in the next menu, check the box telling the wizard that the program ran OK in Windows 98/Me. The wizard then asks you about display settings for that program (if that's a problem for Windows XP). XP will then launch that program with the new settings and ask you to confirm whether or not it worked. If it did, let the wizard know and from now on that program will run with those settings.

Also take note that some programs have minimum memory or storage requirements. Your PC can probably handle most of the programs you want to use, but be sure to check. Some games and graphic programs may require a certain level of graphic board.

What's Everyone Else Using?

I know it sounds strange to suggest that you do what everyone else does. (What ever happened to being your own person?) But when considering what software to buy, there are some good reasons to pay attention to what others are buying.

People who have used a program for a while can give you insights that you wouldn't have thought to ask about. A program might have a lot of important features, but it might also have a really annoying way of organizing its commands or dialog boxes. Or it could have other problems that might make it a bad choice. Ask everyone you know what they would recommend. You'll probably quickly find one or two top choices. One cautionary note, though: People often prefer the program they learned first. So you might want to casually ask what other programs they've used or how long they've been using the program they recommend.

In almost every software category there are one or two runaway bestsellers. The best-selling program isn't necessarily the best one on the market, or the best one for your own needs, but it is an important signpost if you need a place to start looking.

Some programs got to be bestsellers because they were the first on the market, so they had a head start; some bestsellers were simply marketed well. However, programs also gain popularity through word of mouth—people try the program and praise it to others, who go out and buy it themselves.

One advantage to owning a bestseller is that there will be lots of help available, both from friends or colleagues who know the program and from the books that are always available about the most popular programs. Another advantage is that you can easily share files with colleagues who are using the same program. Although it's often possible to share files between different programs, it's always easiest when the person who needs your file is using the same software.

What Do Reviewers Say?

Computer magazines and most daily newspaper have reviewers who put new products through rigorous tests. Trust me, I'm one of them! By all means, take advantage of our work. If the program isn't covered in a current issue, check the publication's Web site to see if you can find older articles. Many publications have a search feature and some provide free access to online reviews.

Where to Find Reviews of Software (and Hardware, Too)

CNET	www.cnet.com
ZDNet (includes *PC Magazine*)	www.zdnet.com
PC World magazine	www.pcworld.com
Byte Online	www.byte.com
Walter Mossberg's *Wall Street Journal* column	www.ptech.wsj.com
Mike Langberg's *San Jose Mercury News* column	www.siliconvalley.com/opinion/techtest/
PCAnswer.com	www.pcanswer.com
The resources section of LittlePCBook.com	www.littlepcbook.com
I write several columns a month which I post on my Web site along with archives of all my old columns that you can locate using the site's search command.	

What Support Is Available?

Try to buy software published by a company that offers free telephone support—it's even better if the number is toll-free. Believe me, you'll use it. These days, a lot of companies offer free support only for the first 90 days or so. In that case, take the software out of its package and try it out right away, because after the free support period is up, you'll have to start paying for help.

Also, check the Help or Support section of the developer's Web site. See if there's a forum where the company answers user questions or lets users answer each other's questions. Does the site offer free downloads of patches, bug fixes, and new versions?

What Do You Use at Work?

If you want to take work home (as if anybody really *wants* to do that), it makes sense to have the same program at home and at the office. You might want to check with whoever is in charge of the computer systems at work about how to get copies of the software for use at home. Sometimes your company can (legally) get you a free copy, or it may buy the program for you or let you use the company discount to buy it. You'll never know if you don't ask.

Is the Price Right?

Of course, cost nearly always counts. And in almost every category, you can find software that is both excellent and reasonably priced.

The low-end programs are not only often a lot less expensive than the high-end ones, but they're sometimes easier to learn and use and they take up a lot less memory and storage space than the industrial-strength programs. If you don't need all the bells and whistles, why pay for them?

Once you've checked all the sources (and your budget), of course, the final choice is up to you.

41 Where to Get Software

Now that you know what you want, where can you find it? There are lots of places you can get software, ranging from the publisher's Web site to office supply stores. There are Web sites that provide free access to shareware programs and you might occasionally be tempted to borrow a program from a friend. Here's the inside story on each option.

The Software Publisher

Usually, when software is reviewed, the publication also provides the phone number and Web address of the software publisher. That may or may not be the best place to buy it.

Some publishers insist on selling their programs at full list price so they won't undercut their retailers. Others offer a reasonable discount. Some software companies don't sell their products directly at all, but they will refer you to a local dealer if you contact them.

Some software publishers will allow you to download a trial version or enter a credit card number to purchase and download a full version. Obviously, it's best to try before you buy if that's possible. If you decide to download the full version, make sure you know how long it will take and find out if there is a refund policy. Also, be aware that you won't get a printed manual (often referred to as *documentation*), though an electronic one may be copied to your hard drive or available online.

Specialty Stores

There aren't too many computer stores around anymore but they're not totally extinct. The good news is that pretty much any store that sells hardware also sells at least some software. The challenge is finding a salesperson who actually knows something about PCs.

You'll also find computers and software at most office supply stores such as Staples, OfficeMax, or Office Depot. The best have knowledgeable staff, good prices, and enlightened return policies. The worst, of course, have none of those things.

Online

Just about anything you can buy at a store can also be ordered online, often from the store's Web site. You can also try the manufacturers' Web sites, and a number of online-only stores that sell software, including Amazon.com and Egghead. AOL users can find software vendors in the Computing Channel (keyword: Computing).

HOW'S THE NEW SOFTWARE?

A REAL DOG — MY HIGHEST RATING.

This can actually be a very convenient way to buy software because you can often get more information about a product online than you can from a catalog or a store. Sometimes you can also see sample screens before you buy, and you can send email

Try Before You Buy:
Shareware, Freeware, and Demo Software

Often, you can actually try out software before you buy it. A whole class of software, called **shareware,** is based on this idea. Shareware is distributed on the honor system. You can get a copy for free, but you're expected to "register" and pay for the program if you find it useful. The registration fee for shareware programs ranges from as little as $5 to more than $150, but the average is about $50—usually far less than the cost of similar commercial programs.

Some shareware programs are slightly disabled until you register, as an extra incentive for you to pay up. A shareware database program, for example, may limit you to a hundred or so listings, whereas the "full-featured" version has no such limit. Other shareware programs have all the features but keep displaying notices asking you to register each time you start them. When you pay the registration fee, you get a version that doesn't nag.

Another class of software, public-domain software or freeware, is actually free. No one ever asks you to pay for these programs, and they're often great, and sometimes even indispensable. Some of these programs were developed at government expense; it's your tax dollars at work, so take advantage of them.

In the last few years, many commercial software publishers have also bought into the try-before-you-buy idea, offering demonstration versions of software that you can order from them or download from their Web sites. Some of these "demo programs" are designed to work for only a certain period of time—usually about 30 days—after which you can purchase the program by forking over a credit card number. Another strategy is to partially disable the program so you get an idea of how it works but can't truly use it. This can include printing something obnoxious on each document you create with the program or not letting you save files, print, or perform other essential tasks.

Sources for Shareware and Demo Software

CNET's Download.com	www.download.com
ZDNet's Hotfile	www.hotfiles.com
CNET's Shareware.com	www.shareware.com

Where to Buy Software

Amazon.com		www.amazon.com
CompUSA	800-266-7872	www.compusa.com
CDW Computer Centers	800-838-4239	www.cdw.com
Office Depot	800-463-3768	www.officedepot.com
OfficeMax	800-788-8080	www.officemax.com
Staples	800-333-3330	www.staples.com
Egghead	800-344-4323	www.egghead.com
MSN eShop		www.eshop.msn.com
PC Connection	800-800-0005	www.pcconnection.com
PC Warehouse	800-727-8673	www.pcwarehouse.com
PC Zone	800-408-9663	www.pczone.com
Yahoo Shopping		www.shopping.yahoo.com

to the dealer if you have any questions or comments. The Web is also the best source for shareware and public-domain software (see sidebar on page 218).

The Five-Finger Discount

I know what you're thinking. You've just paid all this money for a computer and now you have to buy software too? In fact, you could easily spend more on software than you did for the computer.

But let's say the guy next door offers to give you a copy of a program that would otherwise cost you about $300. You wouldn't get the manuals, but for about $20 you can buy a book that will teach you the program. Should you accept the gift?

Legally, you shouldn't. Commercial software is copyrighted, which means it's illegal for its users to distribute copies. A copyright protects the people who own the rights to the software and the creative people who make it. Creating a piece of software is an expensive business, and the practice of illegally copying software (known as *piracy*) deprives companies of the money they've earned.

Many software companies vigorously defend their copyrights. So does the Software Information and Industry Association, a trade organization that monitors the illegal use of software and helps fight piracy. The association's legal department says it tends to go after businesses that buy a single copy of a program and distribute it throughout the organization. It also investigates claims that people are illegally reselling copyrighted programs.

If you have "borrowed" your neighbor's installation CDs, chances are you won't be awakened one night by the FBI pounding on your door. But there are plenty of other good reasons (besides the legal and moral considerations) to buy your own copies of software. If you run into a serious problem you can usually only get help from the software company if you're a registered owner. If there's a bug in the program and you're not on the list of registered owners you may never learn about it. I wouldn't dream of trusting my tax records or business information to a program that I didn't legally own.

What's more, some software companies now require you to register or activate your software. Microsoft, for example, requires activation for Microsoft Office, Windows XP, and other products. If you have a pirated copy, you might be able to install it OK, but it could stop working after a specified period of time if you don't activate it. If it was already activated by the original owner, your activation could be denied. I'm not thrilled with this practice because it can also affect legitimate users, but it's one more reason not to install bootleg software.

Rules for Buying Software

Don't Pay the Full Retail Price

Software publishers generally establish a "suggested retail price" for their programs, but who says you have to pay it? Prices of popular programs are often heavily discounted, sometimes by 50 percent or more. Check ads or visit software Web sites to see what people are really paying.

Get the Right Version

Every piece of software goes through several versions as its manufacturer adds features and fixes bugs. The version number or name usually comes after the product name, as in "Microsoft Office XP" or "Quicken 2002."

I've seen ads for software at extremely attractive prices, but when I called or visited the dealer, I discovered that the software was out of date. Make sure you know what the latest version is before you order software. (You can find out with a quick call to the software company or a visit to the company's Web site.) There's nothing wrong with using an older version of software if you don't need the new features, but if you're not getting the latest version, you should be getting a substantial discount as well as an opportunity to upgrade to the new version at a reduced price.

Try to Get a Money-Back Guarantee

It's not easy, but if you call around, you might be able to find a dealer that will give you a full refund if you're not happy with a software program. Many stores refuse to accept returns because they think people are buying programs, making copies, and returning the original as a way of stealing the software. Fortunately, some dealers have more enlightened policies. Don't accept a guarantee that's limited to replacing a defective disk or CD. If the program doesn't work right, chances are that the problem isn't the disk, but rather bugs in the program, an incompatibility with your system, or documentation that's too poorly written for you to understand.

Buy with a Credit Card

Even if the company you buy from has a good return policy, it's always best to buy computer products with a credit card. Most bank cards have a dispute clause that allows you to get a refund on a product you're unhappy with, and some now double the warranty for products purchased with the card. It also makes refunds easy if a return is necessary.

42 Installing and Uninstalling Software

When you get a new program, your first task is to install it on your computer. "Install" is an ominous-sounding term that evokes images of a service person with a truck, a set of tools, and specialized skills. But installing programs is generally quite easy, especially now that most software comes with a special installation program.

Usually, an install program for an application program creates new folders, copies the application files from the original CD-ROM to your hard disk, and makes any necessary changes to your Windows configuration. The installation program prompts you for the information it needs to configure the software so that it works on your machine. In most cases, the install program runs automatically when you first insert the CD-ROM.

If you download the software from the Internet, the process is the same, except that you'll be working from a file rather than a CD.

Uninstalling

As I said in Chapter 30, if you have a program that you don't want anymore, don't just erase the files. The proper way to go about uninstalling a program is to use the Add/Remove Programs tool

The READ.ME File

Sometimes the installation program will create a file on your hard disk called README or README.TXT. This file contains information that the programmers discovered too late to include in the manual. Here you'll find any late-breaking news about additional features, features that work differently from the way the manual describes them, and any known bugs or incompatibilities with other software or hardware. You might not understand some of the information in the READ.ME file (no one understands it all), but it's a good idea to scan through it anyway, just in case there's something that's important to you.

To open the README file, just double-click it. Usually the file is in ASCII (plain text) format, so WordPad or some other program on your disk will open it automatically. If that doesn't work, open it with any word processing program.

Register Your Software but Opt Out of Junk Mail

When you open a software box, most likely a registration card will fall out. It's usually a post-card that asks you to fill in your name and address, along with some other information that will be useful to the software company's marketing department, and return it to the company. They're like the warranty cards you get with many consumer items. I don't know if it makes any sense to register your new toaster, but it is a good idea to register your software. Some software lets you register online by filling out the questionnaire onscreen.

Registering software makes you eligible for benefits that you can't get any other way. To begin with, registering makes you eligible for a free upgrade if serious bugs are found in the program. Second, registered users receive information on program updates and generally get a discount on new releases. Some companies require you to be registered in order to use their telephone support lines.

As you fill out the registration information, look for any boxes to check or uncheck regarding what they will do with the information. Most companies "offer" you the opportunity to be bombarded with marketing material, but also offer you the chance to opt out. Personally, I get enough junk mail and I bet you do, too. Pay attention to these boxes so you don't unwittingly get put on some company's list of suckers. All you have to do to register is fill out the form or enter the information on the screen. If you don't want to fill in the marketing information, just leave it blank. Your name and address will still make it into the database.

from the Control Panel. A wizard will lead you through the rest of the procedure; all you have to do is answer the questions it asks and do what it tells you to do. (If it asks you whether it's OK to restart the computer, say Yes.)

Sometimes, though, Windows tells you that it hasn't quite completed the uninstall and that you have to remove some items yourself. Usually that means that it couldn't erase the folder that contains the program files. Remember I told you never to delete a program folder? Well, this is an exception. Go ahead and delete the folder—but first make sure you're deleting the right one. When in doubt, leave it alone. It might waste a small amount of disk space, but that's better than disabling your computer or another software program by getting rid of the wrong files.

If for some reason the program you want to remove doesn't show up in the Add/Remove Control Panel, you'll have to delete the files manually. It's not the neatest way, but it's the best you can do without a special utility.

43 Digital Music and DVD Movies

CD-ROMs, MP3s, DVDs—
WHY ALL THE ABBREVIATIONS?

FASTER AND COOLER.

ACRONYM—
COMPOOP.

There was a time when PCs were all work and no play, but those days are over. Today's PCs not only let you play computer games, they also double as complete home entertainment and creativity centers. They can play audio CDs and DVD movies, copy music files from a CD, download music files from the Internet, even let you make your own CDs and DVDs.

Almost anything you want to do with music or movies can be done with an application program that comes with XP. It's called Microsoft Windows Media Player, and I'll give you some tips on using it here, as well as an overview of programs from other companies that can do similar things.

Microsoft Windows Media Player

Windows Media Player is a very versatile program. It can play both audio and video and can also copy audio files between your PC's hard drive and a CD-ROM drive.

Here's what it can do:

- It can play music files on your hard drive or on a standard audio CD in your CD drive. It can also play MP3, Windows Media Audio (WMA), and other audio files.

- It can play certain types of video files, including DVD movies.

- It can help you organize your library of songs and videos.

  Personally, I find Media Player a bit clunky in this regard, but it will search all your drives, find all your music, and create a series of "albums" and play lists. It tries to group songs logically by artist and often succeeds. Unfortunately, overriding its decisions isn't as easy as it should be.

- It can copy music from a CD to your PC's hard drive.

  If you copy files from a standard audio CD to your hard drive, Windows Media Player will convert them to WMA format, which saves disk space. WMA is Microsoft's competing standard to MP3. Although they're similar, Microsoft argues that WMA is superior to MP3. Not all players that play MP3 will also play WMA files, though several companies are developing software that will allow you to use Windows Media Player to create MP3 files as well. For information on this, visit the Plug-in page at www.littlepcbook.com.

- It can copy music from your PC to a standard audio CD.

  Standard audio CDs use a special standard, known as Red Book audio (more on audio formats in a moment). Fortunately, Media Player can automatically convert MP3 and WMA files to standard CD files as it copies them.

Windows Media Player makes it very easy to make your own audio CDs (often called *burning a CD*). It will even convert the music files to the proper format as it copies them. Of course, to make your own CDs, you have to have a CD-R or CD-RW drive.

First, insert a blank CD-R into your drive. Then open Media Player, go to Media Library, and right-click any files you wish to copy. If you wish to copy multiple files, you can click on the top of the list and then Shift-Click on the bottom of the list and it will highlight all files in between. Finally, select Copy to Audio CD. You'll see a list of all the songs you've selected for your CD in the left panel. If you want to add more, you can go back to Media Library and continue the process.

But be warned: At the bottom of the screen, you can see approximately how many minutes of audio you're about to record. Most CDs can hold 74 to 80 minutes, so don't select more songs than will fit on your CD. If you've added too many songs, the excess ones will say Will Not Fit. You can delete those (or any others) by unchecking them.

When you're ready to make the CD, click the red Copy Music button in the upper right corner of the Windows Media Player window. Media Player will start converting the songs to the proper format. If it fails for any reason it will say An Error Occurred. Watch it carefully because if you cancel the process before it actually starts writing to the disc (after all the converting is done), you might be able to save the disc and start again without the file that caused the error.

Alternative Free Media Players

Besides Windows Media Player, there are several other players that you can download. Typically the companies that offer these players give away a one that's pretty good and sell an even better one.

These are the leading media players:

- **RealOne Player (www.real.com).** This program does just about everything Windows Media Player does and also creates MP3 files. The software is free but you can also purchase a monthly subscription service for enhanced content and extra features.

- **MusicMatch Jukebox from MusicMatch (www.musicmatch.com).** An excellent free player that not only plays music but also records both WMA and MP3 files to CD. For $19.95 you get the Plus version that records at up to twice the speed.

CD Writing Errors: How to Make a Coaster

Copying CDs is not an exact science. Sometimes, for no apparent reason, the CD simply doesn't work. In fact, it happens often enough that there's a special word for a failed CD. It's called a "coaster," because about all you can do with a failed CD is put it under a drink to protect your table. If you're especially creative, perhaps you can also use it as small Frisbee or lipstick mirror, but once you mess up a CD-R, you can't record over it. Fortunately, the discs are pretty cheap these days so it probably won't drive you to the poor house.

If you get a lot of bad CDs, there are a couple of possible reasons. First, you may be using poor-quality CDs. You don't necessarily have to buy the most expensive CD-Rs on the market, but the cheaper ones do tend to fail a lot more.

You may have a problem with your hardware or software. Also, running another program while you're burning a CD can cause problems.

Finally, there are some files that can't be copied because of copy protection. Some CDs, for example, have protection in them that prevents you from copying them. Some other media files are embedded with digital rights management software that prevents copying.

- **WinAmp from NullSoft (www.winamp.com).** A good overall music player.

- **Sonique from Team Sonique (www.sonique.com).** Like other media players, it handles MP3 and most other formats. Sonique is known for coming up with cool user interfaces.

- **QuickTime from Apple (www.apple.com).** Mostly used for playing movies recorded in the QuickTime format.

Creating Your Own MP3 CDs

Since MP3s are compressed, you can store about 10 times as much music on a single CD using this format. And the process is exactly the same as for copying any other files to a CD. You don't even need to use Windows Media Player if you want to create a CD that plays MP3 files.

Before you do this, however, be aware that most regular CD players can only play regular audio CDs and won't play MP3s, though you can now buy CD players that play MP3, WMA, or both. I bought a portable CD player that plays MP3 files for $69— just a bit more than I would have paid for a regular portable player. I can now store up to 10 hours of audio on a single CD that cost about 50 cents. Not a bad deal.

Getting Digital Music

There are a number of ways you can get your hands on digital music to play on your PC or record to CD. The two most common are copying music files from CDs and downloading files from the Internet.

Copying files from CDs you own is perfectly legal as long as it's for your own personal use. But downloading music has been a controversial topic. You've no doubt heard about Napster and all of its legal battles. Napster is a service that allows people to use special software to share music over the Internet. The service was basically shut down by court order after a number of record companies filed a lawsuit. Napster had plans to re-emerge, but as I was finishing this book it wasn't clear whether that would happen. In the meantime, several other services emerged to take Napster's

Audio Formats

Let's review the different types of audio files that you can record and play.

A standard CD is in a format called *Red Book audio* or *CD-DA* (for compact disc-digital audio). Every CD that you buy from a store is in this format. If you place a CD in a CD-ROM drive and look at the files, they will have the extension .CDA, indicating that these are CD-DA files.

You may have heard of something called a *Wave file* (.wav); this is the standard way that Windows stores uncompressed audio. If you want to play a Wave file on a standard CD player, you first have to convert it into a CD-DA file. Fortunately, Windows Media Player will do this for you.

MP3 and *WMA* are special "compressed" formats. Music recorded or copied to an MP3 or WMA file sounds almost as good as a CD-DA file, but it only takes up about a tenth as much memory. (The actual amount of compression varies by format, and you can also choose to compress the audio less to get better sound quality, but at one-tenth, only a true audio expert with good ears and very good equipment can tell the difference between a CD-DA file and an MP3 or WMA file.) That means you can store more of these files on CD or on your hard drive. It also means you can download a file or send it to someone over the Internet.

place and, as you might expect, the recording industry made noises about those as well.

I don't know how all of this will be resolved but I do know that it's fun to be able to download your favorite music from the Internet. On the other hand, the people and companies that create and market the music have rights, too.

There are many downloading services that aren't likely to run afoul of the copyright laws because they operate with the blessings of the copyright holders. In fact, the recording industry is setting up its own download site and many record companies already allow you to download music.

Where to Download Music

Any site listed here, especially those that aren't sanctioned by the recording industry, may or may not be in business by the time you read this. Let's face it: The recording industry is working hard to eliminate piracy, and some of the sites listed could make it possible for people to exchange copyrighted files without the permission of the copyright holder.

Where to Download Music

2Look4.com	www.2look4.com
AudioPhilez	www.audiophilez.com/
eMP3Finder	www.emp3finder.com
eMusic	www.emusic.com
Epitonic	www.epitonic.com/
FindSongs	www.findsongs.com
Lycos MP3 Search	www.mp3.lycos.com
MP3.com	www.mp3.com
Music4Free.com	http://www.music4free.com/
Musicgrab.com	www.musicgrab.com

On the other hand, some of these sites are totally above-board and comply fully with the copyright law. So don't assume that just because it's a download site there's something illegal going on. Also, not all MP3 files are free. MP3.com and eMusic.com for example, sell MP3 music and pass on part of the revenue to the artist or the label.

In addition to these sites, most record labels and many artists have their own sites and it is common for them to provide free samples or allow you to purchase music online. You can find links to record labels and other file sharing services at www.littlepcbook.com.

File-Sharing Services

These services allow peer-to-peer sharing of music and, in some case, videos, text, and other types of files. Napster is the most famous, but there are others that grew in popularity while Napster was having legal problems. Once again, there is a chance that these services will

The famous Napster cat listens to music on headphones. But is that cat a criminal?

not be in business by the time you read this. I do not condone the illegal copying and distribution of copyrighted work (see the sidebar, "Copyright Issues") but there are legal and legitimate uses of these services which is why I have included them in this book.

File-Sharing Services

Aimster	www.aimster.com
AudioGalaxy	www.audiogalaxy.com
BearShare	www.bearshare.com
Gnottella	www.gnotella.com
Gnutella	http://gnutella.wego.com
Kazaa	www.kazaa.com
iMesh	www.imesh.com
LimeWire	www.limewire.com
Music City's Morpheus	www.musiccity.com
Napster	www.napster.com

File-Sharing Security Warning

Be very careful about your own security if you use a file-sharing service. Most of these services require that you download and run software on your machine to access the files. Certain types of file-sharing software turn your machine into a server which means that others can access files on your machine. This can usually be turned off or restricted so that, in theory, it only provides access to certain types of files. I would never knowingly allow the public to access any files on my machine. It's an invitation to hackers. Besides, if you have music files or any other copyrighted works on your machine and are sharing those files, you could get into serious legal trouble because distributing copyrighted material is often considered an even more serious offense than downloading it.

Also beware of "spy ware." Some of these programs are actually capable of revealing information about you to marketing companies that contract with the publisher. Yet another issue: Many of these file-sharing services allow you to download video and graphics files that might contain pornography. Don't say I didn't warn you. (See Chapter 51 for advice on how to detect spy ware.)

Copyright Issues

I'm an author, not a preacher, so I'm not going to lay any moral trips on you about what you should or shouldn't do. But it is important to realize that there are copyright laws in place that limit what you can legally do. It's also important to realize that artists and those who invest in artists have financial needs, families, and rights, too. Before you start downloading music, giving away or selling CDs you copy, or, for that matter, making unauthorized copies of software, you should think about how you would feel if someone did this to the product of your work. Enough said.

If you're interested in learning more about copyright laws, check out the U.S. Copyright Office Web site at www.copyright.gov.

Digital Audio Players

If you have MP3 files on your PC, you can listen to them on your computer or copy them to a device that's designed to play MP3 files. There are plenty of these on the market from companies like Creative Labs, Intel, and Philips. Most of these MP3 players come with internal memory that stores your MP3 files. The player connects to your PC, usually with USB, and comes with software that you can use to download MP3 files from your PC to the device.

Handheld devices that run the Microsoft PocketPC also have the ability to play MP3 files. By far the most cost-effective way to listen to MP3 files away from your PC is to get a CD player that also plays MP3 files. There are also home decks and even DVD players that play MP3 files, as well. Aiwa, Kenwood, Panasonic, and several other companies now make CD players for the car that play MP3 files, too. Think of it: You could drive from Los Angeles to San Francisco or Washington, D.C., to Boston on a single CD full of MP3 files and still have enough music left over to go on a two-hour tour once you arrive.

Watching DVD Movies

Many desktop and laptop PCs come with a DVD drive and some even come with a DVD burner. In theory, a DVD drive can be used to run software that's delivered on DVDs, but the software industry hasn't really jumped on the DVD bandwagon so there aren't all that many titles. Hollywood, however, has embraced DVDs big time and virtually all new movies that are released on VHS tape are also released on DVD. Even some old classics are being re-released on DVD, often remastered with better video and sound and lots of extra features.

Any PC with a DVD drive can also play DVD movies. I don't often watch a movie on my desktop PC because I have a DVD player attached to the TV in my living room, but I do sometimes watch movies on my laptop when I travel. Unfortunately, I've never been able to get through an entire movie on a single battery charge, but if you carry an extra battery you might get to watch a movie on a flight. I also sometimes watch movies from hotel rooms, with the laptop plugged into an outlet. And I've even been known to let my kids watch movies from the backseat of the car on long car trips. We bought a $30 "inverter" that allows us to plug the laptop into the car's cigarette lighter. The kids won't look out the window if they're watching a movie, but it keeps them from asking, "Are we there yet?"

"FAST-FORWARD THROUGH THIS PART.
IT'S JUST CONVERSATION."

44 Creating Digital Video

Steven Spielberg and Ron Howard can rest easy. Despite all the technology at my disposal, I'm not about to displace them as world-class film makers. But with a digital video camera and a PC, it's now possible for ordinary people to make some extraordinary home movies. We've come a long way since the days of the 8 millimeter camera. For that matter, we've come a long way since those first home camcorders.

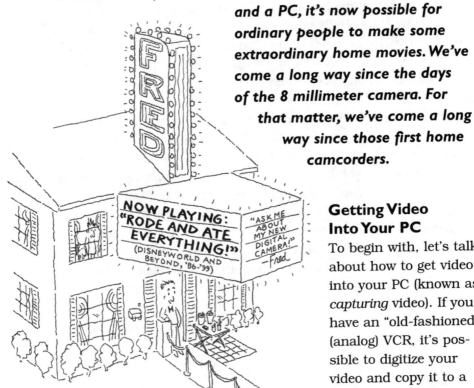

Getting Video Into Your PC

To begin with, let's talk about how to get video into your PC (known as *capturing* video). If you have an "old-fashioned" (analog) VCR, it's possible to digitize your video and copy it to a PC. But if you're in the market for a new video camera and think you might want to take advantage of digital editing, by all means get one of the relatively new digital video cameras that connects to a PC using a FireWire port. You'll also need a FireWire adapter for your PC. (See Chapter 14 for more about FireWire ports.)

Once you connect your digital video camera to your PC, you can move video in either direction between the two devices. You can use the PC to rewind, fast forward, and play the digital tape. You can even locate a specific scene on the tape.

Capturing Analog Video

If you have an older camcorder or if you want to digitally edit older, non-digital tapes (such as VHS), the process is a little more complicated. It's still possible to capture those scenes to edit on your PC, and there are a number of ways to do it.

An S-Video jack is standard on most recent video equipment.

One option is to get a PC graphics card with either a standard RCA or S-Video input. Both are pretty common on most recent video equipment so it's pretty easy to connect the video player or recorder to the PC's graphics card. ATI (www.ati.com) is one of several companies that make graphic boards with S-Video inputs.

Another option is to get an analog-to-digital converter. An inexpensive (about $70)—although limited—solution is Studio Online from Pinnacle Systems, which comes with a special cable that connects your camcorder's audio and video jacks to the PC's USB port. You don't need a FireWire card or any other hardware. The package also comes with a simple but relatively powerful program that can capture, edit, and output videos. The problem with the system is that to get data through the USB port fast enough, you must compress it—which means the image loses resolution and can look choppy.

A more expensive—but far more elegant—solution is Hollywood DV Bridge from Dazzle. This $300 hardware and software combination requires a FireWire port and converts the video from analog to digital before it pumps it into the PC. The result is a cleaner, smoother picture that looks about as good as if it had originally been recorded in digital video. In addition to creating files you can view on your computer, the device has video and audio out ports so you can record your production on a standard VCR.

Finally, you could get a digital video camera with analog input jacks and use the camera itself to convert the video. That way you not only have the ability to convert your old analog tapes to digital, you have digital video for all your new footage.

PCs Built for Video

If you're in the market for a new PC, consider one with a built-in FireWire port. Or if you want to go all the way, consider a system built with video editing in mind. Several PC makers offer complete systems that come with video-editing software. Some even have DVD recorders that let you create your own DVDs that can be played on most standard home DVD players. Although many companies offer such systems, Sony's line of Vaio Digital Studio PCs are especially well tuned for this purpose.

Video-Editing Software

Once you capture video into your PC, the fun—and the work—begins. I say "work" because editing video can be very time-consuming. Whether you find it to be a job or a joy depends on your interest level and how you like to spend your time. Video-editing software can be used to do just about anything you can imagine. You can edit scenes to make them shorter, move scenes around and insert titles, compensate for flaws in your footage, and add all sorts of special effects or a sound track to a movie. Even the most rudimentary video-editing software has plenty of things to keep you busy.

Windows Movie Maker

Speaking of rudimentary, Windows XP comes with a very basic video-editing program called Windows Movie Maker. There are plenty of programs on the market that are far more sophisticated, but before you spend money on new software (or even invest in hardware) you might want to give Movie Maker a spin. It's good enough to give you a feel for what you can do with a PC and some video. You'll find Windows Movie Maker on the Accessories menu. If you don't find it there, go to the Help and Support system and search for "movie."

The nice thing about Movie Maker is that you can practice your video editing skills right now. Not only do you already have the software, you also have some sample video clips to edit. And if you have or can borrow a digital video camera, you can immediately start importing some clips using Movie Maker.

The program allows you to rearrange your clips in any sequence you want, cut the clips to eliminate material you don't want, add transitions between clips, and even add narration that you can synchronize to your video. Check out the program's Help menu to get a feel for what it can do and how it works.

Windows Movie Maker is a simple way to learn the basics of movie making.

More Advanced Video-Editing Software

Though Movie Maker is a good starting place, it's not the be-all and end-all when it comes to digital video editing. You'll be able to get a lot more done if you get a full-featured program like Studio DV from Pinnacle Systems (www.pinnaclesys.com), Video Studio from Ulead (www.ulead.com), or VideoWave from MGI Software (www.mgisoft.com). These programs typically cost less than $100. Last time I checked, Studio DV came bundled with a FireWire card, which is a good, economical way to get everything you need except the camera and the talent. But don't worry about the talent. Just have fun.

Distributing Your Video to the World

There are many ways to get that video project of yours to others (assuming they want to watch it). One way is to output your project file as a highly compressed video file that you can upload to the Internet. Most video-editing software supports at least one of these compressed video formats (MPEG and RealVideo are the most common) that create files small enough to upload to a server. Be careful, however, to keep your videos short—very short. Even short movies can take a pretty long time to upload or view online. Besides, people's attention spans may not be as long as you think.

If you don't want to put your video on the Internet, you have several other options. Obviously, you can record your movies back onto video tape. If you have a digital camcorder you can record them on the digital tape the camcorder uses. If your PC has a video card with S-video or RCA outputs, you can hook up your PC to a standard VCR.

You can also save your movies on a CD-ROM if you have a CD burner. That way they can be viewed on anyone's PC. And if you have a DVD burner, you can make your own DVD movies that can be played on most standard home DVD players.

Burning Your Own DVD

Some PCs now come with a DVD burner built in, but you can also buy an external drive if you want to make your own DVDs. There are a number of competing technologies. The one that looks most promising is the DVD+RW standard supported by Hewlett-Packard, Dell Computer, Sony, Philips Electronics, Mitsubishi, and other companies. The other competing standards include DVD-R and DVD-RW. The difference between DVD+RW and DVD-RW is that one has a plus symbol and the other a hyphen. Seriously, there are real differences, but it isn't clear yet which one will take off and become the standard. Maybe it will have been decided by the time you read this. Let's hope so.

In any case, burning a DVD is a bit like burning a CD, except that the discs and the drives are more expensive (at least for now). Also, commercial DVDs are encoded with special software that prevents copying.

Digital Photography 45

Film isn't dead just yet, but digital cameras are coming on strong. And there's a good reason for it. For one thing, you never have to buy film or take your pictures in for developing. Instead, you store your pictures in the camera's memory and then transfer them to your PC's hard disk. Need a print? You can use an inkjet printer to make a print that looks almost as good as one you'd get from a professional film lab. And if you really want a professional print, you can order it online, directly from within Windows XP.

"OKAY, I'M GETTING YOU FRAMED, NOW SMILE, WAIT, MAYBE I'LL ZOOM IN...HEY, DO I NEED THE FLASH? KEEP SMILING, LOOK RELAXED, STOP WOBBLING...OKAY, ON THREE..."

Where Are Your Photos?

When you import pictures, they will usually go into a folder that's inside your My Pictures folder (which you access directly from the Start menu). If you're not sure where your photos are, start by checking in the My Pictures folder and any folders inside of it. Chances are you'll find them there.

In Chapter 21, I introduced you to digital cameras and discussed the different types of memory cards they use. If you have a camera with one of those removable cards, you can buy an adapter that will let you use that same memory card in your PC. Hewlett-Packard, for example, makes a line of PhotoSmart printers with built-in slots for common types of memory cards. SanDisk (www.sandisk.com) makes ImageMate and SecureMate digital-memory card readers that connect to your PC's USB port. Install one of these relatively inexpensive devices and you can read or write to a CompactFlash or SmartMedia card from your PC.

Many digital cameras come with cables that connect either to your PC's serial port or USB port. If you have a choice, go for the USB port because it's faster and more versatile.

Kodak's line of EasyShare cameras work with an optional docking port. The port, which plugs into the USB port and an electrical outlet, charges the camera's internal batteries and allows you to easily transfer data from the camera to the PC.

Working with Photos from XP

As you may recall from Chapter 27, Windows XP's special My Pictures folder has special attributes, such as showing you thumbnail images of your photos directly within the folder. Also within the folder, without having to load any special software, you can do other things with the photos, including renaming, deleting, and printing them.

The photo tools built into XP are actually quite useful. In fact, without having to launch any special software you can rotate pictures 90 degrees to the left or right and increase or decrease

Printing Pictures from Within My Photos

To print a picture, you can double-click the small icon and, when the picture shows up larger, click the printer icon.

OR

Right-click and select Print.

Here's the neat part: in addition to printing a single picture, you can also print two 5x7 prints on a single page, a group of 3x5 or 4x6 pictures, or an entire page of wallet-size photos. Considering that high-quality photo printing paper can cost as much as $1 a sheet, this is a nice way to get more for your money. Besides, it encourages you to share your photos.

the image preview size. You can't use XP's built-in tools to do any serious editing like adjusting for imperfect lighting or getting rid of red-eye. Other features included in most photo-editing programs include cropping (cutting out the portions of a photo you don't want) and the "cloning tool," which lets you remove blemishes and other material by painting over them in such a way that you can't tell they were removed.

Photo-Editing Programs

Once you've imported the pictures to your PC, you can work with them using tools built into the operating system or a third-party photo-editing program. Most digital cameras come with a free editing program so before you buy anything see what you already have. It may be perfectly adequate.

As you might expect, there are many photo-editing programs that you can buy, such as Paint Shop Pro from Jasc Software, PhotoDeluxe from Adobe Systems, and PictureIt from Microsoft. All of these programs let you clean up scanned snapshots, eliminate red-eye, get rid of scratches, and correct for color, sharpness, brightness, and contrast. Some, like Adobe's PhotoDeluxe, have templates and other features that you can use to create greeting cards, banners, calendars, and other projects.

My favorite photo-editing program is Paint Shop Pro from Jasc Software. This $99 program, which has been around for more than a decade, has more power than I know what to do with. Paint Shop Pro is a direct competitor of the leading graphics program, Adobe Photoshop ($609), but it's a lot cheaper and easier to use. It's more expensive than Adobe's PhotoDeluxe ($49) and other consumer-level photo-editing programs, but it's almost as easy to use and far more powerful. To be fair, Adobe recently introduced a streamlined version of Photoshop called Photoshop Elements ($99) that's competitively priced and a bit less complicated than the professional edition of Photoshop.

What I like about Paint Shop Pro is that you can generally get started right away, without having to wade through too many complex options. Most people just want to capture images from digital cameras or scanners, resize them if necessary, crop out any extraneous elements (such as that ex-boyfriend), remove red-eye, clean up a few blemishes, and print out pictures. You can do that with just about any photo-editing software, including the software that typically comes with digital cameras and scanners. But with Paint Shop Pro, you also have room to grow in case you want to do something more sophisticated, such as make subtle changes to the color of portions of the images or create collages by layering one image over another.

Types of Photo Files

There are a number of different formats used to store photos.

JPEG is the most popular format (it stands for stands for Joint Photographic Experts Group). The files will have the extension .jpg. What's important to know about JPEG is that it is a "lossy" compressed file format. That means that it saves space on your hard drive and (if you upload them) on the Internet because the file is compressed or made smaller. *Lossy* means that you do lose quality when you compress with JPEG. But the good news is that most people will never notice the difference between a JPEG file and an uncompressed file.

TIFF, or Tagged Image File Format, is an uncompressed file format. The files will have the extension .tif. TIFF files typically take up about 10 times the disk space of JPEG files. Most scanners and some digital cameras will save TIFF files, but most digital cameras standardize with JPEG. Although the quality of TIFF is better than JPEG, most people won't notice the difference. Still, professional photographers and serious amateurs who want the best possible quality from their digital photographs are likely to purchase expensive digital cameras that create TIFF images. For the rest of us, JPEG is fine.

EPS stands for Encapsulated PostScript. These files are used primarily by photographers who plan to print their images on high-end printers that use the PostScript language. A handful of high-end photo-editing programs, most notably Adobe Photoshop, support EPS, but the rest of us aren't likely to use it.

Other file formats you may come across include GIF and BMP. Also, most graphic image-editing programs have their own proprietary formats, but they can all open and save files in at least one of the standard formats.

If you want to learn a lot more about digital photography, I recommend the free online Kodak Digital Learning Center, which you can find through the Resources section of w.littlepcbook.com. As you might expect, it's a bit biased toward Kodak products and technology, but the information is accurate and clear. Besides, you're smart enough to make up your own mind as to what type of digital camera to get.

Photo Paper

Ever wonder why color inkjet printers are so cheap? The reason is that the companies that make them also sell ink and paper. If you ask Epson, Hewlett-Packard, Canon, or Lexmark, they'll tell you that their paper—the paper made especially for their printers—is far superior to any other paper.

That's nonsense. Do you think Hewlett-Packard actually makes paper? Of course not. They buy it from a major paper manufacturer, as do all of the other printer companies. (I wouldn't be surprised if they all bought their paper from the same company.) I've used

Canon paper on HP printers and vice versa and have never had any problems. In fact, there are lots of companies that make photo paper, so shop around. That's not to say that there aren't qualitative differences. I recommend you start off by purchasing relatively small packs from various companies and seeing which works best for you.

For Ink, Get the Real Thing

What I said about paper doesn't apply to ink. I don't recommend that you use an off-brand of ink in your inkjet printer, nor do I recommend that you refill your own ink cartridges from those kits you can buy. The wrong type of ink can jam your printing heads and cause serious damage. I know lots of people who've had problems when they tried to save a few bucks with off-brand ink.

Greeting Cards and Other Creative Projects

46

There is no end to the creative projects you can do with a PC. Whether it's creating a special wedding invitation or a birthday card, printing a Welcome Home banner, designing a calendar for your family, or creating your own business cards, you can do it with a PC, an inkjet printer, and some simple software.

I almost don't know where to begin. If you can imagine it and if it can be done on paper, you can probably do it with your PC. And the software for this type of project is getting cheaper and easier to use all the time.

For most of us, the closest we'll come to a career in the graphic arts is designing our own cards for special occasions. Now a whole category of popular software has popped up to let us do just that.

First, let me admit that when I've used my PC to custom-design a card for my wife, Patti, she thanked me, but I've noticed that she seems more excited when I hand-write a note or buy a printed card. When I asked her about this, she admitted that she thinks printed cards look better and handwritten notes seem more thoughtful.

Professionally printed greeting cards do look better. But with the correct software, a good inkjet printer, and high-quality card stock, you can do a pretty good job with a PC. When you make your own cards, you can create a more personal greeting and even add photographs. And they're great for procrastinators like me who remember they need a card after it's too late to go to the store.

Greeting Card Software

There are two kinds of computer-generated greeting cards. Those that are printed on paper and those that you read online. (Well, I suppose there are others, but these are the ones we'll discuss here.) Your PC is well equipped to create both kinds. There are lots of software programs designed to create greeting cards, including American Greetings CreataCard from The Learning Company, Hallmark Card Studio Deluxe from Sierra Home (www.sierrahome.com), and Greetings from Microsoft. Each of these programs makes it easy to design your own cards, invitations, calendars, and other print projects.

Each of these programs comes with a wide selection of premade graphics, designs, sayings, and other elements that let you assemble a greeting card for just about any occasion. Each program also lets you import your own graphics—including photos—and enter your own text. And they all allow you to send your greeting by email.

You can also get a more versatile program that includes other special projects besides greeting cards. PictureIt Publishing from Microsoft, PrintArtist from Sierra Home, and PrintShop Deluxe from The Learning Company are excellent multipurpose programs that can be used to layout anything from a bumper sticker to a novel. They have plenty of templates for greeting cards, stickers, and a lot more.

Greeting Cards on the Web

There are numerous Web sites that let you send a greeting card over the Internet. It's totally paperless. Your recipient gets an email with a link to a special Web page that contains the greeting card that you created. There usually isn't a charge for the service, but you and the person you're sending the card to may be exposed to some advertising.

The most comprehensive of these sites is BlueMountain.com. You can send just about any type of card you want, for any occasion imaginable.

Get the Right Stock

The stock you use will go a long way towards helping you with creative projects. I'm not talking about the type of stock you buy on the New York Stock Exchange—I mean the special types of paper you can buy for stickers, banners, decals, and the like. Most printer makers also offer greeting card paper for PC, as do Kodak and some paper companies.

Avery (www.avery.com) has all sorts of labels and stickers, including blank decals. One of the best places to get ideas is the PaperDirect Web site (www.paperdirect.com), which lists hundreds of different types of paper stock. You can also get stock from your local office-supply store or online from Staples (www.staples.com) and OfficeMax (www.officemax.com).

Label Printer

I realize that this is a bit of a luxury item, but I love my label printer. I have a little Dymo LabelWriter (www.dymo.com) on my desk that's connected to the USB port of my PC and I use it to print labels for just about everything—envelopes, CDs, cell phone, and other things I can lose. You name it, I put a label on it. It only prints labels and it only prints on special label stock that costs about a nickel a label. These printers start at about $180 so they're not exactly cheap, but they are useful.

47 Personal Finances

HELLO, NEW YORK?
BUY LOW,
SELL HIGH!

HELLO, CHICAGO?
DON'T BUY FROM
NEW YORK.

Your computer can't make you wealthy, but it can help you better manage the money you already have. After all, computation—which most of us haven't done since high school, and which is what computers do best—is what finance is all about. Financial management packages are relatively inexpensive, and I've found that they save me lots of trouble.

Organize Your Finances

Quicken, from Intuit, is one of the best-selling programs of all time for the PC. It's an inexpensive, all-around personal finance program that helps you pay your bills and keep track of various accounts, as well as stocks and mutual funds, and see how you're doing at managing your money for retirement and other financial goals. Another program with similar features is Microsoft Money from Microsoft. The prices for these programs vary slightly, but they're typically about $35 to $50. You'll pay more for the "deluxe" versions, which add some multimedia files providing extra help

Check Out Online Banking Before
Investing in Financial Software

Before investing in personal finance software, find out what online services your bank offers. Some banks provide basic account-management programs online for free. Also, not all financial institutions are set up to work with all financial software. (I'll tell you more about online banking in Chapter 56.)

and financial advice but really don't have all that much more functionality.

Both programs let you keep track of income and expenses, allowing you to pay a bill by filling out a form onscreen that looks like a check. The programs keep track of your income and expenses in a register that, not surprisingly, looks like a check register. You can print out reports detailing things like each expense category and income source.

Now that American Express and many banks that issue Visa and MasterCard accounts provide electronic statements, these programs can also manage your credit cards. I get all my credit card statements online, letting me record all the expenses in Quicken automatically—a real time-saver at tax time. You can also use Quicken and Money to manage your investment accounts with certain online brokers, including Fidelity and Schwab.

Both programs also let you connect to the Internet to pay bills electronically. You enter the information in the program, and instead of printing the check, the software transmits the check order over the Internet. I know what you're thinking—you don't want your personal financial information going through the Internet. Well, I can't tell you that anything is 100 percent safe, but I've been doing online banking for years and I never worry about security. The odds of someone stealing my information over the Internet are probably lower than of someone stealing my wallet or going through my trash. One nice thing about electronic banking is that it can handle recurring payments automatically. I've set up the program to pay my mortgage and car payments every month.

Making Tax Time Less Taxing

There are lots of advantages to using a computer to do your taxes. First of all, the software does all the arithmetic for you, eliminating a lot of human error. Also, tax preparation programs can automatically sort and add all of those receipts you're keeping in shoe boxes. Once the receipts are entered in the program, the program keeps them all straight.

Another useful feature of tax programs is that they include all the forms that most taxpayers need. You don't have to order forms or even search around your desk. You just bring them up in the program, fill them out onscreen, and print them to send them in. Most programs can also be used to file your returns electronically, although that requires paying a small fee to another company.

The programs carry forward data from each form and schedule to the appropriate line of the 1040. If you use a personal finance program such as Quicken or Microsoft Money to keep track of your finances during the year, you can import your financial data into any of these tax preparation programs.

The leading tax preparation programs are TurboTax from Intuit and TaxCut from Block Financial Software. It's hard to recommend one program over another because each developer upgrades the software annually to try to outdo the competition. TurboTax and TaxCut almost always come out the top two in reviews, so I'd go for either of them. Tax preparation programs typically cost about $40.

Although these programs have a lot of help features, don't expect quite the level of strategic advice you can get from a good tax professional. Nevertheless, they will help you better understand which deductions you're entitled to and how to enter them on the forms.

Doing Your Taxes on the Web

Both TurboTax and TaxCut also offer a service that allows you to do your taxes on the Web. The process is similar to using the software, but all of your data and the programs you'll use are on a Web site. There are some advantages to doing it this way.

Garbage In/Garbage Out

The Internal Revenue Service doesn't mind you using a tax preparation program. In fact, the IRS likes it when people use tax preparation software because that tends to cut down on errors. Nevertheless, the tax payer, not the tax preparation software company, is responsible for any errors in a return.

- First, it's usually cheaper. When companies don't have to bother manufacturing and shipping software they can charge less.

- It can be more convenient if you work both at home and in an office because you can always access your data stored on the tax service's Web site.

- You don't have to worry about getting the latest software or backing up your data. The service takes care of that.

There are also some advantages to buying the software.

- You can use it for as many returns as you like at no additional charge. With the online service, you pay by the return.

- You don't have to be online to do your taxes. That means you can work on them from an airplane or a park bench or when your Internet connect is down.

- PC software is faster than working over the Web.

Regardless of whether you use the stand-alone software or do your taxes on the Web you can now file electronically which not only saves paper, it also saves time. Some online tax services charge a small fee for electronic filing, but in return, you'll get your refund faster.

48 Games

Millions of people love to use their PCs to play games. And PC games are not just for kids, either. Adults—especially young men—are the major force behind many PC games.

I have to admit, I'm not much of a game player. My idea of having a good time with a PC is surfing the Net, checking my email, chatting online with my friends, listening to music, or writing something in my word-processing program. So I had to learn a little bit more about the topic in order to give you an idea of what's out there.

One of the best places to learn about PC games is Gamespot.com, a Web site that provides news, reviews, and playing tips about all types of games including those for PCs and consoles such as PlayStation, Nintendo, and Microsoft xBox.

Windows XP, is "great for games," according to Gamespot.com founder Vince Broady. Because it's a new operating system, there may be some compatibility issues with older games, but, Broady predicts that, "it won't take very long before all the game makers have XP versions available."

Check out Gamespot.com for all sorts of gaming information.

Game Ratings

The rating system established by the Entertainment Software Review Board (www.esrb.org).

 EARLY CHILDHOOD — Content may be suitable for persons ages 3 and older. Contains no material that parents would find inappropriate.

 EVERYONE — Content may be suitable for persons ages 6 and older. May contain minimal violence and some comic mischief or crude language.

 TEEN — Content may be suitable for persons ages 13 and older. May contain violent content, mild or strong language, and/or suggestive themes.

 MATURE — Content may be suitable for persons ages 17 and older. May contain mature sexual themes or more intense violence or language.

 ADULTS ONLY — Content suitable only for adults. May include graphic depictions of sex and/or violence. Not intended for persons under the age of 18.

 RATING PENDING — Product has been submitted to the ESRB and is awaiting final rating.

Ratings

Most commercial games these days are rated, just like movies. As with movies, the ratings are a guideline for parents, not an absolute rule. You'll have to decide for yourself what your kids can handle, since only you know what values you wish to instill.

There has been some talk about the role of video games in teen violence. While there's no credible evidence that violent games cause children to commit acts of violence, there is certainly evidence that playing certain types of games leads to more aggressive behavior. My advice to parents is to get to know the games your children play. Don't overreact if the game has a bit of violence, but watch for signs that could indicate problems. (After all, the Westerns I watched as a kid had plenty of shooting, and I'm no homicidal maniac.) If your children are obsessed with games, even gentle games, or exhibit inappropriate behavior, you might consider changing their software and media diet.

Genres

Broady divides the gaming world into several categories or genres: action, real-time strategy, simulations, sports, driving, and role-playing.

Action games, sometimes called "first-person shooters" typically thrust the player into the role of a would-be superhero assigned to take out an enemy or save civilization. Perennial bestsellers in this category include Quake (from ActiVision), Doom (GT Interactive), Half Life (Sierra Online), and Unreal (GT Interactive). The games listed above are all rated Mature 17 are considered to contain a great degree of "realism," which is often a euphemism for "gory graphics." Online gaming arenas often feature this type of game, and the players there are usually intense and quick. Parents should be especially cautious about letting their kids play this type of games.

Real-time strategy games feature a combination of resource management and combat strategy—usually the player commands troops, develops technologies, and helps develop a culture. Some notable examples include Red Alert (Westwood Studios), StarCraft (Blizzard Entertainment), and Age of Empires (Microsoft), all rated Teen 13+. These games are extremely refined, according to Broady. They contain a strong multiplayer element and can also be very addictive, though they aren't as violent as the first-person shooters.

Simulation games generally let you build a world where things happen even when you're not actively managing them (the exception is the "flight simulation" subgenre, which lets you pretend you're flying an airplane). Examples include Microsoft Train Simulator

If you have a budding Bill Gates in your family, I recommend Monopoly Tycoon.

(Microsoft), SimCity (Electronic Arts), Roller Coaster Tycoon (Hasbro Interactive), Monopoly Tycoon (Infogames), and Black and White (Electronic Arts). The games listed here are all rated for Everyone (except Black and White, which is rated Teen 13+). They are very sophisticated and quite challenging. Your job is to subtly influence an environment over time rather than complete a mission as in the strategy and action games.

Sports games are exactly what they sound like: simulated sports. Notable sports games include Madden NFL (Electronic Arts), NHL Hockey (Electronic Arts), NBA Live (Electronic Arts), and my favorite Virtual Pool (Interplay), all rated for Everyone. In these games you're simulating the action on the field. You won't get jostled or injured by these sports contests, but you will have to exhibit good strategy and hand-eye coordination to win.

Driving games like Nascar Racing (Electronic Arts) and Motor City Online, both rated for Everyone, let you hear the engines roar as you wind around curves and compete with fellow drivers. They often use accurate replicas of real race cars on real courses. The Nascar game even has a replay mode that lets you review your race after it's over, to help you improve your techniques.

Role-playing games let players create their own characters who make friends and go on quests. Popular games include Ultima Online (Origin Systems), Everquest (Sony Online Entertainment), WarCraft (Blizzard Entertainment), and Asheron's Call (Microsoft). The games listed here are all rated Teen 13+, except for Ultima Online, which is rated Mature 17. These kinds of games represent the most dramatic new development in gaming according to Broady. They have taken a very addictive, sophisticated genre that is brought it to life onscreen. Some of the most popular games include an online mode, where your character can interact with other people's characters and develop relationships that some-times turn into real (not just online) friendships.

Children's Software

It almost goes without saying that kids love computers, and not just for games. Fortunately, there are lots of great programs for children, includ-ing many that fit into the "edutain-ment" category, which lets kids have fun while they learn lessons, skills, and values.

A great source of independent reviews of kids' software is ComputingWithKids.com, a Web

The Reader Rabbit series is a classic favorite.

site operated by Jinny Gudmundsen. The site has reviews from her syndicated column, and not only describes programs but rates them as well.

Some programs to which Gudmundsen gives five stars are Blue's Reading Time Activities (Humongous), JumpStart Phonics (Knowledge Adventure), Blue's Treasure Hunt (Humongous), and Freddi Fish 5: The Case of the Creature of Coral Cove (Humongous). Gudmundsen also gives the thumbs-up to some of the titles from the Carmen Sandiego Series (The Learning Company) such as Carmen Sandiego's Great Chase Through Time, where children trace Carmen Sandiego back through history.

The Reader Rabbit series from The Learning Company and the Math Blaster programs from Knowledge Adventure are also great programs for young children. They were around when my kids (now teenagers) were little and I suspect they'll be around for some time to come.

This section only scratched the surface of all the cool things you can do with a PC. (For more ideas, check out www.littlepcbook.com.) The beauty of computers is that they are infinitely expandable with both hardware add-ins and software. And with all the great programs on the market today, you can do almost anything imaginable on your computer—except maybe teleportation.

So far, the Internet is the closest thing we have to teleportation and in the next section, we'll beam you up for a tour.

Now that you have your PC all set up and know a thing or two about software, it's time to take a journey. No, I'm not running you out of town; I want you to join me on a tour of the World Wide Web and all the other things that the Internet has to offer. As you probably already know, the Internet is changing the way all of us live our lives. Whether you're choosing a movie, booking a flight, buying a book, or investing in the stock market, the Internet can help you out. It's becoming the world's marketplace and changing the way we communicate, as email, online chat, and personal Web pages become part of our daily lives.

Exploring the Internet

four

49 Internet Basics

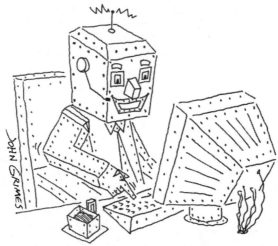

"SIR, YOUR QUESTIONS ARE FAR TOO IMPORTANT TO BE TRUSTED TO JUST ANY ROBOT."

Before we get started with our explorations, I'm sure you have some questions. Well, here's (almost) everything you ever wanted to know about the Internet and how it works.

What Is the Internet?
The Internet is a global network of computers. Any computer connected to the Internet can communicate with any other computer connected to the Internet. Think of it like a worldwide highway system. You can get from any highway to any other highway, though not necessarily via a direct route. The Internet even has rules of the road, called protocols, that determine how data gets from one connected computer to another.

How Did the Internet Get Started?

The Internet began life in 1969 as the Arpanet, a network designed to let government researchers across the country share computer resources. More and more universities and government agencies were added to the network over the '70s, and in the late '80s it was opened to commercial traffic.

No one owns or even governs the Internet now. It's a decentralized network that is supported by the companies and institutions that access it. Network administration (such as deciding on new types of domains) is overseen by a committee called ICANN (www.icann.org).

How Does Information Travel on the Internet?

Information sent over the Internet can travel directly from your ISP to that of the person you're communicating with, but often it travels an indirect route. In fact, messages are sometimes broken apart into smaller pieces or packets. Each packet may travel a different route to its destination. Then all the packets are reassembled into the single message. This is called packet switching, and you'll sometimes hear real geeks refer to the Internet as a "packet-switched network."

The Internet can handle all types of digital data including text, numbers, programs, illustrations, photographs, audio, animation, and video. Anything you can view on a computer screen or hear through computer speakers can be transmitted over the Internet. But it's not (yet!) possible to transport objects or people.

What Is Bandwidth?

Think of the Internet as a system of pipes that carry data. Little pipes can carry only a small amount of data, but larger pipes can carry more data. **Bandwidth** refers to the size of the metaphorical pipe, or the amount of data that can be handled at any one time. So more bandwidth not only means that more people can use the Internet at the same time, it also means that people can work with larger files. Text and numbers take up relatively little bandwidth but audio takes up more and video a great deal more. A single photograph can take up as much bandwidth as thousands of words, making the old adage, "a picture's worth a thousand words," a bit of an understatement.

What Is the World Wide Web?

The World Wide Web has become extremely popular because it is easy to use and provides many different types of information. The key to the Web is hypertext, which was developed in 1989 by Tim Berners-Lee at CERN, the European Laboratory for Particle Physics in Geneva, as a way to coordinate information around the world. It's a system that uses what we now call **hyperlinks** or just plain links, which transfer users from one Web page to another with the click of a mouse.

As the Web developed, graphics were added to the hyper-linked documents, and **Web browsers** were introduced that made accessing documents easier still. Creating the documents, or Web sites, however became more difficult, so that an entire industry grew up around it. Now a Web site can be as little as one page or a vast number of pages, containing enormous quantities of information. The Encyclopedia Britannica, for example, is a single Web site (www.eb.com) that contains as much information as the multivolume printed edition. Still, every Web page has its own unique address or **URL** (for "uniform resource locator").

How Are Web Sites Created?

A Web page is created using a programming language called HTML (for "hypertext markup language"). This sounds complicated but it really isn't. HTML is basically ordinary text with some tags or commands that tell it how to display the text or graphics and how to link to other sites. It's not that hard to learn HTML, but these days you don't have to know anything about it to create a Web site. Numerous programs on the market let you create Web pages

just as if you were using a word processing program.
In fact, most modern word processing programs, including
Microsoft Word and WordPerfect, can also be used to create
and edit Web pages.

How Do I Find Web Sites?

There are numerous **search engines** that you can use to find
places on the Web. A search engine is itself a Web site that is
designed as an interface to a database that searches for information on other Web sites. There are basically two types of search
engines. Directories like Yahoo are a compendium of sites entered
by people. Automated search engines like Google and AltaVista
use software called a crawler or spider to search the entire Web
and catalog the information. Then you can search that catalog
on the site by typing the word or words you're interested in. The
advantage of crawlers is also their disadvantage: They include
everything. So these search engines will show you a list of every
site that contains the word you're looking for. Often that includes
many sites that aren't really related to your topic.

Many search engines have both a directory service and a
crawler. But whatever search engine you use, be sure to check
out its help system for rules, tips, and syntax. Most search
engines use Boolean logic. which allows you to narrow or broaden
your search with terms like AND, OR, NOT, or NEAR. If you type
"united OR airlines" (most search engines don't care about capital-
ization) you will get sites that use either word. If you type "united
AND airlines" you will only get sites that use both words. If you
type "united NOT airlines" you'll only get sites that mention
"united" but don't mention "airlines." When in doubt, consider
putting your words in quotes. With some search engines typing
"united airlines" in quotes will give you only sites where the two
words appear next to each other.

What Else Can I Do on the Internet?

The World Wide Web is only one of many services available over the Internet. The most popular Internet service is electronic mail, commonly known as email. Anyone connected to the Internet can send mail to anyone else on the Net. Other very popular services are chat and instant messaging. Unlike email, chat sessions are "in real time," which means you can "speak" and "listen" at the same time. Anything you type in a chat will instantly be displayed on the screen of anyone else who is tuned into the same "channel" as you. An instant message, on the other hand, isn't necessarily public. It can be between two people or a small group of people who have agreed to exchange real-time messages. (More on this in Chapter 52.)

Another feature is newsgroups, which are forums or bulletin boards. One person posts a message and others respond. Everyone can read what everyone else says and you don't all have to be in the same time zone or online at the same time. Newsgroup messages are saved, so that people can look at them and respond at any time. You can use special software to access newsgroups or use Internet Explorer or Netscape (click Mail and News on the Internet Explorer Tools menu). You can also access newsgroups on the Web at www.deja.com.

Last, but not least, the Internet lets you transfer files from one computer to another using **FTP** (for "file transfer protocol"). You can also use the Internet to listen to audio or watch videos. It's even possible to use the Internet as a voice or video phone system.

Getting Online 50

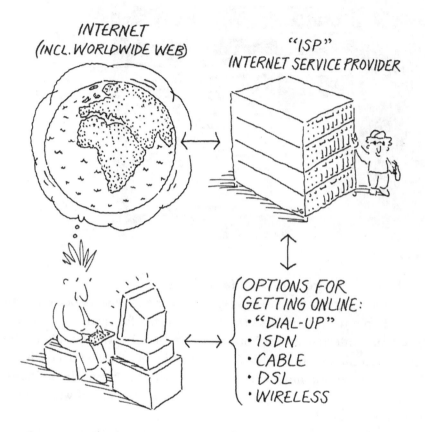

INTERNET (INCL. WORLDWIDE WEB)

"ISP" INTERNET SERVICE PROVIDER

OPTIONS FOR GETTING ONLINE:
- "DIAL-UP"
- ISDN
- CABLE
- DSL
- WIRELESS

So now you know the basics about the Internet. But how do you actually get online?

Well, there are basically two ways to get on the Internet. The majority of home users connect to one of these services by using a computer equipped with a modem to dial in over a regular phone line, but an increasing number now have high-speed access using technologies such as DSL or cable modems (see Chapter 20 for more on this). And there are two choices when it comes to service providers: America Online (AOL) and all the other Internet Service Providers (ISPs).

The AOL welcome screen.

AOL: The 800-Pound Gorilla of ISPs

The reason I give AOL equal weight to everyone else is because, as far as home users are concerned, it accounts for nearly half of all U.S. home Internet users. You might say it's the McDonalds of the Internet: Millions and Millions served! Why is AOL so successful? Well, its marketing muscle is enormous. Just think of the millions of CD-ROMs that not only come with the necessary software but offer free online time.

But there are other reasons why AOL is so popular. For one thing, the company makes the Internet relatively simple and straightforward. All you need is a PC and an AOL installation CD (in fact, the AOL software is preinstalled on many computers.) AOL goes beyond just making it easy to get on the Internet, though; AOL has proprietary content that is available only to its subscribers, but it also provides access to the broader Internet. Other Internet service providers generally provide a connection to the Internet but no special data. The AOL content is presented clearly and is easy to navigate, because it's logically organized in to channels such as Autos, Careers, Games, Health, and Kids Only. Of course, you can find the same type of information on the Web using another ISP, but AOL does make it easy.

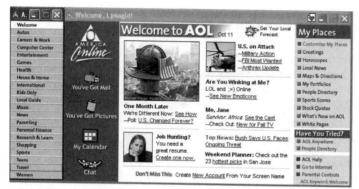

AOL's channels are listed to the left of the welcome screen.

Another key factor to AOL's success is AOL's success. I know that sounds redundant but on the Internet success tends to breed success for a number of reasons. For example, one of biggest hits on AOL is its instant message service, which makes it incredibly easy for subscribers to find and chat with each other. AOL also offers celebrity chats, held in an "auditorium" available only to subscribers. Even though there are sometimes thousands of participants, the auditorium experience is interactive for all because the audience is divided into rows where members can carry on a side conversation while the "speaker" is answering the questions of the lucky ones whose questions actually made it through.

One thing I like about AOL is that it offers dial-up access from just about everywhere. If you're traveling within the United States, chances are AOL has a local access number (AOL keyword: access). If you're out of the United States in a major city, there's probably a number you can call for an additional charge (typically $6 an hour but sometimes more).

AOL is not the cheapest service around. Last time I checked, the company was charging $23.90 a month for unlimited access. In fact, at a time when many ISPs were going out of business, AOL raised its fees and wound up growing in the process.

Watch Out for Those "Free" Offers

They're starting to die down, but for a while, PC companies were offering free or low-cost PCs for anyone willing to sign up for a three-year contract with a particular ISP. Be careful. If the ISP charges $20 a month, you're on the hook for $720 for the service. That's OK if you really like the service and want to keep it for three years. But in technology, three years is an eternity. Who knows what will come along later that might tempt you away from that binding contract? If you do take the bait, make sure there's a way out that you can live with.

Speaking of free, another trend that seems to be going away is free ISPs. For a while companies were offering free services in exchange for making you look at advertising. Well, advertising didn't turn out to be such a great money maker after all, so many of these companies are dropping their free service. If you find one that offers free service, read the fine print very carefully and consider what you'll do if the company goes out of business or drops its free service.

Plenty of Other Choices

Although AOL dominates the consumer marketplace, it's hardly the only game in town. There are plenty of other ISPs. Whether you use a national provider such as EarthLink, Microsoft Network, or AT&T WorldNet or a small, regional company (perhaps your local phone company), once you're connected you have access to all the public resources of the Internet. There was a time when AOL and similar online services such as Prodigy and CompuServe were much easier to use than plain ISPs, but that's no longer necessarily the case.

When you use an ISP, you do give up that friendly AOL interface, but many users find that they prefer the interface you get with a standard ISP. Most ISPs expect you to use a browser such as Internet Explorer or Netscape Navigator to access the Net. They also expect you to access your email via a program like Outlook Express (which comes with Windows), Eudora, or Outlook. Some ISPs also encourage their users to access their mail via the web. Personally, I like using Internet Explorer as my interface to the net. I find that it's faster than AOL's interface and I've customized my home page and my bookmarks so that everything is right there for me. I'll explain how to do all that in Chapter 53.

Get reviews of ISPs all over the world at www.thelist.com.

If you haven't decided yet which ISP to use, ask people in your community for their advice. Which company offers the best prices and the best service? Pay special attention to customer support. Can you reach them on the phone? The most frustrating thing about having your Internet service go down is wondering if it's a system wide problem or something on your end. For a listing of ISPs around the world and reviews, check out The List at www.thelist.com.

In Chapter 20, I covered the difference between dial-up and broadband. Most of the major national carriers offer both types of service. Many ISPs offer DSL, as well, sometimes with better customer service than the phone company.

The mechanics of getting online depend on your ISP. If you use AOL, it's totally automated. Just install the AOL software and it will locate your modem and sign you on. The same can be true with other ISPs, too: Many of them provide software to help get you through the process.

XP Connection Wizard

If your ISP doesn't provide you with software to automate the task, you're still OK because XP has a relatively easy to use New Connection wizard.

1. Go to the Widows Control Panel (from the Start menu) and select Network and Internet Connections.

2. Select Set up or change your Internet connection.

3. Click Setup to start the Wizard.

4. Check Connect to the Internet.

At this point, Microsoft will be really helpful and offer to let you select from a list of ISPs. If you go with that option, it should come as no surprise that the default selection is Get online with MSN. (In case you haven't realized, "MSN" stands for "Microsoft Network.")

If you select Other, you'll get to another screen that gives you yet another chance to sign up with MSN (Microsoft doesn't give up easily). You then have the option of clicking on an icon that will dial a special number to provide you with "offers" from other ISPs. When I tried it, I got the message, "No offers available in your area at this time." Of course, there's always MSN. How convenient.

Assuming you already have an account with an ISP, you can choose "set up a connection manually." The wizard will ask you a fairly clear set of questions. Enter the data and, with any luck, you'll be able to sign on to your ISP. Before you start this, though, make sure you know a few things.

- The phone number your computer dials to get to the ISP (not the phone number to talk to your ISP)

- Your user name

- Your password

- Your user name

Bear in mind that user names and passwords can be case-sensitive, so if you don't get through on your first try, check to see that you capitalized everything correctly.

"THIS CAN'T BE GOOD."

You've probably heard some horror stories about the Internet. Yes, it's true—people do get into trouble online. On the other hand, millions of people use the Internet every day and most do just fine. You just need to understand the risks and take appropriate precautions.

Internet Safety for All Ages

When you or your children are online, you're out in public. That's the first thing parents need to understand when coping with the difficult issue of how to protect their children when they visit the Internet. So what's a parent to do? As a practical issue for parents, you need to prioritize your concerns, pick your battles and come up with a reasonable strategy to deal with whatever problems arise.

I think almost all parents would agree the safety of their children is the first priority. That's why it's so important that children understand the Internet is something like a city street, where there are interesting buildings and people, as well as danger.

As I'm sure everyone realizes by now, no one really knows who you are online. That 13-year-old girl could actually be a 15-year-old boy or a 45-year-old man. Make sure your children understand not to reveal anything about themselves that would allow someone to track them down. That includes the obvious, such as full name and address, but also less obvious details such as phone number, name and location of school, and where parents work. Children should be taught that when they're talking with someone in a chat room or an instant message session, they're interacting with a stranger unless they're positive they really know that person in the "real" world.

It's also a bad idea for your child to reveal his or her email address, but that's sometimes difficult to prevent, unfortunately, especially for America Online users. By default, the screen name that appears in AOL chat rooms and instant message sessions is also your email address. One solution is to create a special screen name that you or your children use whenever entering a chat room. Another trick for instant messaging is to download the AOL Instant Messenger software and register to use a different screen name for that program instead of your regular AOL screen name.

It's never a good idea for kids to get together with someone they meet online. If, for whatever reason, your child feels that it's absolutely imperative to get together with someone they've "met" online, make sure it's in a public place, like a restaurant, at a reasonable hour, and that Mom or Dad is present. That doesn't give you an iron-clad assurance that all will be well, but at least you'll get a rough idea of the person's age, gender, and demeanor.

Speaking of age, don't assume this advice applies only to pre-adolescents. Teens are victimized at a far higher rate than young children, especially when it comes to sex crimes, according to the

National Center for Missing and Exploited Children. Teens are especially vulnerable to exploitation because they're often going through emotional growing pains that make them easy prey for "sympathetic" and "understanding" individuals who are only too happy to give them a warm shoulder to lean on. In most cases, teens who get into trouble through Internet contacts are lured away from home. (In fact, this cautionary advice even applies to adults. Both women and men have been assaulted or otherwise victimized by predators they met online.)

Then there's the more complicated question of exposure to pornography—complicated because, to begin with, most sexually explicit material is not illegal. Just because something isn't appropriate for children to look at doesn't give the government justification for a broad prohibition. How parents respond depends on many factors, including the age of the child. Young children, for example, aren't likely to be looking for porn, but they are more likely than teenagers to be troubled if they stumble upon it. However, I suspect that many more teens find it because they're looking for it.

There are a number of filtering programs you can install that will block access to "inappropriate" sites. Generally, you can configure the software to block the types of sites you object to, such as sexually explicit sites or sites that condone racism, sexism, and other forms of oppression. Some filters even allow you to specify the levels of nudity that are acceptable. Filtering programs almost always have a password that parents can enter to get around the filter when they're online or to modify the level of filtering.

For more on Internet safety, please visit SafeKids.com, a Web site I maintain as a public service.

But filters are not a panacea. For one thing, they can block sites that shouldn't be blocked and allow access to sites that may be objectionable. Also, it's important to teach kids to exercise their own judgment online. It's good training for later life and it helps them learn to protect themselves.

Protection from Hackers

As I've said before, when you're connected to the Internet, you have a door that the rest of the world can use to enter your computer. The question is whether that door is open and whether you're vulnerable to an attack.

Kids' Rules for Online Safety

(from SafeKids.com)

- I will not give out personal information such as my address, telephone number, parents' work address or telephone number, or the name and location of my school without my parents' permission.

- I will tell my parents right away if I come across any information that makes me feel uncomfortable.

- I will never agree to get together with someone I "meet" online without first checking with my parents. If my parents agree to the meeting, I will be sure that it is in a public place and bring my mother or father along.

- I will never send a person my picture or anything else without first checking with my parents.

- I will not respond to any messages that are mean or in any way make me feel uncomfortable. It is not my fault if I get a message like that. If I do I will tell my parents right away so that they can contact the Internet service provider.

- I will talk with my parents so that we can set up rules for going online. We will decide upon the time of day that I can be online, the length of time I can be online, and appropriate areas for me to visit. I will not access other areas or break these rules without their permission.

- I will not give out my Internet password to anyone (even my best friends) other than my parents.

- I will be a good online citizen and not do anything that hurts other people or is against the law.

The good news is that XP has built-in firewall software that, to a limited degree, protects you from a hacker trying to break into your PC. But it's far from foolproof. (The term **firewall,** by the way, comes from the automotive industry; a firewall is the shield between the engine and the passenger compartment. On a network, a firewall acts as a barrier to someone who tries to break in.) The Windows firewall only protects you from people trying to break in, not from software running on your PC that sends information out.

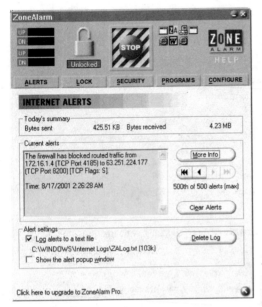

The personal edition of ZoneAlarm from Zone Labs takes only a few minutes to download and install and will keep you safe.

Here's an example. Let's say you download a program or someone emails you a program that, once it's run, starts sending files from your PC to a hacker. I'm not saying it's likely, but it is possible and it would get by Microsoft's firewall software.

For extra protection, it's a good idea to get a third-party firewall program that not only keeps people out but keeps software on your machine from sending out personal information. Fortunately, one of the best firewall programs is free. The personal edition of ZoneAlarm from Zone Labs takes only a few minutes to download and install and will keep you safe. There are also commercial firewall programs such as Norton Internet Security and McAfee Fireware but they do the same thing as Zone Alarm.

Protection from Scam Artists

I wish there were a piece of software that could protect you from scam artists, but unfortunately that's up to you. My best advice is simple: If something sounds too good to be true, it probably is. Be very careful about any offers you get by email or come across on the Web, unless they're from a reputable source that you know

The Federal Trade Commission's "Dirty Dozen"

12 Scams Most Likely to Arrive by Email

- Business opportunities

- Bulk email

- Chain letters

- Work-at-home schemes

- Health and diet scams

- Effortless income

- Free goods

- Investment opportunities

- Cable descrambler kits

- Guaranteed loans or credit on easy terms

- Credit repair

- Vacation prize promotions

For more information, click on the Scams link at www.littlepcbook.com/resources.htm.

and trust. I don't think anyone is trying to sell swamp land in Florida anymore, but there are all sorts of other dodgy offers out there, ranging from a hot stock that's about to make a few people rich to some miracle diet or cure.

Protection from Everyone Else

Let's face it, anyone who has physical access to your PC has access to what's on it. There is no surefire way to completely protect your private stuff, but there are ways to greatly minimize the chance that someone can see what you're up to.

Let's start with the basics. Internet Explorer has a History function that keeps track of where you've been on the Web (for more detail about Internet Explorer, see Chapter 53.) That can be good, but if you don't want someone in your household or place of business to know where you've been, you'll have to cover your tracks.

One way to do that is to "purge the cash" or delete the History data. That's pretty easy to do.

1. From the Tools menu of Internet Explorer, select Internet Options.

2. Click Clear History.

3. When asked to confirm, click OK.

Clear AutoComplete if you don't want Internet Explorer to complete strings of text for you.

Another thing you can do is to clear AutoComplete. The AutoComplete feature turns on a system in Explorer that automatically completes strings of text. So, if you've consistently entered the name John Smith into a Web form, the next time you type "Jo" it will automatically fill in "John Smith." Again, that's a convenience, but it means that anyone else using your PC can figure out what you've entered.

This is only a little more complicated to clear out than History is.

1. From the Tools menu of Internet Explorer, select Internet Options.

2. Click the General tab if it isn't already showing (it should be).

3. Click the Content tab.

4. Click AutoComplete.

5. Click Clear Forms.

This won't wipe out any of your data, but it does mean that you'll have to re-type information in forms, so only do it if you have something you want to delete. You can also turn AutoComplete off so Internet Explorer will no longer remember what you type. You can do that within the same AutoComplete dialog box by unchecking the items Web addresses, Forms, and User Names and Passwords on forms.

Cookies

Cookies are a much maligned feature of Web browsers. While some people worry that they can be used to track what you do on the Web, they are, for the most part, a convenience for you. For example, I have a (free) subscription to the New York Times Web site (www.nytimes.com), so of course I have to identify myself with a username and password before I enter the site. Rather than having to type that each time, I've allowed the Web site to place a cookie that contains that information on my machine. Now, whenever I visit www.nytimes.com, the site checks the cookie, which tells it that I'm a registered user, saving me the trouble of logging on.

In theory, a cookie could be used to help track your behavior but, in theory there are a number of things that could track you both on and off the Internet, including the license plate on your car or the fact that your home has glass windows. Just because it's possible for you to be tracked doesn't mean that you are being tracked.

That's not to say that you might not be tracked or otherwise spied upon. Even paranoids have real enemies. But I would consider the source. If you think the *New York Times* has nothing better to do than keep track of what you're doing on the Web, then you ought to take every possible precaution. Personally, I'm willing to take that chance. But I'm not willing to take any chances on Web sites whose owners are unknown or not trusted. On those sites, I too am paranoid.

The fact is, most people whose privacy is violated on the Internet actually disclose the information that leaks out. Whether that's giving your credit card to a site that you can't vouch for or entering in personal information in a chat room, what you type can come back to haunt you.

I don't worry much about cookies myself, but if you do, you can delete them easily.

1. From the Tools menu of Internet Explorer, select Internet Options.

2. Click the General tab if it isn't already showing (it should be).

3. Click Delete Cookies.

4. Confirm it by clicking OK.

Also, while you're in this area, check out the Delete Files button. That deletes temporary files on your machine that someone could use to determine where you've been on the Net.

Email, Instant Messaging, and Online Chatting

52

Email is rapidly becoming the primary way the world communicates. That's not to say there's no longer any need for the postal service, but more and more people are relying on email for sending rapid business and personal messages. And now that instant messaging and online chatting are becoming popular, you can really use your PC to communicate with just about anyone.

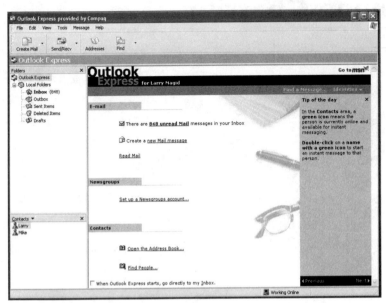

Outlook Express is the email program that ships with Windows XP.

Email

For everyone other than AOL users there are basically two ways to send and receive email within Windows XP. You can use an email program like Outlook Express (which comes with XP), Outlook (which comes with Microsoft Office), or Eudora (which you can download), or you can send and receive your email from a Web site like Microsoft's Hotmail, Excite, or Yahoo.

Outlook Express and Microsoft Outlook

As you might suspect, Outlook Express and Microsoft Outlook appear to be pretty similar. The interfaces look almost the same, and both offer easy-to-use email programs that are powerful enough for most users. The main difference between the programs is that Microsoft Outlook, which does not come with Windows but does come with some versions of Microsoft Office, also has a calendar, a contact-management system, and some other features.

Outlook Express is just an email program, but it does work with the Windows Address Book, so you can store people's email addresses as well as their names, phone numbers, and addresses in the Address Book and Outlook Express can access them.

To run Outlook Express, go to the All Programs section of the Wndows XP Start menu and select Outlook Express. The first time you run it, it will probably ask for your email address and information about your email account, so make sure you have that information handy. Your ISP should have provided the information for you. If not, you can usually get it from the Support section of your ISP's Web page or, if necessary, by calling the company's tech support department.

If Outlook Express doesn't prompt you when you start it up (or if you want to change your email information or add another account), you can use the New Account wizard to set things up.

1. Select Accounts from the Tools menu.

2. Click on the Mail tab (near the top).

3. Click Add and then select Mail.

4. Type your name or whatever else you want displayed when people get your email.

5. When it asks for your email address type your entire address, for example, jack@earthlink.com.

    Here's where it can get tricky.

6. The next question asks for your Incoming POP3, IMAP HTTP server. You need to get this information from your ISP. Typically it's something like pop3.isp.com or mail.isp.com (where isp.com is the name of your ISP), but check with your ISP to be sure. You'll also need to know the route for outgoing mail, which is usually either smtp.isp.com or mail.isp.com.

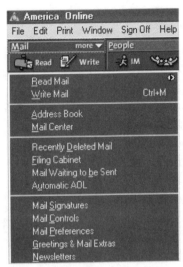

The Mail menu lets you send and receive AOL mail.

AOL Mail

AOL users can use the same programs as everyone else, but they can also send and receive email from within the AOL software or from the AOL Web site (www.aol.com).

AOL email is pretty straightforward. You access it from the Mail menu within the AOL software. You can write or read email or make additions or changes to your address book.

Web-Based Email

Accessing your email on the Web has some advantages and some disadvantages. To begin with, not every email service offers Web-based email though many, including AOL, do. Another problem is that the email isn't stored on your PC but on a server somewhere. That means you can't read and respond to email while you're offline (for example, on a plane if you have a notebook PC) and it can be a bit slower to interact on the Web than to work with a program like Outlook Express or Outlook.

One advantage of Web-based email is that it's usually pretty easy—you don't have to mess with configuring an email program. Another advantage is that you can access your email from any computer, even a public one at a library or Internet café.

Of course, you can have it both ways. You can have a regular email account with your ISP that you access from software and you can have another account at a Web-based service. Most Web-based email systems also allow you to read email from your regular account by providing them with the same type of information that you would use to configure an email program.

Hotmail, from Microsoft, is the leading Web-based email service. That's partly because it's one of the oldest (Microsoft acquired it several years ago), but it's also because Microsoft markets it heavily, even encouraging you to sign up for Hotmail when you install XP.

Other free email services include Yahoo Mail and Excite Mail, which you can access from their main sites (www.yahoo.com and www.excite.com). A company called MailStart (www.mailstart.com) charges $10 a year for Web-based email, but it really lets you have your cake and eat it too. You can access any account you wish from MailStart's server.

Instant Messaging and Chatting

If you want to learn about instant messaging and chatting, just ask a teenager. My daughter practically lives in AOL's instant messaging system and, apparently, so do most of her friends. When we were traveling on the East Coast (we live in California) looking at colleges for her, she stayed up 'til the wee hours of the morning so she could chat online with her friends on the West Coast.

There are several ways you can engage in instant messaging. The most popular service is AOL Instant Messenger, which is part of the AOL software and also available as a separate free program called AOL

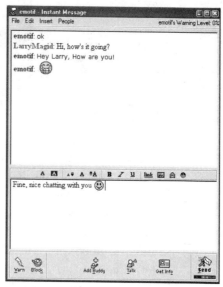

AOL Instant Messenger lets you chat with your fingers instead of your voice.

Instant Messenger (AIM). You can download the software from AOL's Web site (www.aol.com).

Microsoft, not wanting to be outdone by rival AOL, has built an instant messaging program into Windows XP. It's called Windows Messenger and chances are you've already come across it when you installed Windows XP. If not, you may still see it pop up from time to time.

Like AIM, Windows Messenger allows two or more people to "chat" using the keyboard. You type in a message and press the Send key and the message is instantly displayed on the screen of the person or people you're chatting with.

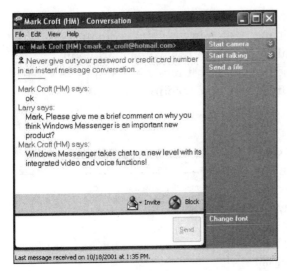

Windows Messenger is the instant messaging program that comes with XP.

Knowing that, be careful before you press the Send key because you can't take it back. Be sure you dreally know who you're chatting with.

Windows Messenger does more that just let you chat with they keyboard. It also lets you chat by talking, using your PC's microphone and speakers, and it allows you to carry on a video conversation if you equip your PC with a camera. You don't need an expensive digital camera just a simple Web camera such as the Logitech QuickCam (which you can purchase for as little as $50).

One problem with using a Web cam or even voice is that it may not work if your PC has a firewall (see Chapter 51, for more about these) to protect you from hackers. Hopefully, Microsoft will have this resolved by the time you read this book, but as I was writing it, I was unable to actually carry on a video session because my router (see Chapter 37) wouldn't allow it.

Logitech's QuickCam is an inexpensive way to have video chats.

Sample Chat Slang Abbreviation

AFK	Away from keyboard
BRB	Be right back
FWIW	For what it's worth
FUBAR	Fed up beyond all recognition (polite version)
GD&R	Grinning, ducking, and running
IMHO	In my humble opinion
LOL	Laughing out loud
PMFJI	Pardon me for jumping in
TTFN	Ta ta for now
ROTFL	Rolling on the floor laughing
WB	Welcome back
YMMV	Your mileage may vary (You may not have the same luck I did)
YWIA	You're welcome in advance

Chat Slang

If you're in a chat and someone types "BRB," and then leaves, don't despair. It means your friend will "be right back."

And, if you tell a joke and the response is "LOL," that's a good sign. It stands for "laughing out loud." ROFL is even better: "rolling on the floor laughing." And there's no greater compliment than "BWL," or "bursting with laugher."

Chat room slang is rapidly becoming a way for kids and even adults to communicate both online and off. I'm not sure if your grandmother will understand you, but millions of people are speaking this new "language," so you may as well learn a few terms.

53 Internet Explorer

Before going any further, let me remind you that Internet Explorer is not the only software you can use to explore the Internet. Explorer does come with Windows and it is free. But Netscape Navigator (www.netscape.com), Opera (www.opera.com), and other browsers are also free, though you have to download them.

There has been a lot of controversy over the years about Internet Explorer. It was one of the issues in the Justice Department's antitrust suit against Microsoft. But, while attorneys and judges battled over Microsoft's future, users started getting accustomed to Internet Explorer, which, after all, is a very good browser.

Setting a Home Page

When you first run Internet Explorer, the first page you'll see asks you to indicate the country you're in and your language. It then takes you to the Microsoft Network's home page. Of course, Microsoft would love for you to keep that as your home page (the first page your browser shows you) because the more people who visit that page every day, the more money Microsoft makes from its advertisers. But you don't have to keep that as your home page. You can go to any Web page you want and make that your home page. And if you change your mind, you can always go back later and set a new home page.

For this example, I'll show you how to make my Web site, www.pcanswer.com, your home page. I admit I'm taking unfair advantage of my captive audience here, trying to get you to make my page your home page. But I'm not a monopolist and, besides, you can substitute any page you want for mine.

1. If you aren't already in Internet Explorer, click the Internet Explorer icon in the Start menu.

2. Type Ctrl-O to bring up a box where you can type in the Web address (or click in the address bar near the top of the browser window and type it there).

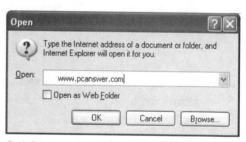

Ctrl-O brings up a box where you can type in a Web address.

3. Type **www.pcanswer.com** (or whatever other site you prefer) and press Enter.

4. To make this your home page, click the Tools menu and select Internet Options.

5. In the first part of the Internet Options area is the Home Page section. Click the Use Current button to make the current page your home page.

Your Favorite Web Sites

In addition to setting your home page, you can add as many "favorite" pages as you like. This is a very powerful feature that all Web browsers share, though only Explorer actually calls them Favorites. It means the browser remembers Web addresses for you, so you don't have to worry about it. Just add a site to your Favorites and you can go back there whenever you like.

You can add Web addresses either to the main part of your Favorites menu or to a folder inside it. It's fast and easy to add a site to the main part, but if you do it a lot you'll soon be overwhelmed. That's why it makes sense to set up subject folders within your Favorites such as news, music, or sports.

To add a site, just click the Favorites menu, select Add to Favorites, and then click OK. You'll see the default name of the page, but you can change it to whatever you want. To insert the address into an existing folder do the same, but before you press OK, click the Create In button and select a folder. You can add folders by clicking New Folder after Add to Favorites, and you can add, change, or move Favorites between folders by clicking Organize Favorites.

Adding Favorites to Desktop or Start Menu

You can also add Favorites to your desktop, Start menu, or even a folder inside your Start menu. Just drag the icon for the page you're visiting to wherever you want your Favorite to show up. The icon is located in the address bar, just to the right of the word *Address*, and it usually looks like an Internet Explorer icon.

If you want to drag it into the Start menu, select it, then left-click to grab it and, without letting go, drag it over the Start menu. In this case, you have to hold it there for a couple of seconds before letting go.

Placing a Folder in the Start Menu

You can also place a shortcut for a folder inside the Start menu and drag items into that folder.

1. Go to My Documents and create a new folder by right-clicking anywhere in the My Documents folder.

2. Select New from the context menu and click Folder.

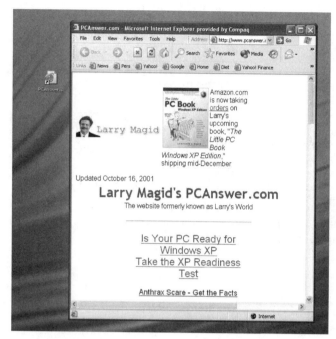

Drag the icon in the Address bar to your desktop, Start menu, or a folder.

3. Give the folder a name like My Web sites.

4. Left-click the new folder, drag it to the Start menu, and let go.

Now when you click the Start menu, you'll see your folder in there. If you want, you can left-click it and drag it up or down. If you decide you don't want it in the Start menu, right-click it and select Remove from list. Remember, removing an icon from the Start menu only removes the shortcut. The folder still exists in your My Documents folder.

Explorer Toolbars

Internet Explorer has a toolbar that you can use to get around the Internet more easily.

Most of the tools on the toolbar are pretty self-explanatory. If you can't remember what one means, hold the cursor over it for a few seconds and a legend will pop up.

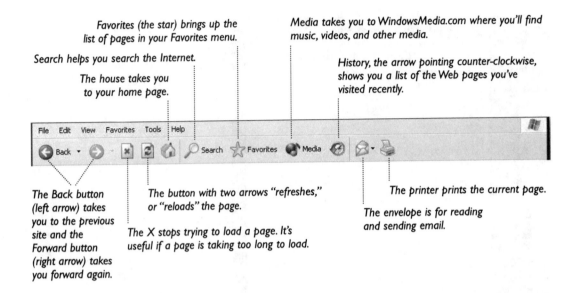

Favorites (the star) brings up the list of pages in your Favorites menu.

Media takes you to WindowsMedia.com where you'll find music, videos, and other media.

Search helps you search the Internet.

The house takes you to your home page.

History, the arrow pointing counter-clockwise, shows you a list of the Web pages you've visited recently.

The Back button (left arrow) takes you to the previous site and the Forward button (right arrow) takes you forward again.

The button with two arrows "refreshes," or "reloads" the page.

The X stops trying to load a page. It's useful if a page is taking too long to load.

The printer prints the current page.

The envelope is for reading and sending email.

History Can Be Friend or Foe

Clicking the History icon shows you a list of the Web sites you've visited recently. That can be very good, because it helps you find your way back to interesting sites you didn't add to your Favorites. But History can also be bad, because anyone who has access to your PC can use it to find out where you've been on the Internet. If that doesn't matter to you, then don't worry about it. But if you don't want someone else in your household or office to know where you've been, you'd better learn how to clear out the History file, as discussed in Chapter 51. Also, if you have kids, you can use History to find out where they've been. It doesn't take the place of the filtering and more sophisticated monitoring programs discussed in Chapter 51, but it's still useful (unless your kids know how to clear the History file, too).

Customizing Internet Explorer

The Internet Explorer View menu lets you choose, among other things, how big the text is on the pages. If you're having trouble reading pages, consider selecting Text Size from the View menu and making the text larger. It will affect text on all pages. If you later decide you don't want it, you can always change it back to Medium.

The View menu also controls which toolbars appear on your screen and allows you to lock and unlock the toolbar.

Toolbar Shortcuts

In addition to adding Web site shortcuts to your Favorites menu, you can also add them to the toolbar. Likewise, you can remove the sites (like Microsoft's own Hotmail service) that Microsoft put there by default. Customizing your toolbar can make it a lot easier to get to the sites you visit often, but don't overdo it. The toolbar isn't that big and you don't want to clutter it up. Use the Favorites menu for all but the most frequently visited sites.

Add a Web site shortcut to the toolbar by dragging the Web page icon from the address bar to the toolbar.

Delete a shortcut by right-clicking it and selecting Delete from the context menu.

Dragging a Bar Around

Here's a nifty trick. Notice how the Web address (in the Address line) takes up a whole line. You can recover that space by moving the Address line up and making it a little smaller.

Start by selecting Toolbars from the View menu and unchecking Lock the Toolbars (if it's checked) to unlock them.

Left-click the word *Address* in the Address bar and drag the entire bar to just right of the Help menu at the very top. Let go of the Address bar and you've now saved some space. If it's too long, left-click and drag Address to the right to make the bar shorter. You can then click the vertical row of dots just to the left of the word *Address* to move the bar over to the left a bit.

When you're done, it's a good idea to lock the Toolbar again so you don't accidentally move it.

Save Space by Shortening Names

You can also right-click an icon and change the text of the shortcut or change the icon. Changing the text can save you a lot of space on the toolbar, because pages often have very long default names and you can shorten them. I've changed Yahoo to Y and Microsoft Finance to $M. I know what they mean and, by making them shorter, I can get a lot more shortcuts on the toolbar.

54 Surfing the World Wide Web

Once you learn how to surf the Web, the world is at your doorstep. In this chapter, you'll learn how to use hyperlinks, search engines, and Internet addresses to navigate the World Wide Web.

Hyperlinks

As I mentioned in Chapter 49, one thing that makes the Web so powerful is its use of hyperlinks, or links, which let you move from one Web page to another just by clicking the link with your mouse.

Looking at a Web page, you should be able to spot the links easily. Hyperlinked text is usually set in blue and underlined, though Web page designers can choose any color and style for their links, even graphics. Most designers want to make their links stand out, so they are usually set in some obvious contrasting color.

Arts & Humanities
Literature, Photography...

When you roll your cursor over a hyperlink, the arrow changes to a pointing hand.

If you're not sure if something is a hyperlink, point at it with your mouse. As the cursor rolls over a hyperlink, the arrow changes to a pointing hand. If Web page designers really want to get fancy, they create more elaborate rollover effects, making links change color or shape, even make sounds. Don't be startled. These are all just ways to get you to click that link.

Search Engines and Portals

The Web has millions of sites covering all kinds of topics, from obscure pop song lyrics to computer hardware catalogs, from the latest research on diabetes to wedding pictures of a happy couple in Saskatchewan, not to mention lots of X-rated material. How do you find your way around this vast universe? One way is to use a search engine as we discussed in Chapter 49. But these only help if you know exactly what you're looking for. If you know what kind of information you're looking for but can't narrow it down to a few key words, you can visit a **portal,** a site that organizes a large number of links by topic.

When you start Internet Explorer, Windows automatically takes you to the Microsoft Network (MSN) home page, which is one example of a portal page. Other well-known portals are Yahoo, Excite, Lycos, AOL.com, and Netscape Netcenter. There are even kid-friendly portals like Yahooligans or Ask Jeeves for Kids. My favorite search engine is Google (www.google.com) because it's both fast and vast

Resources

AltaVista
www.altavista.com

America Online
www.aol.com

Ask Jeeves for Kids
www.ajkids.com

Excite
www.excite.com

Google
www.google.com

Lycos
www.lycos.com

LookSmart
www.looksmart.com

Microsoft Network
www.msn.com

Netscape
www.netscape.com

Yahoo
www.yahoo.com

Yahooligans (for kids)
www.yahooligans.com

For an up-to-date listing of portal sites, visit www.littlepc.com.

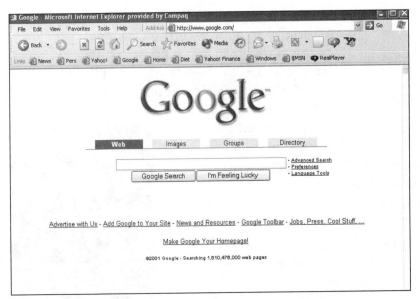

Google.com is my favorite search engine.

and doesn't bombard you with too much advertising. I sometimes use Yahoo (www.yahoo.com) when I want a well-organized directory of sites. LookSmart (www.looksmart.com) is also quite good.

Some portal sites let you customize the page you see to show the kind of information that's of particular interest to you, such as sports scores, stock quotes, local news, or links to specific types of Web content. Getting all that updated personal information is fun, but these pages are just starting points for all the exploring you're about to do on the Web.

To use a search engine, you just type one or more words into a text box (usually located at the top of the page) and then click the search button. (The button may be called different things on different sites, but it should be clear enough.) The search engine software will scan its database of sites and return a list of pages that match your search terms. The list is hyperlinked, so you can begin exploring by simply clicking on the links of pages that interest you.

Some Web sites are case-sensitive, which means that you must type the URL exactly as it was given to you, with the same use of

Web Addresses

Every page on the Web has a unique address, referred to as a URL (sometimes pronounced "earl") or Universal Resource Locator. If you type that address in your browser's Address Bar, the browser will take you to that page.

The first part of a URL is always *http://,* but you don't actually have to type those characters in most browsers, so you'll often see Web addresses with that part left off, as in this book. (In case you're wondering, http stands for "hypertext transfer protocol." You already know what hypertext means, so you can probably figure out how they wound up with that term.) The next part of an address, often, is www (short for "World Wide Web"). These characters are optional in the latest browsers, too, so sometimes people don't mention them, either.

The next part of the address, though, the **domain name,** is important. The domain name comes in two parts. The first part is usually the organization's name or an abbreviation of it, such as bankamerica, latimes, ucla, etc.

What follows is the kind of domain, called the **top-level domain**. If the Web site is for a company, it's .com (for commercial). For educational organizations it's .edu. Military organization use .mil, and government agencies use .gov. Organizations are usually .org. The Internet governing group, Internet Corporation for Assigned Names and Numbers (www.icann.org), has approved additional domains including .aero (for aerospace), .biz for business, .coop for cooperatives, .info for information services, .museum for museums, .name for individuals, and .pro for professionals. (See the list of top-level domains on the next page.)

So what does that all add up to? Well, http://www.ibm.com is IBM's website. UCLA's is http://www.ucla.edu. And the Web site for the President of the United States is http://www.whitehouse.gov.

uppercase and lowercase characters. If you get an error message or end up at the wrong Web site, check the address carefully; chances are, the problem is just a typo.

The first few times you use a search engine, you may be startled to see a result that reads something like, "We found 332,714 pages that matched your search," along with a list of tons of links, many of which have nothing to do with your topic. The good news is, most search engines put the most likely matches at the top of the list.

Every portal conducts searches differently, though. You can make your searches more exact by knowing the quirks of each one. Most of the portal pages offer tips for effective searching, so be sure to read

Common Top-Level Domains

.com	Commercial (though there are no real restrictions on its use)
.org	Non-profit organization (though companies, individuals, and families sometimes use it)
.gov	Government
.mil	Military
.aero	Air-transport industry
.biz	Businesses
.coop	Cooperatives
.info	Unrestricted use
.museum	Museums
.name	Individuals
.pro	Professionals such as accountants, lawyers, and physicians

them. For more tips on searching, check out Larry's Concise Guide to the Internet on my Web site at www.pcanswer.com/primer.htm.

But wait—there's an even easier way to do an Internet search! Type your search terms in Internet Explorer's Address Bar and you'll be automatically redirected to a search engine, which will return a list of matching sites.

One last note: Be aware that some unscrupulous people create Web sites (often containing "adult" material) at domain names that are very similar to those of popular sites. They might take a government site's name and change the .gov to .com or misspell the name of a site just a bit to catch people who make typos. What bothers me about this is that it's very easy for children to stumble onto sites like these. I'm a strong believer in the First Amendment and the right to express yourself freely, even if I don't like what you're saying, but I don't think that includes the right to trick people into visiting your site.

Using Microsoft.net   55

One of most controversial, yet potentially powerful, aspects of Windows XP is Microsoft's decision to link it to the company's "Dot Net" (.Net) strategy. In a nutshell, Microsoft.net takes advantage of the company's operating system to engage you in commerce.

Eventually, Microsoft will start offering software packages, including versions of Microsoft Office, that run over the Internet instead of on your PC. That way, instead of buying Microsoft Office, you subscribe to it and can use it over the Internet from any machine.

In the meantime, .Net allows you to shop at MSN and partner Web sites by simply entering your Microsoft password. Your credit card and shipping information is stored by .Net, so you don't have to retype it for every merchant.

And, perhaps more importantly, you can use .Net to store your files on the Internet. Because it's so closely integrated into the operating system,

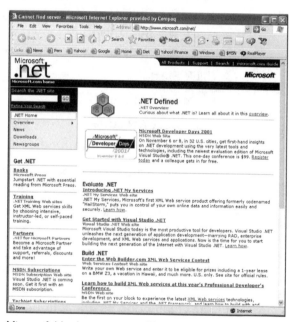

Microsoft.Net lets you store files remotely on the Web.

you can set up a folder on .Net that looks to you as if it's on your local hard drive, but it's actually on a server, possibly thousands of miles from you.

There are, of course, all sorts of privacy implications with this strategy. Your decision of whether to use it should be based, in part, on whether you trust Microsoft to provide an adequate level of security and abide by its own privacy policies (which say that Microsoft won't look at your personal data). Try as they may, Microsoft and many other companies sometimes fail to protect their networks against invaders. I do use Microsoft Web folders to store some of my data, but the data I'm storing is not highly secret. I wouldn't be happy if I found out someone had access to it, but it wouldn't devastate me, either.

Setting Up a .Net Folder

In order to use this service, you need to sign up for a Microsoft.net Passport account. This provides you with access to a variety of services offered by Microsoft and its partners. To sign up for a Passport account, use the .Net wizard in the User Accounts area of the Control Panel.

1. Click Start.

2. Click Control Panel.

3. Click User Accounts.

4. Click Change an Account.

5. You will be asked to choose an account. You must choose the account that you're currently logged onto.

6. You will then be asked, "What do you want to change about your account?" Select "Set up my account to use a .Net Passport."

The Passport wizard will now launch and ask you to enter your email address and a password. The email address is your regular email address and will now become your user name for .Net, but the password doesn't have to be the one you use for that email account. This password will only be for .Net, and can be anything (as long as it's at least six characters long and doesn't include spaces). The wizard will ask you a few more questions, and when it's done, you'll have your Passport account.

Once you have a Passport account, you can add it to My Network Places.

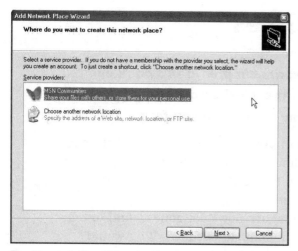

The Network Place Wizard will create an account for you.

1. Select My Network Places from the Start menu.

2. Click Add a Network Place to start the Network Place wizard.

3. Select MSN Communities and click Next.

   You may have to wait a few minutes while XP fetches some data from the Internet. If you're not online, it will try to connect you to the Internet.

4. You should now have an icon for Web sites on MSN in your My Network Places area.

   If you click that icon, you'll be able to create new folders and actually drag files into those folders to be stored on the Web. You can even drag a file from your hard drive to this folder. Then, you'll be able to access those files from your computer or from someone else's as long as you remember the username and password to get into your Passport account.

56 My Favorite Sites

Finally, I get to write my favorite chapter in this book and tell you about my favorite sites. At the risk of overusing the word "favorite," I'm opening up my Favorites menu for you.

In case you haven't noticed, I'm pretty excited about the Internet. I've been interested in the online world for more than 20 years and have tried every conceivable online service out there, but there's nothing like the World Wide Web.

True, many of the "dot coms" are now "dot gones," and to tell the truth, I'm not surprised that some have failed. Why would anyone want to buy pet food online when just about everyone lives near a pet food store?

But some online businesses do make sense, like using the Internet to buy movie tickets and find out what's playing. It certainly makes sense to make travel arrangements online because it's easier and offers far more options than the old-fashioned way. Buying and selling stocks and mutual funds is easier online, too, though you have to careful.

And while I like to be able to buy books online, I also love to shop at my local bookstore. Still, Amazon.com and Barnes & Noble (bn.com) have great search engines that make it very easy to locate the books you want. The same is true for music and other products. And while I love to read the news online, it doesn't take the place of sitting down with the morning paper and a cup of coffee.

Personally, I think there will continue to be plenty of "brick-and-mortar" stores, even as e-commerce continues to grow. The Web is here to stay, at least until someone comes up with something better.

Getting the News Online

I'm a news junkie. Of course, I'm a journalist, which partially explains my interest in the media, but I probably spend more time looking at news sites than at any other type of sites on the Web.

No Need to Type in the Addresses of These Sites

All the sites mentioned in this book—and then some—are listed as hyperlinks in the resources section of www.littlepcbook.com. So rather than typing each URL, visit the Web site and "click" your way to them. If you like them, you can follow the directions in Chapter 53 to add them to your own Favorites menu.

Newspaper Web Sites

Naturally, I'm partial to the *Los Angeles Times* (www.latimes.com) and *San Jose Mercury News* (www.sanjosemercury.com) Web sites because I write columns for those newspapers. But I also spend a lot of time at the *New York Times* (www.nytimes.com), *Washington Post* (www.washingtonpost.com), and *Wall Street Journal* (www.wsj.com) sites. With the exception of the *Wall Street Journal*, which charges an annual fee, all the major newspaper sites are free, "at least at the moment. Given the sorry state of Internet advertising revenue, it wouldn't surprise me if some of these sites start charging for access.

One thing I like about reading newspapers on the Web is that you can search past issues. In many cases, you'll have to pay to read the old articles that you retrieve but at least you can perform the search for free.

Another thing I love about reading newspapers on the Web is that, wherever you live or happen to be, you can always get your home-town paper (or any out-of-town paper) online. If there's a big story out of Israel, I can read about it in the English language edition of the *Jerusalem Post* (www.jpost.com). If there's news from the United Kingdom, I can read about it in the London *Times* (www.thetimes.co.uk), the *Guardian* (www.guardian.co.uk), or another British paper. You won't just find big city newspapers online. Many small town, college, and even high school newspapers are online. For a listing of my favorite sites and a global directory of newspapers around the world, check out www.littlepcbook.com.

The *New York Times* has a great Web site.

The CBS MarketWatch Web site provides invaluable financial news.

TV News Web Sites

Let's not forget TV news. Because they already report the news 24 hours a day, broadcast organizations are well-positioned for the Internet. When important national or international news breaks, I turn my TV to CNN, NBC, or Fox, and if I'm online I point my browser to the same sources. The stories on the broadcast news sites are usually pretty fresh, even if the reporting is a bit less thorough than what you'll find in a newspaper source.

Radio Station Web Sites

Thousands of radio stations around the world broadcast live over the Internet, playing every conceivable musical format, from punk to classical music, as well as news and information. You'll even find the old radio dramas, modern comedy, and more. Many local TV and radio stations have their own Web sites, too. For breaking news, community updates, and regional music, these are terrific resources. Often, the URLs match up with the call letters. For example, www.kcsm.org is the Web site for KCSM, a great Jazz station in San Mateo, California.

Leading News Sites

ABC News	www.abcnews.com
Boston Globe	www.bostonglobe.com
CBS News	www.cbsnews.com
Christian Science Monitor	www.csmonitor.com
CNet Tech News	www.news.com
CNN	www.cnn.com
Financial Times	www.ft.com
Fox News	www.foxnews.com
Los Angeles Times	www.latimes.com
MSNBC	www.msnbc.com
New York Times	www.nytimes.com
Newsweek Magazine	www.newsweek.com
San Jose Mercury News	www.sv.com
Time magazine	www.time.com
USA Today	www.usatoday.com
Wall Street Journal	www.wsj.com (annual fee)
Washington Post	www.washingtonpost.com

And, like those out of town newspapers, you can listen to radio stations from around the world. A few years ago, before my family took a trip to Australia, I started listening to Australian radio stations, just to get in the mood and to pick up on the accent. Stations were easy to find and they came in loud and clear. No worries.

You can use just about any search engine to locate these stations, but there's a great one just for radio stations: Radio Locator (www.radio-locator.com) can ferret out any station in the world. To listen to radio on the Web, you need either RealPlayer (which you can download at www.real.com) or the Windows Media Player (which comes with XP). Some radio stations require one and some require the other, so I recommend having both players.

Where to Find Online Radio Stations

Classical Music	http://classicalwebcast.com	Lists classical music radio stations online
Radio Locator	www.radio-locator.com	Finds any radio station in the world, online or offline
Radio Tower	www.radiotower.com	Searches by format to find any type of station
Real Networks Guide	http://realguide.real.com	A guide to stations that broadcast in Real Audio
Windows Media Guide	www.windowsmedia.com	A guide to stations that broadcast using Windows Media
Yahoo's Broadcast	www.broadcast.com	Finds Internet radio and TV stations

My Favorite Online Radio Stations

BBC	www.bbc.co.uk	The venerable British Broadcasting Service now broadcasts its World Service and other programs from its Web site
Bloomberg Radio (WBBR NY)	www.bloomberg.com/wbbr	Business news comes from the source, Bloomberg news
CapitalFM	www.capitalfm.com	The United Kingdom's largest commercial music station offers a bit of news (including my tech reports)
National Public Radio	www.npr.org	This is where to find all of NPR's commentary, news, and cultural reports on the Web
Radio Disney	www.radiodisney.com	Here's where the kiddies can come for online programming

Moviefone tells you what's playing and lets you buy tickets online.

Movies on the Web

Are you thinking of taking in a movie tonight? You could go through the newspaper, but it might be faster to check online.

Moviefone (www.moviefone.com) and Fandango (www. fandango.com) have listings for movie theaters throughout the United States. In many areas you can also purchase tickets online. There is a surcharge (typically about $1 a ticket), but it can be worth it if you can avoid the lines and assure yourself a ticket before the movie sells out. So far, booking your ticket online won't reserve your seat, but that may be coming soon.

And if you want to find movie trivia on the Web, check out the Internet Movie Database. It features tons of movies, both old and new, with biographical information about the entire cast. My wife and I saw *Proof of Life* on video and couldn't remember the name of the actor who played Peter Bowman. I went to www.imdb.com, typed in the name of the movie and now I know everything there is to know about David Morse—his age, birth place, and complete "filmography" of all of the movies and TV shows that he's ever appeared in or directed.

Dot Bomb Disclaimer

In this age of "dot bombs," there is always the chance that some of the Web sites listed in this chapter will be out of business by the time you read this. For example, I had planned to include iCAST.com in this section, but when I went to the site I found the following message: "Sorry you missed us! iCAST Corporation has closed down its Website and is in the process of winding down the business." Even big-name players have had trouble trying to make it on the Web screen. Entertaindom from Time Warner and Pop.com, backed by Steven Spielberg, have also closed down.

Watching Movies Online

Believe it or not, it's now possible to watch full-length Hollywood movies on the Internet from your PC, just as you do on cable or satellite TV. It's not exactly the same experience as sitting on the couch in front of your TV. Still CinemaNow.com and a handful of other online movie sites are giving it a try. In August 2001, Metro-Goldwyn-Mayer, Paramount, Sony Pictures, Universal Studios, and Warner Brothers jointly announced plans to launch an online movie site to test market their films.

Resources

AtomFilms
www.atomfilms.com

FilmSpeed
www.filmspeed.com

RobotFilms
www.robotfilms.com

Meanwhile, there are plenty of short-subject movies you can watch online, and one of the best places to find them is AtomFilms (www. atomfilms.shockwave.com). You'll get better picture and sound quality if you have a high-speed broadband connection, but it is possible to watch a film even with a 56K modem.

The Small Screen

The ubiquitous *TV Guide* also has a Web site that is more useful in many ways than the printed version. Type in your Zip code and indicate whether you're watching broadcast, cable, or satellite, and you'll get a customized listing of what's on TV. Unfortunately, I still have trouble finding programs I like to watch, but no Web site can solve that problem.

In addition, most TV stations and all networks have their own Web sites with lots of information about programming. Some even let you watch live programming.

Finding Phone Numbers, Addresses, and Maps

Here's the 411 on finding phone numbers: You no longer need to call 411, which means you don't have to pay a fee to your phone company every time you want to look up a number.

Watch short films online at AtomFilms.

What's more, you can also get the address of any residence or place of business, plus a map to get you there.

There are a number of sites where you can look up numbers. My favorite is www.switchboard.com, because it's easy to use. It lets you search the entire United States, even if all you have is the person's last name. You can narrow down the search by entering the first name or initial, as well as the state or city. There is also a separate business search which lets you search for businesses by name or category. Of course, it won't find unlisted numbers and it may not be completely up to date, so if it's really important and you can't find it on switchboard.com, you can try other services or—if you're desperate—call directory assistance.

InfoSpace (www.infospace.com) has all the usual White Pages and Yellow Pages services, plus a reverse directory in which you can enter a phone number to find the subscriber's name and, if listed, address. You'll also find the same service at www.reversephonedirectory.com.

Resources

AT&T Anywho
www.anywho.com/

InfoSpace
www.infospace.net

Switchboard
www.Switchboard.com

Yahoo People Search
http://people.yahoo.com/

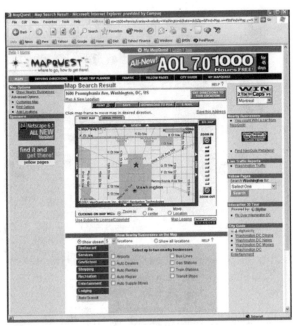

Get maps and directions online at Mapquest.com.

Maps and Directions

I'm directionally challenged. Even with a map, I have a hard time finding things. One solution is to use one of the Internet mapping services. You can enter any location in the United States and get a map of that area. If you enter two locations, you can get a map plus turn-by-turn driving instructions from door to door. I find the instructions to be quite useful, but I never rely on them completely.

The computer-generated maps aren't always up to date and there is always the possibility that you'll be asked to drive over a river without a bridge or travel a long and circuitous mountain road when you could have easily used a freeway. Laugh if you must, but both of these have happened to me while trying to follow computerized directions. Most of the time, online directions are accurate, but double-check them before you hit the road.

Travelling With the Web

I wouldn't consider getting on a plane without checking out one of the online travel services. I like to compare prices from different airlines and see if I can save a few bucks on my fare.

Resources

Mapquest
www.mapquest.com

Yahoo Maps
http://maps.yahoo.com

Maps on Us
www.mapsonus.com

Switchboard
www.switchboard.com

For example, I travel to Washington, D.C. a lot, but it turns out that flights to nearby Baltimore are considerably cheaper. The airline might not tell you that, but some online travel services let you look for flights to airports within 25, 50, or 100 miles of your preferred airport. This feature saved me $400 for two tickets on a one-way flight from D.C. to Boston by routing me from Baltimore to Manchester, New Hampshire, instead. Sure, it meant an extra hour of driving on each end, but it was quite a savings.

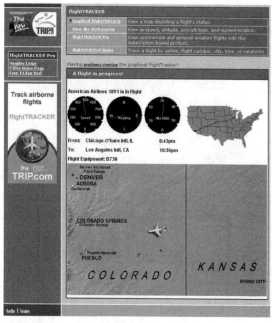

Trip.com lets you track flights in progress, so you know exactly when the plane is going to land.

Travel Sites

Expedia	www.expedia.com	Provides booking information on virtually all airlines, plus hotels and car rentals
Hotel Discount	www.hoteldiscount.com	Offers good discounts at hotels in major cities
Orbitz	www.orbitz.com	Owned by major airlines and features flight information on virtually all airlines, plus hotels and car rentals
Travelocity	www.travelocity.com	Features booking information on virtually all airlines, plus hotels and car rentals
Trip.com	www.trip.com	Tracks flights while in the air

Getting Healthy On the Web

I'm not a medical doctor and I don't play one on TV. Yet, as a parent, a husband, and a hypochondriac, I sometimes find myself acting as a medical sleuth, searching health-related Web sites in search of explanations, cures, or advice about a wide variety of ailments.

Medical information on the Internet is a mixed blessing. On the plus side, there is plenty you can learn. But on the negative side, there is also plenty of misinformation.

One problem with doing your own medical research is that almost any symptom can point to several illnesses. The general health sites will usually focus on the most common causes of symptoms, but they don't spare you the possibility that it could be something worse. According to WebMD (www.webmd.com), for example, a headache can be caused by muscle tension or a brain tumor. A cough can be the result of a common cold or possibly lung cancer.

I've had some sleepless nights contemplating all the things that might possibly be wrong with me or my family. When I do find something alarming, I often print it out and take it with me when I visit my doctor. Sometimes I'll even email it to my doctor. As it turns out, I'm not alone. According to a 2001 survey, 64 percent of us discuss Internet findings with our physicians, and 14 percent email our concerns.

Dr. Judith Murphy, a Silicon Valley pediatrician, estimates that one quarter of her patients have come to her armed with information they found online. "Many people use it to learn about a specific condition. It's increased the availability of information and it's very positive and helpful," she says.

Still, there are patients who come to her with needless worries. "People who are anxious or hard to reassure have a tendency to focus on the small probabilities of something disastrous," Murphy adds. "Some parents have expressed worry over conditions that I've never seen in my 19 years of practice."

Murphy does find the Internet extremely useful for people with very rare conditions or diseases. "When someone does have

Health Sites

Dean Edell's Health Central	www.healthcentral.com	Medical advice, plus information on food and nutrition
Dr.Koop.com	www.drkoop.com	Good overall information for consumers
Mayo Clinic	www.mayoclinic.com	Advice from the venerable clinic
Medline Plus	www.medlineplus.gov	Advice for consumers, including drug charts
U.S. National Library of Medicine	www.nlm.nih.gov	Health information for consumers and medical professionals

something quite rare, the Web can offer lots of information that is useful to both me and the patient. It hooks people up to a virtual community of others who are dealing with something quite unusual."

Despite my tendency to become alarmed about what I read online, I've generally found worthwhile information. Some of the more useful sites include former Surgeon General C. Everett Koop's site (www.DrKoop.com), Dr. Dean Edell's www.HealthCentral.com, WebMD, and the Mayo Clinic's www.mayoclinic.com

In addition to finding out about conditions, symptoms, and procedures, the Net is a great place to find out about drugs. Like most families, we have prescription drugs in our medicine cabinet, and in most cases, the pamphlets that come with most of them are nowhere to be found. Fortunately, you can find information about virtually any prescription or over-the-counter drug at most of the health Web sites. You can find even more if you enter the drug's generic or brand name in a search engine like www.google.com.

There are also government-funded medical databases, including PubMed (www.pubmed.com) and Medline Plus (www. medlineplus.gov). Medline Plus is, for most people, a far more useful compendium of medical information. Aimed at both consumers and professionals, it has a database of prescription and non-prescription medicines, listed by both brand and generic names.

You can also find information in forums and newsgroups. Deja.com is a Web-based newsgroup search engine that makes it easy to locate information on virtually anything. But before you go off to newsgroups to learn about medical conditions, remember that anyone can post to a newsgroup, and you have no way of determining whether the person actually knows what he or she is talking about.

Tracking Money on the Web

The good news about investing online is that it's quick and easy. The bad news about investing online is that it's quick and easy. If you decide to trade online, be aware that the moment you hit the Submit button, you've made a trade, whether you meant to or not. I realize that's pretty obvious, but I've made mistakes that have cost me money because I wasn't being careful enough. Once I bought high and sold low, not because of bad timing or bad luck but because I just hit the wrong button. Silly me.

The Motley Fool helps you laugh your way to the bank.

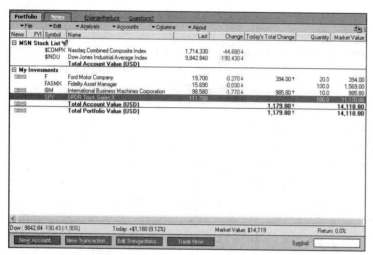

MSN Investor gives you up-to-the minute information on all of your holdings.

Having said that, there are some great online sites that not only let you invest your money but also help you with the information you'll need.

One of the most popular investment Web sites is The Motley Fool (www.fool.com). It has a slightly irreverent and sometimes humorous approach toward investing and money. Despite the yuks, Motley Fool is serious when it comes to providing solid advice.

The Street (www.thestreet.com) is another serious investment site with some of the best advisors in the business. But remember that the "best" advisors aren't always right, as the millions who lost money in dot-com stocks can testify.

Why I Trust Bill Gates with My Money

Bill Gates gets some of our money whenever we buy a Windows PC. But Microsoft also has a way of keeping track of money with its MSN Investor Web site (www.investor.com). What I like about Investor is that it will track my portfolio based on my investments with online brokers.

If you have online accounts with Fidelity, Charles Schwab, or other major online brokerage houses, Investor can track your investments in real time. Give Investor your account number and password and it looks up the information for you. True, it means revealing confidential information to Microsoft, so you have to decide whether or not that bothers you. It doesn't bother me because I really don't think that Gates or anyone else at Microsoft bothers to look at my financial status. Other Web sites, including Yahoo Finance, do the same thing.

Speaking of online brokerage houses, it makes sense to set up an online account with your broker even if you have no interest in trading online. Why? Because you can get up-to-the minute information about the status of your account, your balances, and trade confirmations. You get the same thing on the phone or in the mail, but tracking it online is faster and easier. Also, when tax time comes around, you can get the reports and statements you need immediately.

Online Banking

Many banks now offer online banking services that let you check your balances and pay your bills online. The bill-paying service usually requires you to enter information about your payees, and then the bank sends the check by mail (or electronically for some large merchants) and deducts the balance from your account.

Be sure to check the bank's policies regarding how the money is deducted. Some banks take it out the moment you place the order, but others wait until the day the money actually changes hands. That's better, of course, because you keep your funds until the last possible minute.

One thing I like about online bill paying is that I can pay my bills days or even months in advance, but still hold on to the money until the last minute. I also like having my regular bills, like mortgage and car payments, paid automatically every month so I don't have to worry about them. I do, however, have to make sure there's enough money in my account to cover the bills.

Paytrust is an interesting service that not only pays your bills but presents them as well. You tell all of your billers to send your invoices to Paytrust instead of to you, and then Paytrust presents the bills to you on a secure Web site. You can have Paytrust pay your bills automatically or can elect to do it one by one online. I have it programmed to automatically pay the minimum balance on all my credit cards. I usually pay the entire balance (avoiding interest), but this way, even if I'm out of town. the minimum amount gets paid so I don't get late fees or any negative remarks in my credit file.

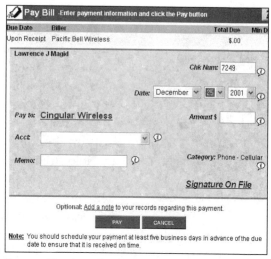

Paytrust, like the online banks, lets you pay bills with onscreen checks.

Keeping It Legal on the Net

For anyone accused of a crime or involved in a major lawsuit, there's no substitute for a good lawyer. But when it comes to drawing up basic legal documents, an attorney sometimes really can be replaced by a computer.

Legaldocs (www.legaldocs.com) lets you choose from a pretty wide variety of forms that can be filled out online. Some are free, but most range in price from $3.50 to $27.75. You create documents by answering on-screen questions, and when you're done, the site generates a document that you can print or copy and paste into a word-processing program. There is no charge to answer the questions and view a summary of your document, but you will be asked for a credit card number before it generates the complete document. The advantage to this is that you

Legaldocs.com lets you fill out legal forms online.

Quicken Family Lawyer

pay only for what you need. But if you think you might need more than one or two documents, you're better off buying a program.

If you have a lot of forms to complete, you may be better off with software that you can run any time you want. Quicken Family Lawyer bears the same name as the Quicken financial software but, unlike the financial software, it is pubished by Nolo Press, a leading self-help legal publisher.

It'sLegal (www.itslegal.com) is a service of The Learning Company. The site has a lot of useful material, including its Legal Information Network, which provides extensive information about wills and trusts, real estate, home ownership, consumer law, family law, employment law, and health and medical issues. The site also has a good selection of links to other legal sites, and a Lawyer Locator in case you need some serious help.

If you're in the process of getting a divorce, check out Split-Up.com (www.split-up.com). This well-crafted site has information about custody, alimony, property division, financial and emotional advice, as well as state-specific information about family law. The site lets you purchase software specifically designed for people involved in a divorce. It also provides a chat area and advice for those who are still trying to save their marriages.

Special Interest Groups Online

No matter what your religion, favorite sport, ethnic background, or political philosophy, you can find like-minded people and Web sites to keep you plugged in. The Web is especially helpful for people who feel isolated geographically. Even if you can't find many people in your area who share your particular interests, there are bound to be plenty in the virtual community.

The best way to seek out whatever you're looking for is in a search engine or a directory. You can probably find it in the Yahoo or LookSmart directories, and if not, you will definitely find it in Web crawlers like Google or AltaVista.

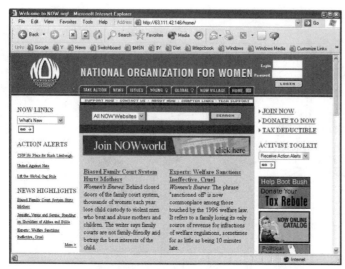

The Web site for the National Organization for Women offers news
with a feminist perspective.

Every major and minor religious group is represented online,
including official sites from the Vatican and the other major religious institutions. Many churches and temples also have their
own Web sites.

If you're into gay rights, women's rights, children's rights or
even left-handers rights, you'll find sites that will put you in touch
with others who can provide you with support and information.
Like a lot of Americans, I have some special interests and I know
how helpful the Web has been.

Now you know the Net! Well, some of it, anyway. I wish I could tell you that we've covered everything there is to know about the Internet, but that would be like standing on a beach in Santa Monica and claiming that you know all there is to know about the Pacific Ocean. The Internet is almost as deep. The good news is that you can learn a great deal just by exploring. Check out as many sites as you can, use the directory services like Yahoo and LookSmart, and don't forget the resources at www.littlepcbook.com.

And, hey, congratulations on getting through **The Little PC Book, Windows XP Edition** *(or on jumping to the last page)! In record time, you've learned everything you need to know to work confidently with your PC. Have a great journey— and lots of fun along the way.*

Glossary

A

Accessibility Options A feature of Windows XP that makes it more accessible to people with visual or physical impairments.

account In a multi-user environment, the information and settings for each person who uses the PC.

Activate Windows An anti*piracy* feature. The process sends information to Microsoft that certifies your copy of Windows.

Add/Remove Programs A section of the *Control Panel* used to add or remove *programs.*

Active Desktop In *Windows 98*, a feature that allows live Web content to be displayed on the *desktop.*

active matrix screen A high-quality *LCD* screen used on *notebook PCs.*

adapter See *expansion board.*

AGP Stands for "advanced graphics port," a high-speed video *port* available in new PCs.

All Programs The icon on the *Start menu* used to access *programs.*

application program A piece of software that does a particular task, such as word processing, database management, or accounting.

ASCII Pronounced "as-key," it stands for American Standard Code for Information Interchange. It's another term for *plain text,* a file format that includes only alphabetic or numerical characters and no format information.

atomic clock An extremely accurate clock used to set other clocks. Windows XP can set your PC's system clock from an atomic clock over the *Internet.*

B

backing up Creating copies of program and data files, in case the original is damaged.

bandwidth The amount of data that can be transferred in a specified amount of time. Usually used for *Internet* speeds, such as "*DSL* has a bandwidth of up to 1.5 *megabits per second*."

baud A term used to describe data-transmission speeds, especially for *modems*. Baud is often used to mean *bits per second* (bps).

beta version A prerelease version of software, sometimes made available to the public so that the software's publishers can get feedback on its features.

bit The smallest unit of measurement for electronic data, a bit (short for "binary digit") is one on or off signal. Eight bits make one *byte*.

bit depth The number of *bits* used to save a piece of graphic information. Generally, the higher the bit depth, the better the quality of the graphic.

bit-mapped graphics Images made up of an arrangement of tiny dots.

board See *expansion board*.

boot To start up the computer. The word is derived from the expression "to pull oneself up by the bootstraps," because the computer uses information stored in its own chips to start itself up.

boot files System files used to *boot* the PC.

browser Software used to navigate the *World Wide Web*.

bug An error in a computer program or system. It got its name when a moth was found on a tube in one of the first computers.

burn Record to a *CD-ROM* or *DVD*.

bus A pathway for moving data inside a computer. It's important to know what bus standard your computer uses so that you can buy compatible *peripherals*.

byte Eight *bits*. A byte is enough information to express a single alphanhumeric character in a file.

C

C prompt See DOS prompt.

cable modem An adapter designed to link a PC to a coaxial cable, offering high-speed Internet access.

cache memory A portion of memory set aside for temporary storage, generally used to speed up processing.

CAD Stands for "computer-aided design": using a computer for product design.

card See *expansion board*.

carpal tunnel syndrome A wrist and hand injury caused by repetitive actions such as typing.

cascading A method of arranging windows on the desktop so they are stacked one on top of another, with only the title bars and left-hand borders of the bottom windows showing.

cascading menus A set of menus and submenus.

CD-R Stands for "compact disc, recordable," a type of CD and disk drive that allows you to record data (once) onto CDs, a well as play back data stored on them.

CD-ROM Stands for "compact disc, read-only memory." CD-ROM discs hold about 650 MB of data and are used to distribute lots of information, such as software, graphics libraries, or reference works. The data on a CD-ROM is permanently etched on the disc and cannot be changed.

CD-RW Stands for "compact disc rewritable," refers to both the *disk drive* and the discs that can be recorded, then modified or erased.

Celeron A *processor*, made by Intel, based on the *Pentium II* but less powerful.

central processing unit The *chip* on a computer's *system board* that does the main processing. For PCs, these chips are based on Intel's *Pentium* chip technology. (Older PCs may use Intel-compatible 386 or 486 chips.) Abbreviated CPU.

channel A special type of *World Wide Web* site designed to be downloaded to your computer on a regular schedule.

chat Real-time, usually text-based, communication over the Internet. See also *instant message.*

checkbox In Windows, a program control that allows you to pick an option by clicking in a box next to the option name.

child window A *window* within a window. *Program windows* may contain several child windows, each containing a separate file.

chip See *processor.*

Classic View A way to configure *Windows XP* so that it looks like previous versions of Windows.

click To press and release the left *mouse button* once to select something on screen.

client On a *network*, a computer or piece of software meant to retrieve files from a central computer called a *server.*

clip art Files containing ready-made, copyright-free images that you can buy on disk or download from the *Internet* and use in your own work.

Clipboard In *Windows*, a temporary holding place for information you cut or copy from a document. Data from the last cut or copy operation is kept on the Clipboard so that you can paste it to a new location.

clock speed The number of cycles per second (*megahertz*) at which a *processor* runs. For any given type of processor, the faster the clock speed, the faster the processor.

close button In *Windows*, the icon at the top right of a window that you click to close the window.

COM The designation for a computer's *serial ports*. The first serial port is referred to as COM1, the second as COM2, and so on. You use the name to tell setup programs where they can find a *peripheral*, such as a *modem* or a *mouse*, that is connected to the computer by a serial port.

command An instruction for the computer. In Windows, commands can be given in many ways: by choosing them from *menus*, by using the *keyboard*, or by clicking buttons and *toolbars*.

command button A Windows program control, activated a command by clicking a button onscreen.

communication protocol A set of rules followed by the software at both ends of a *modem* connection, creating a common language for online communication.

computer-aided design See *CAD.*

Contact-management software A type of *personal information manager* designed for salespeople and others whose business relies on client contact. The software keeps a record of telephone contacts as well as names and addresses.

context menu In *Windows*, a *menu* that appears when you *right-click* an object.

context-sensitive help Online help that gives information for the current task. For example, if you call up help while using a dialog box, a program that offers context-sensitive help will automatically show a help window for that particular dialog box.

Control Panel The area off the *Start menu* where you configure your system, *install* or uninstall *hardware* or *software*, and perform other routine functions.

cookie A small file saved to your *hard drive* by a Web sites. Usually used to store passwords and other information so that you don't have to enter it each time you visit the site.

CPU See *central processing unit*.

CRT Stands for "cathode ray tube." See *monitor*.

cursor keys On a *keyboard*, the keys, labeled with arrows, that move the Windows *insertion point* (or "cursor") around the screen.

D

database Any collection of information, such as a phone book or a company's inventory. On a computer, you use a *database management program* to create and control databases.

database management program Software designed to handle large amounts of information on a computer.

DDR Stands for "double data rate," a faster memory based on *SD-RAM*.

desktop In Windows, the main interface, which you see when you first start your PC. It can hold the tools and files you use to do your work, but in *Windows XP* the *Start Menu* is the preferred location for tools and files.

desktop publishing Using a personal computer to lay out and produce complex documents.

dialog box In *Windows*, a box from which you choose command options.

digital camera A camera that stores pictures in memory instead of on film. Digital images can be downloaded to a PC for editing and printing.

digital video camera A type of home video camera that uses memory instead of film and usually connects to a PC with a *FireWire* port. Digital video can be stored, edited, and played on a PC.

digital flat-panel interface A special graphics port that sends digital graphics data, suitable for use by *flat-panel displays*, instead of the analog data designed for *CRTs*. Abbreviated DFP interface.

digital rights management Software, generally used on CDs, that prevents copying.

DIMM Stands for "dual in-line memory module," a device designed to plug into a computer's *system board*, that holds *memory* chips. See also *SIMM* and *RIMM*.

directory 1. In *DOS*, a section on a disk, like the file folders in Windows, in which you keep a related set of files. 2. A list of the files on a disk.

disc An alternate spelling for *disk*, usually used to refer to *CD-ROMs* and *DVDs*.

disk An object with a magnetic surface on which information is written for storage. Most PCs have a *hard disk* that stores the bulk of the user's data. *Floppy disks* and other removable media are used to distribute files to others and to *back up* hard disk data.

disk cache An area in *memory* used to temporarily store information from the disk drive. Its use speeds up operations because the computer can access memory faster than it can access the *disk*.

disk defragmenter See *fragmented*.

disk drive The *hardware* device that reads information from a *disk*.

display See *monitor*.

display adapter A set of chips, often on an *expansion board*, that translates data into video information for a monitor.

docking station A hardware base that adds extra ports and other features to *subnotebook PCs*.

document A file created with an *application program*.

domain name The name used to identify the computers at a particular location on the *Internet*. Companies and other entities can register domain names with a central Internet authority so that computers all over the world can access their *servers* by using the domain name.

domain name service Software run by *ISPs* that routes Internet messages to known *domain names*.

DOS See *MS-DOS.*

DOS command line See *DOS prompt.*

DOS prompt The line *MS-DOS* displays when it's waiting for a command. On most computers it will be some variation of C:\>. (The letter names the current *disk drive.*)

dot matrix printer A type of *printer* that produces characters and illustrations by striking pins against an ink ribbon, much like a typewriter. Unlike an *inkjet printer* or *laser printer,* a dot-matrix printer can print on forms with carbon copies.

dot pitch A measure of the closeness of the tiny red, green, and blue dots that make up each *pixel* on a color *monitor.*

double-click To press and release the *mouse button* twice in quick succession. Double-clicking an icon generally opens the object (program or file).

dragging Moving the mouse with the *mouse button* pressed down, usually in order to move an object or select a string of text.

DRAM Stands for "dynamic random access memory." DRAM is what people usually mean when they just say "RAM" or "memory."

drawing program A program that creates *object-based graphics,* that is, pictures from collections of individual geometric shapes.

drive A: A PC's first *floppy disk* drive.

drive B: A PC's second *floppy disk* drive.

drive bay A space in a PC designed to hold extra *disk drives.*

drive C: A PC's *hard disk.*

driver A small program that runs *peripheral hardware,* such as a *printer* or *scanner.*

drop-down list In Windows, a list of options for a *field* that appears when you click an arrow next to the field.

DSL Stands for "digital subscriber line," a technology for sending digital messages at high speeds over phone wires.

DV See *digital video camera.*

DVD Stands for "digital versatile disc," a *storage* technology that looks like a *CD-ROM* but holds much more information—4.7 to 17 *gigabytes.* It's also becoming a popular medium for movies.

DVD+RW A *DVD* writing standard supported by some, but not all, PC companies.

DVD-RAM 1. A *disk drive* that can play and record both *DVD* and *CD-ROM.* 2. A special type of DVD stored within a case, that only works with special drives.

DVD-RW A *disk drive* that can read, record, and modify *DVDs* which can then, in theory, be played on any PC or television DVD system.

E

EDO RAM Stands for "extended data output random-access memory," a type of high-speed *memory.*

email Short for "electronic mail," a method of sending messages over a *network* such as the *Internet.* The addressee receives the message almost instantaneously.

ergonomic keyboard A type of keyboard designed to reduce the risk of repetitive stress disorders, such as carpal tunnel syndrome, that can result from too much typing.

error message A message displayed by a piece of software to inform you that something has gone wrong.

Ethernet A technology designed to link computers over high-speed *local area networks.*

expansion board Boards that add processors to the *system board* give the computer extra functions. Expansion boards are installed in a computer's *expansion slots*.

expansion slot A place set aside on a computer's *system board* where *expansion boards* can be added to give the computer extra functions.

F

Favorites menu A menu in Internet Explorer and parts of *Windows XP* that stores Web pages or files you designate for quick access.

field 1. A place in a *dialog box* where you type information. 2. An information category in a *database*.

file A collection of data with a name attached, saved on a computer's *disk*.

file extension Three characters following a period at the end of a file name. The file extension usually indicates the *file format* or the program used to create or modify the file.

file format The kind of data a file holds. Any *application program* can read and save only certain file formats. The file format is usually indicated by the *file extension*.

firewall Hardware or software designed to keep intruders from invading or damaging your computer.

FireWire A technology designed to link *PCs* and *peripherals*, such as *disk drives*, that require high-speed connections. Also called 1394 or IEEE 1394.

Flash card A storage technology designed for use in digital cameras and other portable devices.

flat-panel display A monitor, usually based on *LCD* technology, that has a flat case, rather than the deep, TV-like form used for a *CRT*.

floppy disk A portable disk consisting of a floppy mylar disk enclosed in a hard shell.

folder In Windows, a method of grouping files saved on a disk. See also *directory*.

folder window A *window* that displays the file system of the PC. Compare *program window*.

font A collection of characters in a certain type style. On PCs, fonts are files, in either *TrueType* or *PostScript* format, that supply outlines for the shapes of the letters.

format 1. To prepare a disk to hold information. 2. The kind of information saved in a file. 3. To add design information to a document.

forum See *newsgroup*.

fragmented Said of a *hard disk* where bits of *application programs* and *files* are scattered around the drive, causing slower performance. Can be fixed using the disk defragmenter program in the Accessories menu.

freeware See *public domain software*.

FTP Short for "file transfer protocol," a method of transferring files between computers.

function keys A set of keys on a PC *keyboard*, usually labeled F1, F2, and so on, that can be programmed to carry out special commands.

G

gigabyte About a billion *bytes* or a thousand *megabytes* of data (1,073,741,824 bytes). Abbreviated GB.

graphical user interface An *interface*, such as that used by *Windows*, that lets the user give commands by manipulating graphical representations of objects, such as files and programs. Sometimes abbreviated "*GUI*."

GUI Pronounced "gooey." See *graphical user interface*.

graphics adapter See *display adapter*.

H

hacker Usually refers to a person who writes or distributes a *virus* or other destructive or invasive *software.*

hand-held computer An extremely small computer made to be carried in a pocket or briefcase. Also called a *palmtop PC.*

hard disk A storage device, either internal or external to a computer's *system unit,* that holds large amounts of data.

hardware The physical components of a computer system. Compare *software.*

hardware interface The technology used to connect *peripherals* to a PC. Some examples are *FireWire, USB,* and *PCI.*

hibernation A power-saving mode in which the PC uses no power at all.

hub A *hardware* device used to connect PCs to a *network.*

hyperlink A method for navigating through documents on the *World Wide Web.* The creator of a Web site can make any graphic or piece of text a hyperlink, so that clicking on it calls up a related Web page.

I

icon A graphic representation of a *file* or a *command.*

IDE Stands for "integrated drive electronics," the most common *interface* for connecting an external *hard disk* to a PC. See also *SCSI.*

ink jet printer A type of printer that creates images on the page with controlled spurts of ink. See also *laser printer* and *dot matrix printer.*

insertion point In *Windows,* an *I*-shaped indicator that shows where any text you type will be inserted. You place the insertion point by pointing to the desired location with the *mouse* and clicking the left *mouse button.*

install The process of adding either *software* or *hardware* to your PC.

instant message To exchange text-based messages over the *Internet* in real time, using a *program* such as AOL Instant Messenger or Windows Messenger. See also *chat.*

integrated program A program that combines features of several application programs in one, usually word processing, spreadsheet, database, graphics, and communications.

interface 1. The rules by which a piece of software communicates with you and you with it. Each piece of software has its own interface, although different *Windows* programs generally have similar interfaces. 2. The method used to connect external devices to a PC. See *PCI* and *USB.*

interlacing For *monitors,* a method of drawing an image on screen in which only every other line of information is drawn in each pass. Compare *noninterlaced.*

Internet A "network of networks" through which computer users can communicate with others around the world, using *email,* the *World Wide Web,* and other services.

Internet filter A piece of software that controls what *Internet* sites can be accessed from a PC.

Internet service provider A company that connects individual PC users to the *Internet.* Abbreviated *ISP.*

ISDN Stands for "integrated services data network," a technology used to send digital information at high speeds over phone wires.

ISP See *Internet service provider.*

J

joystick A *pointing device* designed for use with games.

K

keyboard The typewriterlike device used to input text and give commands to a computer.

keyboard shortcut A method of giving *menu* commands using the *keyboard* instead of a *mouse*.

kilobyte A unit of data equal to 1024 *bytes*. Abbreviated K or KB.

L

LAN See *local area network*.

laptop PC A relatively small, battery-operated PC, with a built-in *monitor* and *pointing device,* typically weighing between four and seven pounds. Also called a *notebook PC*.

laser printer A type of printer that produces images on paper using a laser beam, similar to the mechanism used for a copier. Generally, laser printers provide the highest-quality black-and-white images available from a desktop printer. See also *dot-matrix printer* and *inkjet printer.*

LCD Stands for "liquid crystal display," a technology used to create flat-panel displays. See *monitor*.

legacy-free PC A PC with no *expansion slots*. Uses *USB* or *FireWire* for *peripherals*.

Linux A public-domain version of the *Unix operating system* software.

local area network A group of personal computers connected by cables and special networking software, so that the computers' users can share files, printers, and other services.

LPT The PC's designation for parallel ports. The first parallel port is LPT1, the second is LPT2, and so on. You use the name to tell setup programs where they can find printers and other *peripherals* connected to the computer.

M

Macintosh A type of personal computer made by Apple Computer. Macintoshes use a different operating system and run different application software than do Windows-based PCs.

Magnifier An accessory that makes Windows look as if you're viewing it through a magnifying glass.

math coprocessor A *processor*, specially designed for speedy math calculations, that is added to the *system board* of some computers. The *Pentium* CPUs have a math coprocessor built in.

maximize/restore button In *Windows*, a button at the top right corner of every window that enlarges the window to fill the screen when it's clicked. If the window is already full size, clicking the button restores the window to its smaller size.

megabit About a million *bits*. Abbreviated Mb.

megabits per second The number of *megabits* that can be transferred (usually over the *Internet*) in a second. Abbreviated Mbps. See also *bandwidth*.

megabyte About a million *bytes* (1,048,576, to be exact). Abbreviated MB.

megahertz The number of cycles per second at which a *processor* works. Abbreviated MHz.

megapixel A million pixels. Used mainly to describe *digital cameras*. Generally, the higher the number, the better the images.

memory The place where a computer keeps programs and data when they are in use. Also called "random-access memory" or "RAM." Compare *storage*.

menu A list of commands displayed by a program.

menu bar In *Windows* programs, the list of *menu* names that ranges across the top of a window.

Microsoft Windows The operating system used by most PCs.

minimize button In Windows, a button at the top right corner of every window that reduces the window to a *Program button* on the *taskbar* when it's clicked.

MMX A technology added to *Pentium* processors to speed up multimedia processing. MMX technology is included in *Pentium II* and later chips.

modem A device that *mo*dulates computer data into signals that can be carried over phone lines, and *dem*odulates data it receives from the phone lines into a form readable by the computer.

monitor The screen on which programs display information. Also called the *display*.

motherboard See *system board*.

mouse A *pointing device* that allows you to give commands and select items on screen in a *graphical user interface*.

mouse buttons Buttons on the top of a *mouse* that you press in order to activate a command. Generally, PC mice have two mouse buttons.

mouse pad A pad used under a *mouse* to make its movements smooth.

mouse port A socket on the back of some computers designed specifically for attaching a *mouse*.

MP3 A *file format* that compresses audio to a file size of about one-tenth. MP3 files can be played on a PC or on special devices called MP3 players.

MS-DOS Stands for "Microsoft disk operating system." Until the arrival of *Windows*, it was the standard *operating system* for PCs.

multiscan monitor A monitor designed to work with a variety of *display adapters*, at different *resolutions*.

My Computer A *Start menu* option that provides access to all *folders* and *files* in the current *account*.

My Documents A *Start menu* option that provides access to all documents in the current *account*.

My Music A *Start menu* option that provides access to all music *files* in the current *account*.

My Network Places A *Start menu* option that provides access to computers on the local *network*.

My Pictures A *Start menu* option that provides access to all image *files* in the current *account*.

N

network Personal computers that are connected so their users can share *files, printers*, and other services. See also *local area network* and *Internet*.

network adapter See *network interface card*.

network computer A computer that has no *operating system*, but provides access to the *Internet* or a *local area network*.

network interface card An adapter that connects a PC to a *local area network*, cable service, or other *network*.

newsgroup An *Internet* service where users can post messages on a given topic. Also called a *forum*.

noninterlaced For *monitors*, a method of drawing the onscreen image that uses a single pass to draw the entire image. Compare *interlacing*.

notebook PC See *laptop PC*. See also *subnotebook PC*.

O

object-based graphics Graphics created from collections of individual geometric shapes that can be manipulated separately.

OCR Stands for "optical character recognition." OCR software translates the shapes of letters from a scanned file into a file readable by *word processing software*.

online service A subscription service that provides *Internet* access offers such features as libraries of information, *shareware* and *public domain software*, *chat* services, and online *forums* where subscribers can post messages to each other.

operating system The software that takes care of basic system activities, such as reading from and saving to disk, so that *application software* can focus on doing its own particular tasks. The main operating system for PCs is *Microsoft Windows.*

option buttons In *Windows*, a set of buttons in a *dialog box* only one of which can be selected at a time.

P

paint program Graphics software that creates *bit-mapped graphics.*

palmtop PC See *hand-held PC.*

parallel port A socket used to attach *printers* and other devices to the computer.

Passive-matrix screen A type of *LCD* screen.

path A string of directory names that tells *Windows* where to locate a particular *file* or *directory.* A path has three parts: the *disk drive* name, the list of *directories* that leads to the designated file or directory, and finally, the file name. The directory names are separated by backslash characters (\).

pathname See *path.*

PC Stands for *personal computer,* but usually refers specifically to a *Windows*-based personal computer.

PC card A credit card-sized *expansion board* for *notebook PCs.*

PC-compatible 1. A *Windows*-based PC. 2. As an adjective, software or hardware that works with a Windows-based PC.

PCI A type of *hardware interface* for PCs.

PCL Stands for "printer control language," a page-description language used by *PC-compatible laser printers.*

PCMCIA card See *PC card.*

Pentium A type of *processor* created by Intel. Subsequent generations in the product line have a number after the name, such as Pentium II and Pentium 4.

peripheral *Hardware,* such as a *modem* or *printer,* that is added to a computer to give it additional functions.

personal computer Any computer made to be used by a single person.

personal information manager A kind of *database* program designed to track names, addresses, and scheduling information. Abbreviated *PIM.*

PIM See *personal information manager.*

piracy Illegally copying or distributing software.

pixel Short for "picture element." On a *monitor,* a pixel is a single one of all the dots of light that make up an image.

plain text See *ASCII.*

pointer An on-screen indicator, controlled by a *mouse* or other *pointing device,* used to select the object you want to work with.

pointing device A *hardware* device, such as a *mouse, trackball, joystick,* or *touchpad,* used to move the *pointer* or *insertion point* on screen.

port A socket used to attach *peripheral* devices to the computer. See also *parallel port* and *serial port.*

portal site On the *World Wide Web,* a site designed to serve as a launch pad for explorations. Portal sites generally provide a *search engine* as well as categorized lists of *hyperlinks.*

PostScript A language created by Adobe Systems, commonly used in desktop publishing applications and high-end laser printers. Like TrueType, PostScript is a font format.

PowerPC The *processor* used in late-model *Macintosh* computers.

printer A *hardware* device that puts text or pictures on paper. See also *dot-matrix printer, inkjet printer,* and *laser printer.*

processor A circuit in a computer that processes information. Processors are attached to the *system board* or to add-on *expansion boards.* See also *central processing unit.*

program Data that is interpreted by a computer's processor to instruct the computer how to behave. See also *application program, utility,* and *operating system.*

Program button In *Windows,* a button that appears on the *taskbar* for each open *program* and *folder window.*

program window In *Windows,* a *window* that displays the *interface* for an *application program.*

Public-domain software Software that its creators give out freely, without asking for payment. Also called *freeware.* Public-domain software is available from *online services, user groups,* the *Internet,* and from companies that sell compendiums of programs. See also *shareware.*

Q

QuickLauch A toolbar that can be installed in the taskbar to provide quick access to *programs.*

R

RAM See memory.

Random-access memory See *memory.*

RD-RAM Stand for "rambus random-access memory," a very fast type of memory used in some high-end *Pentium* 4 systems.

RealAudio An audio format for use over the *Internet.* Requires the RealPlayer from RealNetworks. Compare *wave file.*

reboot To turn off a computer and start it again, or to restart it by pressing the Ctrl, Alt, and Del keys, or the Reset key. Often necessary when a computer freezes up. Many computers also provide a reset button that reboots the computer without turning off the power.

Recycle Bin In Windows, a storage area on the desktop that holds deleted files. Like other icons, the Recycle Bin can be opened so that its contents can be viewed. Emptying the Recycle Bin deletes its contents once and for all.

refurbished PC A used PC that has been professionally checked and is sold at a discount price.

registration card A postcard used to register software with the publisher. Being phased out in favor of registration over the *Internet*.

registry A part of the Windows operating system that stores information about every piece of installed software.

removable storage A storage system, such as floppy disks, CD-ROMs, and Zip drives, in which the disk is separate from the disk drive.

residential gateway See *router*.

resolution For printers and scanners, resolution is measured in dots per inch; for monitors, it's measured by the number of pixels on the screen. The higher the number, the sharper the image.

right-click To quickly press and then release the right mouse button. In Windows, right-clicking an item generally calls up a menu that lets you act on the item.

RIMM Stands for "Rambus in-line memory module." A device, designed to plug into your computer's *system board*, that holds *memory* chips. See also *DIMM* and *RIMM*.

router A *hardware* device that allows several computers to share an *Internet* connection.

S

save To record work onto a disk for permanent storage. Until work is saved, it exists only in *memory* and will be lost if the computer is turned off or its power is otherwise interrupted.

scanner A device that translates a graphic image into a computer-readable file.

screen saver A software *program* that displays graphics when the computer has been idle for a few minutes.

scroll bar In *Windows*, a control that appears whenever a window contains more than it can show at one time. Clicking the scroll bar moves the window contents up or down to show more.

SCSI Stands for "small computer systems interface," a method of connecting external hard drives and other *peripherals* to a PC. Pronounced "scuzzy."

SD-RAM Stands for "synchronous dynamic random-access memory," a type of memory used in some computers.

search engine Software that searches through a file system—on a computer or on the *Internet*—to find files related to specified subjects.

select To choose the object that the next command will act on, usually an object is selected when you *click* on it.

serial port A socket used to attach *peripherals* to the computer. Usually the serial ports are used for a *mouse* or a *modem*.

server On a *network*, a computer or a piece of software that provides files or software services to other computers, called *clients*, on the network.

shareware Software that is distributed for free, but which you're asked to pay a nominal fee for if you keep using it after an initial trial period. Shareware is usually distributed over the *Internet* and can be freely copied among friends and co-workers. See also *public-domain software*.

shortcut In *Windows,* an icon that acts like a copy of another icon, but takes up much less room on disk. Shortcuts for *printers, files, folders,* or any other object can be kept on the Windows *desktop,* allowing easy access to that object without removing the original file from its original location on the disk.

SIMM Stands for "single in-line memory module." A device, designed to plug into your computer's *system board,* that holds *memory* chips. See also *DIMM* and *RIMM.*

sleep mode See *standby mode* and *hibernation.*

slot See *expansion slot.*

software Computer programs. Compare *hardware.*

sound card An *expansion board* that increases the sound capabilities of your computer. Used with games, educational software, multimedia CDs, and music applications.

spreadsheet A type of *application program* designed for working with numbers. A spreadsheet's *interface* is patterned after an accountant's worksheet, with the data arranged in rows and columns.

standby mode A power-saving mode where the PC uses very little power.

Start button In *Windows,* a button on the left side of the *taskbar* that when clicked, opens the *Start menu.*

Start menu In *Windows,* a menu on the *taskbar* that lets you start programs, open files, get help, and carry out other useful tasks.

startup disk A floppy disk that holds the DOS or Windows boot files so it can be used to start the computer if the hard disk isn't functioning properly.

startup menu A menu that appears during the PC's startup process if there is a problem loading *Windows.*

status bar A section of a *window* that includes information about its contents.

StickyKeys An *accessibility option* that allows certain *commands* to be performed using one key instead of two.

storage Where you keep files not currently in use. It usually refers to a computer's *hard disk*. Compare *memory*.

submenu In *cascading menus*, a *menu* that appears when you click a main menu command.

subnotebook PC A particularly small *notebook PC*, usually weighing 4 pounds or less.

suite A set of several software applications sold as a unit.

surge protector A device that protects a computer from electrical surges. (The computer plugs into the surge protector, which plugs into an electrical wall outlet.)

SVGA Stands for "Super VGA." A graphics standard that supplies a monitor with a *resolution* of 640-by-480 pixels up to 1024-by-768 pixels.

system board The main board in the computer's *system unit* that holds the *central processing unit*, *memory*, and other circuitry. Also known as a *motherboard*.

system icon An *icon* at the top-left corner of every window that, when clicked, displays the *system menu*.

system menu A *menu* that appears when you click the *system icon* in any window, letting you close, resize, or move the window.

system requirements The *hardware* configuration required to run an *application program*. Always check an application's system requirements before you buy it, to make sure your computer can run it.

system unit The box on a desktop PC that holds the computer's workings, including the *system board* and *disk drives*.

T

tab In dialog boxes within *Windows* and Windows applications, a label that marks a "page" of options in the *dialog box*.

tape cartridge A memory medium used mostly for *backing up* data.

taskbar A bar that extends across the bottom of the *Windows desktop*, providing access to the *Start menu*, the system clock, and *program buttons*.

TCP/IP The *communication protocol* used for the *Internet*.

terabyte About a trillion *bytes*. Sometimes abbreviated TB.

text box In *Windows*, a box into which you type information.

text editor A simple word processor that creates files in *ASCII format*.

TFT Stands for "thin film transistor," used to describe an *active matrix screen*.

theme A way to personalize the look and feel of *Windows XP*.

thread In a *newsgroup*, a group of messages responding to the same original posting.

thumbnails 1. A smaller version of an image. 2. A *folder* view that shows small images of the *files*.

tiling A method of arranging windows on the *desktop* so the windows are placed border-to-border and no part of any window is hidden.

title bar The bar that extends across the top of every window, holding the window's name plus the minimize, maximize, and close icons.

titles Similar to ordinary *icons*, but larger and showing more information, such as *file* size and the name of the *application program* used to create it.

toggle A control that is either "on" or "off." In *menus*, toggle commands usually have a checkmark or bullet next to them if they are "on," and none if they are "off."

toolbar In *Windows* and Windows *application programs*, a bar of buttons that extends across the top of a window. Each button on the toolbar activates a common command.

Tools menu A menu that controls various *program* options, such as *network* configuration and *folder* options in *Windows XP*.

ToolTip A box that sometimes appears when you hold the *pointer* over an onscreen object, such as a button in a *toolbar,* that names the object you're pointing at.

top-level domain The part of a *domain name* that describes the type of organization the domain name belongs to. Common top-level domains are .com for commercial, .edu for educational, and .gov for government.

touchpad A *pointing device* used on many *notebook PCs.* You move the *pointer* onscreen by moving your finger over the touchpad.

trackball A pointing device consisting of a rotating ball embedded in a base, that can be used instead of a *mouse.*

trial version An *application program,* usually limited in function, that is free to try out. Similar to *shareware.*

Trojan horse An seemingly harmless *program* that is actually destructive. Similar to a *virus.*

TrueType A *font* format used by *Windows.* See also *PostScript.*

U

uninterruptible power supply A device that provides power to a computer for a few minutes even after the main electricity fails. Abbreviated UPS.

Unix A type of operating system.

UPS See *uninterruptible power supply.*

URL Stands for "universal resource locator," a string of characters that identifies a file on the Internet.

USB Stands for "universal serial bus," a *hardware interface* used to connect *peripherals* to a PC. The newer USB 2 standard is faster than USB 1, but still backward compatible with it.

user group A group of computer users who band together to offer each other help with computer problems and other computer-related services.

utility An *application program* designed to manage the computer itself, providing functions such as checking for viruses or backing up a hard disk.

V

vector graphics See object-based graphics.

V.90 A communication protocol used to control communications between 56K modems.

vertical refresh rate The number of times per second that a monitor's screen is redrawn from top to bottom, measured in Hertz (Hz). The higher the number, the less flicker on screen.

VGA Stands for "virtual graphics array." A graphics standard that offers 640-by-480-pixel color resolution.

virus Software designed to cause damage to computers or files. Viruses generally enter your computer system through files you receive on floppy disks or over networks. Compare *Trojan horse* and *worm*.

VRAM Stands for "video random access memory," a bank of memory on a display adapter that provides a place for the board to process graphics information.

W

wave file An audio file format developed by Microsoft. Compare *RealAudio*.

Web See World Wide Web.

Web cam A type of *digital camera* used to broadcast video over the *Internet*.

Web browser See *browser*.

window A frame on the computer's screen that contains a file, an application, or a group of icons.

Windows The *operating system* used by most PCs.

Windows 2000 A version of Windows designed for businesses, now replaced by Windows XP Professional.

Windows 3.1 The first widely adopted version of Windows.

Windows 95 A version of Windows released in 1995.

Windows 98 A version of Windows released in 1998.

Windows CE A version of Windows designed for hand-held PCs.

Windows Explorer A feature in *Windows XP* that allows easy access to *files* and *folders* on the *hard drive*.

Windows Millennium Edition A version of Windows released in 2000. Now replaced by Windows XP Home Edition. Also called Windows Me.

Windows NT A version of Windows designed for networked PCs.

Windows registry See *registry*.

Windows Tour A feature of Windows XP that provides an audio-visual introduction.

Windows XP The newest version of Windows, released in 2001. Has two versions: Windows XP Professional and Windows XP Home.

Windows Media Audio The audio file format used by Windows Media player. Abbreviated WMA.

Wintel Short for "Windows" and "Intel," the two technologies that define PC-compatible computers.

wizard A software tool that leads you through a complicated process.

WMA See *Windows Media Audio.*

word processing software A type of application program that enables users to write, edit, and format text and, often, incorporate graphics.

workstation Another word for personal computer. Usually it refers to especially powerful PCs.

World Wide Web An *Internet* service that lets publishers post multimedia content. Users view the content in a *browser* and navigate by clicking *hyperlinks.*

worm A type of virus that gets into a machine and executes all by itself. Worms usually affect servers and other machines attached to a network, but they can also infect PCs. See also *Trojan horse.*

wrist rest A soft pad that sits in front of the *keyboard* to support your wrists as you type; it helps guard against wrist injuries associated with extensive keyboard use.

write-protecting Using a device on a floppy disk to ensure that nothing can be saved to the disk.

WYSIWYG Pronounced "wizzy-wig." Stands for "what you see is what you get." Used to refer to *application programs* that can display a document on screen exactly as it will be printed.

X Y Z

XP see *Windows XP.*

Index

? (question mark), in dialog box, 130
2Look4.com, 230
2Wire, 186
3Com, 186
3D graphics adapters, 61
10BaseT wires, 184
386 processor, 7, 43
486 processor, 7, 43, 45
802.11b technology, 38, 185–186
8088 processor, 43
80286 processor, 43

A

abbreviations, chat slang, 287
About option, Help menu, 12
Accessibility accessories, 177–178
Accessibility Wizard, 144, 148, 177
accessories
    computer, 94–97
    Windows, 177–182, 212
accounts. *See* user accounts
action games, 254
Activate Windows accessory, 180
activation, software, 180, 220
active matrix screens, 36, 63–64
adapters, 29. *See also* specific types
Add/Remove Programs tool, 136–137,
    222–223
Add to Favorites command, 290
Address Book, Windows, 211
Administrator account, 121, 142, 143
Adobe
    PhotoDeluxe, 241, 242
    Photoshop, 242, 243
    Photoshop Elements, 242
    tech support, 13
Advanced Micro Devices, 7
AGP slots, 60–61
AIM, 285
Aimster, 231
airline reservations, 310–311
Aiwa, 232

All Programs icon, 27
Alpha Memory, 48
Alt key, 70
AltaVista, 263, 295
Amazon.com, 17, 217, 219, 302
AMD, 7, 44
America Online. *See* AOL
analog-to-digital converter, 235
anti-virus programs, 200
antitrust case, Microsoft, 19–20, 112, 288
Anywho, 309
AOL
    alternatives to, 265, 268–269
    children's safety considerations, 272
    Computing Channel, 217
    email, 284
    getting connecting with, 269
    instant messaging, 285–286
    monthly fee, 267
    popularity of, 266–267
    portal site, 295
    sending faxes via, 87
AOL.com, 295
APC, 97
Apple Computer, 7, 228
application software, 5, 19, 211.
    See also software
arrow keys, 71, 72
Ask Jeeves for Kids, 295
**Association, Software Information and
    Industry,** 220
Association of PC User Groups, 15
ATI, 235
AtomFilms, 308, 309
atomic clocks, 144
AT&T Anywho, 309
AT&T WorldNet, 268
attachments, email, 199
audio CDs
    creating, 225–226, 228
    playing on PC, 137, 225, 226, 228
audio controls, 137–138, 179
AudioGalaxy, 231

AudioPhilez, 230
Auto Save command, 172
AutoComplete feature, Internet Explorer, 278–279
Automatic Update tab, Control Panel, 138–139
Avery, 247
AVI files, 92

B

Back-UPS Office 350, 97
backing up, 191–194
    hardware options, 53, 54, 192–193
    importance of, 191
    over the Internet, 194
    software options, 192, 193
Backspace key, 70
Backup, 194
backup power, 97
bandwidth, 261–262
banking, online, 249, 316–317
banners, 247
Barnes & Noble, 17, 302
batteries
    camera, 91
    laptop, 38, 141
battery backup system, 97
BearShare, 231
beeping, 110, 111
Berners-Lee, Tim, 262
bill-paying services, 249, 316–317
bits, 47
Block Financial Software, 250
BlueMountain.com, 247
Blue's Reading Time Activities, 256
Blue's Treasure Hunt, 256
BMP files, 243
books, computer, 16–17
Boolean logic, 263
booting, 110
brand-name computers, 40–41, 44
Break key, 71
brightness control, monitor, 111
broadband connections, 29, 84, 200–201
Broderbund Software, 13
Brother printers, 77, 80, 81
browsers. *See* Web browsers
bulletin boards, 10
bumper stickers, 246

burning
    CDs, 225–226
    DVDs, 238
bus, 45
Byte Online, 214
bytes, 47

C

C drive
    cleaning up, 139
    viewing contents of, 119–120, 159
cable modems
    availability of, 84
    and Ethernet cards, 58, 84
    and hackers, 200
    and IP addresses, 187
    and routers, 188
    speed of, 84
cache, disk, 45
cache memory, 44–45
Calculator accessory, 182
calendars, 246
camcorders, 92
cameras
    digital, 90–93, 239–240
    digital video, 234–235
    Web cam, 9.1–92, 286
Canon
    cameras, 91
    printers, 77, 80, 81
Caps Lock key, 70
capturing, video, 234, 235
cards. *See* expansion boards; greeting cards
Carmen Sandiego Series, 256
Carpal Tunnel Syndrome, 94, 95
cartridges, printer, 81
case, removing PC, 102
Category 5 wires, 184–185
cathode ray tubes. *See* CRT monitors
CD-DA format, 229
CD-R discs/drives, 54, 153, 226
CD-ROM discs/drives, 29, 52, 53, 54, 225
CD-RW drives, 29, 52, 54, 153, 192–193
CD Writing wizard, 153
CDs
    backing up to, 192–193
    burning, 225–226
    copying files to, 153
    playing audio, 137, 225
    writing errors, 227
CDW Computer Centers, 219

Celeron processor, 43
central processing unit. *See* CPU
CERN, 262
chairs, computer workplace, 104
Character Map accessory, 180
chat
    abbreviations/slang, 287
    services, 264, 267, 272, 285–286
check boxes, 129
children
    and online safety, 271–274, 275, 298
    search engines for, 295
    software for, 211, 256
chips, 43, 47
CinemaNow.com, 308
Cisco Systems, 186
classes, computer, 17–18
Classic view, Windows, 134, 135
Clean Desktop Now command, 114
clicking, 116, 124–125
Clipboard, 168
clock, computer, 144
close box, 130
close button, dialog box, 130
Close command, 175–176
CNET, 214, 218
"Code Red" worm, 198
command buttons, 129
Command Prompt accessory, 182
commands, 123–131
    keyboard shortcuts for, 128
    menu, 126–128
    mouse, 123–125
    toolbar, 130–131
Communications accessories, 178
communications software, 211
CompactFlash cards, 91, 240
Compaq Computer, 9, 13
Compaq Works, 33
Compatibility Wizard, 213
CompUSA, 219
CompuServe, 268
computer courses, 17–18
computer desks, 104
computer magazines, 10, 15–16, 214
Computer Shopper, 16
computer stores
    buying hardware/software from, 30, 217
    getting help from, 15
    list of, 219

Computer User, 16
computers
    advice for first-time users, 4–5
    books about, 16–17
    choosing, 40–42
    compared with other home appliances, 5
    connecting via networks, 183–186
    factors affecting speed, 43–45
    getting help with, 8–18
    installing new hardware, 138, 141
    laptop vs. desktop, 34–35
    naming/renaming, 138
    new vs. used, 32–33
    protecting from power surges/outages,
        96–97
    removing case, 102
    setting up, 98–101
    sharing, 121–122
    shutting down, 203–205
    starting, 110–111, 194–195
    system components, 28–29
    types of, 6–7
    when to buy, 32–33
    where to buy, 30–33
    workspace considerations, 104–105
ComputingWithKids.com, 256
connectors, 55–58
contrast control, monitor, 111
Control Panel, 134–144
    accessing, 27
    purpose of, 134
    settings
        accessibility options, 144
        add/remove programs, 136–137
        appearance/themes, 134–136
        date/time/language/regional, 144
        performance/maintenance, 138–141
        printers/other hardware, 141
        sound/speech/audio, 137–138
        user accounts, 142–143
    switching to Classic view, 134, 135
cookies, 279–280
copiers, 77
Copy command, 72, 150–151, 167–168, 172
copy protection, 227
copyright
    laws governing, 232
    for music files, 229, 231
    for software, 219–220
Corel, 13
courses, computer, 17–18
Covad, 84

CPU
386, 7, 43
486, 7, 43, 45
8088, 43
80286, 43
Celeron, 43
identifying type/speed of, 138
major manufacturers, 7, 44
Pentium, 7, 43, 45, 48
purpose of, 43
speed, 43–44
crashes, program, 22, 173, 195
crawlers, 263
CreataCard, 246
Create Shortcut command, 164, 165
Creative Labs, 232
CRT monitors, 28, 56, 63
Ctrl-Alt-Delete, 195
Ctrl key, 70, 72
cursor keys, 71
Customize Desktop command, 114
Cut command, 72, 150–151, 167–168, 172
CyberPatrol, 273

D

D-Link, 186
daisy chaining, 56
Dantz Development Corp, 193
database management software, 211
Date options, Control Panel, 144
Dazzle, 93, 235
DDR memory, 48
decals, 247
defragmenting, 140
Deja.com, 264, 314
Del key, 71, 72
Dell, 9, 13, 33
demo software, 218
department store, buying PC from, 30
desks, computer, 104
desktop, Windows, 112–114
adding items to, 113, 290
changing appearance of, 134–136
cleaning, 114
closing vs. minimizing windows, 176
and Microsoft antitrust case, 112
showing, 133
XP vs. earlier versions, 26, 112
desktop PC. *See also* computers
components of, 28–29

contrasted with laptop, 34–35
setting up, 98–101
desktop publishing software, 211
DHCP server, 187–188
dial-up modems, 83, 265
dialog boxes, 129–130
digital audio players, 232
digital cameras, 90–91, 100, 239–240
digital music, 228–231
digital photography, 239–244
digital sound, 138
digital subscriber line. *See* DSL
digital video cameras, 234–235
DIMM, 47
disabilities, configuring Windows to accommodate, 144
disaster prevention/recovery, 191–202
backing up, 191–194
fending off hackers, 200–202, 274–276
preventing viruses, 198–200
restarting computer, 194–195
restoring system, 196–198
unerasing files, 198
discount store, buying PC from, 30
disk cache, 45
disk drives. *See also* specific types
cleaning up, 139
names for, 121
viewing contents of, 27, 119–120, 159
Disney Interactive, 13
display adapters, 62–63, 67
display resolution, 65
displays. *See* monitors
divorce Web site, 318
docking stations, 37, 38
documents
cutting and pasting data between, 167–168
editing, 167–169
saving, 171–174
sharing, 121–122
storing, 27
Documents and Settings folder, 117, 121–122
domain names, 297
DOS command prompt, 182
"Dot Net" strategy, Microsoft, 299–301
dot pitch, 66, 67
dots per inch, 78
double-clicking, 116, 124–125
Download.com, 11, 218
dpi, 78

dragging, 125
DRAM, 47
DriverGuide.com, 11
drivers, 10–11, 24, 101, 146
driving games, 255
DrKoop.com, 313
DSL modems
    and Ethernet cards, 58, 84
    and hackers, 200
    and IP addresses, 187
    and routers, 188
DSL service, 84, 85
"Dummy" books, 17
DVD burners, 238
DVD/CD-RW combo drives, 29
DVD discs/drives, 52, 54, 233
DVD movies, 233
DVD-R drives, 29
DVD-ROM drives, 29
DVD+RW standard, 238
Dymo LabelWriter, 247

E

EarthLink, 268
Easy CD Creator, 54, 193
EasyShare cameras, 240
Edell, Dean, 313
Edit menu, 160, 167–170, 172
eFax, 87
Egghead, 219
electrical surges, 96
email, 281–285
    advantages over fax, 86–87
    attaching files to, 199
    popularity of, 264, 281
    scams, 277
    software for sending/receiving, 19, 268,
        282–283
    and viruses, 199
    Web-based, 284–285
eMP3Finder, 230
Empty Recycle Bin command, 198
eMusic, 230
Encapsulated PostScript, 243
Encyclopedia Britannica, 262
End Task command, 195
energy-saving features, 140–141
Enter key, 70
Entertainment accessories, 179–180

entertainment software, 211
Entertainment Software Review Board, 253
Epitonic, 230
EPS files, 243
Epson
    printers, 80, 81
    tech support, 13
ergonomic keyboards, 69
Esc key, 70, 72
eShop, 219
Ethernet, 29, 38, 58, 184–186
Eudora, 268, 282–283
Excite, 282, 285, 295
Exit command, 176
expansion boards, 29, 102–103
expansion slots, 29, 59–61
Expedia, 311
Explorer, Windows, 151–152. *See also*
    Internet Explorer
extensions, file, 150, 154–157, 174
eyestrain, 104, 105

F

Fandango, 307
FAQs, 9
FatBrain, 17
Favorites menu, 160–161, 290
fax modems, 29, 83–84, 86–87
faxing
    with multifunction device, 77
    via AOL/Internet, 87
file extensions, 150, 154–157, 174
file formats
    photo, 242–243
    video, 92
File menu, 160, 167, 172
file-sharing services, 230–231
File Transfer Wizard, 180–181
files, 149–158
    backing up, 191–194
    changing program associations, 158
    closing, 175–176, 203–204
    copying, 113, 150–151, 153
    creating, 160, 167
    making shortcuts for, 164–165
    moving, 150–151
    naming, 157
    opening, 150
    printing, 174–175
    restoring deleted, 198

files *(continued)*
    saving, 170–174
    searching for, 152–153
    sharing, 121–122
    showing hidden, 119–120, 149, 155
    viewing, 162–163
FilmSpeed, 308
filtering software, 273–274
financial management software, 211,
    248–251
Find and Replace command, 169
Find command, 169, 172
FindSongs, 230
firewalls, 201–202, 275–276
Fireware, McAfee, 276
FireWire
    cards, 38
    contrasted with USB, 58
    and hard disks, 50
    ports, 53, 236
    purpose of, 58
floppy disks/drives, 29, 52–53
folders, 159–165
    accessing, 27
    copying, 113
    creating, 159–160
    making shortcuts for, 164–165
    menus/controls, 160–163
    naming, 27, 160
    placing in Start menu, 290–291
    restricting access to, 143
    searching for, 117, 152–153
    sharing, 121–122
    viewing, 162–163
fonts, 79, 170
Format menu, 170
forums, 10
fragmentation, disk, 140
Freddi Fish 5, 256
"free" PC/ISP offers, 268
freeware, 218
Frequently Asked Questions, 9
ftp, 264
function keys, 70

G

game software, 252–256
    and 3D graphics adapters, 61
    genres, 254–256
    ratings, 253–254
    Web site, 252

    and Windows XP, 22, 252
Gamespot.com, 252
Gateway Computer, 13
gateways, 186, 188
GB, 29, 47
Gibson Research, 201
GIF files, 243
gigabytes, 29, 47
Gnottella, 231
Gnutella, 231
Google, 9, 263, 295–296
graphics accelerators, 63
graphics adapters, 60–61, 63, 66
graphics software, 211
greeting cards
    software for creating, 246
    supplies, 247
    Web sites, 247
Greetings, Microsoft, 246
grounded outlets, 101
Guardian **Web site,** 303
Gudmundsen, Jinny, 256

H

hackers, 147, 200–201, 274–276
Hallmark Card Studio Deluxe, 246
hand-held computers, 7
hard disk, 49–51
    contrasted with memory, 49, 51
    defragmenting, 140
    freeing up space on, 139
    IDE vs. SCSI, 50
    purpose of, 29, 49
    recommended size for, 49–50
    speeding up, 45
    viewing contents of, 119–120
hardware. *See also* specific types
    getting help with, 8–18
    installing/uninstalling, 138, 141
    manuals, 8
    reviews, 16, 214
    serial numbers, 12
    Web sites, 13
headphone jacks, 57
Health Central, 313
health Web sites, 312–313
hearing-impaired, configuring Windows
    for, 144
help
    hardware/software, 8–18, 215
    Windows XP, 145–148

Help and Support menu, 145–148
Help key, 72
Help menus, 8, 12
Hewlett-Packard
    printers, 77, 80, 81, 240
    tech support, 13
hidden files, 119–120, 149, 155
History feature, Internet Explorer,
    277–278, 292
Hollywood DV Bridge, 93, 235
Home Edition, Windows XP, 24, 192
home electronics store, buying PC from,
    30–31
home gateways, 186, 188
home movies. *See* movies
home page, 289
home phone line alliance, 186
hot swapping, 58
Hotel Discount, 311
Hotfile, 218
Hotmail, 282, 284–285
HPNA, 186
HTML, 262–263
hubs, 184
Humongous Entertainment, 13, 256
Hungry Minds, 17
hyperlinks, 262, 294–295
HyperTerminal, 178
hypertext, 262

I

"I Love You" virus, 198
IBM
    compatibles, 6
    refurbished computers, 33
    tech support, 13
ICANN, 261
icons, removing from desktop, 114
IDE interface, 50
IEEE 1394, 58
iLink, 58
image-editing software, 211, 243
image files, 118
ImageMate, 240
iMesh, 231
InfoSpace, 309
ink cartridges, 244
inkjet printers, 76, 77–78, 81, 243–244

Ins key, 71
instant messaging, 264, 267, 272, 285–286
Intel
    digital audio players, 232
    processors, 7, 43, 44
IntelliEye mouse, 73, 74
IntelliMouse, 74
interlacing, 66
Internet, 260–264. *See also* World Wide Web
    accessing via TV, 7
    backing up files to, 194
    connecting to, 83, 84, 136, 265–270
    defined, 261
    features, 264 (*See also* specific features)
    how it works, 261–262
    magazine devoted to, 16
    origin of, 261
    privacy considerations, 277–280
    safety considerations, 271–274, 275
    scams, 276–277
    search engines, 9, 263, 295–298
    sending faxes via, 87
    sharing connection via networking,
        186–188
    software (*See* Web browsers)
    as source of hardware/software help,
        9–10
Internet Explorer, 288–293
    adding Favorites, 290
    Address Bar, 298
    AutoComplete feature, 278–279
    customizing, 292–293
    History feature, 277–278, 292
    and Internet searches, 295, 298
    and ISPs, 268
    and newsgroups, 264
    setting home page, 289
    toolbar, 291–292, 293
    and Windows, 19, 288
Internet Guard, 273
Internet Movie Database, 307
Internet protocol, 187
Internet Service Providers. *See* ISPs
Intuit, 13, 248, 250
investment Web sites, 314–315
invitations, 246
Iomega, 53, 193
IP addresses, 187–188
ISA slots, 60
ISDN, 85
ISPs, 265, 268–269
It'sLegal, 318

J

J2 fax service, 87
Jasc Software, 241
Jerusalem Post **Web site,** 303
Joint Photographic Experts Group, 242
joules, 96
joysticks, 75
JPEG files, 242
.jpg file extension, 242
JumpStart Phonics, 256

K

Kazaa, 231
KB, 47
Kenwood, 232
Key Tronic, 69
keyboard holders, 104
keyboard shortcuts, 128, 172
keyboards, 68–72
  choosing, 68
  common functions, 72
  connecting, 68
  desktop vs. laptop, 35, 36
  ergonomic, 69
  and hand/wrist pain, 94–95, 104
  onscreen, 178
  purpose of, 28
  typical layout, 70–71
kids. *See* children
kilobytes, 47
Kingston Memory, 48
Knowledge Adventure, 256
Knowledge Base, 146
Kodak
  cameras, 91, 240
  Digital Learning Center, 243

L

LI/L2 cache, 45
label printers, 247
LaCie, 53
Langberg, Mike, 214
Language options, Control Panel, 144
LANs, 7, 58, 183–186
laptop PC, 34–39
  component considerations, 36–39
  contrasted with desktop, 34–35
  notebook vs. ultralight, 36–37
  power-saving schemes, 141

  upgrading, 35, 36
  watching movies on, 233
Larry's Concise Guide to the Internet, 298
laser printers, 77, 78, 79–80
Lawyer Locator, 318
LCD monitors, 28, 56, 63–64, 67
Learning Company, 246, 256, 318
Legal Information Network, 318
Legaldocs, 317–318
Lexmark printers, 77, 80, 81
lighting, workspace, 105
LimeWire, 231
line in/out ports, 57
links, 262, 294–295
liquid crystal displays. *See* LCD monitors
Little Mac Book, The, vi
LittlePCBook.com, 214, 295
local area networks. *See* LANs
Log Off command, 205
Logitech
  mouse, 74
  QuickCam, 286
London Times **Web site,** 303
LookSmart, 295
Los Angeles Times **Web site,** 303
lossy compression, 242
Lycos, 230, 295

M

Macintosh computers, vi, 6, 7
MacMillan USA, 17
magazines, computer, 10, 15–16, 214
magnetic media, 52
Magnifier accessory, 177
mail-order PCs, 31–32
MailStart, 285
Maintenance Wizard, 148
manuals, hardware/software, 8, 9
Mapquest, 310
Maps on Us, 310
Math Blaster, 256
Maxtor, 53
Mayo Clinic Web site, 313
MB, 47
McAfee
  anti-virus software, 200
  firewall software, 276
Media Player, 19, 224–226
Medline Plus, 313

megabytes, 47

megapixels, 90

memory, 46–48
and computer speed, 44–45
contrasted with hard disk, 49, 51
determining available, 12, 138
measurement units, 47
purpose of, 46
recommended amount of, 46–47
types of, 47–48
where to buy, 48
and Windows XP, 22, 46–47

memory cards, camera, 91, 240

memory leaks, 22

memory space, 22

Memory Sticks, 91

menu bars, 126

menu commands, 126–128

menus
expanding, 166–167
for folders, 160–163
how to read, 127
types of, 126

Messenger, Windows, 285–286

MGI Software, 237

mice. *See* mouse

microphone jacks, 57

Microsoft
antitrust case, 19–20, 112, 288
ergonomic keyboards, 69
Greetings, 246
IntelliEye, 73, 74
IntelliMouse, 74
Internet Explorer (*See* Internet Explorer)
Knowledge Base, 146
Money, 248–249
Network (*See* MSN)
Outlook (*See* Outlook)
Outlook Express (*See* Outlook Express)
PictureIt, 241
PictureIt Publishing, 246
tech support, 13
Windows (*See also* specific versions)
contrasted with Macintosh operating system, 6
Control Panel, 27, 134–144
giving commands in, 123–128
identifying installed version, 12, 138
programs included with, 19–20, 212
purpose of, 19
taskbar, 132–133
version history, 20–21
xBox, 252

Microsoft.Net, 299–301

MicroTimes, 16

Minolta printers, 80

Missing and Exploited Children, National Center for, 273

mobility aids, 144, 178

modems, 82–87
connecting, 56
and phone service, 83–84
purpose of, 29, 82–83
speed of, 83, 84–85
types of, 83, 84–87

monitor platforms, 105

monitors, 62–67
brightness/contrast controls, 111
buying, 66–67
connecting, 56, 67, 99
desktop vs. laptop, 35, 63–64
and image quality, 66–67
interlaced vs. noninterlaced, 66
multiscan, 63
positioning, 105
purpose of, 28
resolution, 64, 65, 66
size options, 65
types of, 28, 36, 63–64
and UPS devices, 97

Mossberg, Walter, 214

motherboard, 43

Motley Fool, 314, 315

mouse, 73–75
alternatives to, 75
buttons, 73, 124–125
cleaning, 74
commands, 123–125
connecting, 73
contrasted with laptop pointing devices, 35
controlling speed, 125
and hand/wrist pain, 94
how it works, 73
optical, 73, 74
pads, 95
ports, 73
purpose of, 28
scroll wheel, 73
techniques for using, 123–125

Movie Database, Internet, 307

Movie Maker, Windows, 236–237

Moviefone, 307

movies
editing, 92
playing DVD, 225, 233

movies *(continued)*
  transferring from analog camera to PC,
    92–93
  on the Web, 307–309
MP3 files
  copyright considerations, 229–230
  finding/downloading, 230
  and Media Player, 225, 228
  and PC speakers, 28
  players for, 228, 232
  storing on CD, 228, 229
MP3 Search, 230
MP3.com, 230
MPEG files, 92, 237
MS-DOS command prompt, 182
MSN
  as alternative to AOL, 268
  eShop, 219
  Investor Web site, 315–316
  and My Music folder, 117
  and Network Place wizard, 301
  portal, 295
  and XP Connection wizard, 270
  and XP desktop, 112
multi-user function, Windows XP, 25,
    121–122
multifunction devices, 77
multiscan monitors, 63
Music City's Morpheus, 231
music files, 28, 117–118, 225, 228–231
Music4Free.com, 230
Musicgrab.com, 230
MusicMatch Jukebox, 226
My Computer, 27, 119–120, 149
My Documents folder, 27, 116–117
My Music folder, 27, 117–118
My Pictures folder, 27, 117, 118, 240

N

naming
  computer, 138
  files, 157
  folders, 160
Napster, 228, 230, 231
Narrator accessory, 177
National Center for Missing and Exploited
    Children, 273
National Institute of Safety and Health, 105
National Library of Medicine, 313
NDC Communications, 186

.Net strategy, Microsoft, 299–301
.Net wizard, 300–301
Netscape
  Navigator, 264, 268, 288
  Netcenter, 295
network adapters/cards, 29, 184
network computers, 7
Network Place wizard, 301
Network Setup Wizard, 189–190
network wires, 184–186
networking, 183–190
  and computer shutdown, 204
  configuring XP for, 136, 188–190
  and hackers, 201–202, 274–276
  hardware requirements, 184–188
  and routers, 186–188
  sharing Internet connection via,
    186–188
  sharing printer via, 79
  wireless, 185–186
New command, 167, 172
New Connection wizard, 270
New York Times **Web site,** 279, 303, 304
news Web sites, 302–306, 305
newsgroup readers, 10
newsgroups, 10, 264, 314
newsletters
  software company, 16
  user group, 14, 15
newspaper Web sites, 303
Nintendo, 252
Nolo Press, 318
Nortel, 186
Norton
  Anti-Virus, 200
  Internet Security, 276
  Utilities, 198
notebook PC, 34, 36. *See also* laptop PC
NotePad, 182
NT. *See* Windows NT
NullSoft, 228
numeric keypad, 71
NumLock key, 71

O

Office Depot, 219
OfficeMax, 219, 247
online banking, 249, 316–317
online services, 83, 266–268
Onscreen Keyboard accessory, 178

Open command, 172
Opera browser, 288
operating systems. *See also* Windows
    contrasted with application software, 19
    for hand-held computers, 7
    purpose of, 19
    Windows *vs.* Mac, 6–7
optical drives, 29
optical mouse, 73, 74
option buttons, 129
Orbitz, 311
Osborne/McGraw-Hill, 17
Outlook, 211, 268, 282–283
Outlook Express, 10, 19, 268, 282–283

P

packet switching, 261
packets, 261
Page Setup command, 170
Paint program, 212
Paint Shop Pro, 241–242
Palm Operating System, 7
Palm organizers, 211
palmtop computers, 7
Panasonic
    CD players, 232
    printers, 80
paper
    greeting card, 247
    photo, 243–244
PaperDirect Web site, 247
paragraph formatting, 170
parallel ports, 56
passive matrix screens, 36
Passport wizard, 300–301
Paste command, 72, 167–168, 172
Paste Shortcut command, 113
Pause/Break key, 71
Paytrust, 316–317
PC, 6. *See also* computer
PC card slots, 37
PC Connection, 219
PC Magazine, 16, 42, 214
PC User Groups, Association of, 15
PC Warehouse, 219
PC World, 16, 42, 214
PC Zone, 219
PCAnswer.com, 214
PCI slots, 60

PCL printers, 79–80
Peachpit Press, vi, 17
Peerless hard drives, 53
Pentium processors, 7, 32, 43, 45, 48
Performance and Maintenance section,
    Control Panel, 138–141
Performance tab, Task Manager, 195
peripherals, 59, 101
personal computers, 6. *See also* PC
personal finance software, 248–251
personal information managers, 211
Philips, 232
phone directories, 309
phone jacks, 57
photo-editing software, 241–242
photo paper, 243–244
photo tools, 240–241
PhotoDeluxe, 241, 242
photographs
    editing, 88–89
    file formats for, 242–243
    printing, 80–81, 90, 241
photography, digital, 239–244
Photoshop, 242, 243
Photoshop Elements, 242
PhotoSmart printers, 240
picture files, 118
PictureIt, 241
PictureIt Publishing, 246
PIMs, 211
Pinnacle Systems, 92, 235, 237
piracy, software, 220
pixels, 65
PlayStation, 252
Plug and Play feature, 138, 141
PocketPC, 7, 232
pointers, mouse, 28
pointing devices, 35, 38–39, 75
portals, 295–298
ports, 29, 55–58
PostScript printers, 79–80
power, backup, 97
power-saving features, 140–141
power strips, 100, 110
power supply, 96–97, 102
presentation software, 211
Print command, 174
Print Screen key, 71
PrintArtist, 246

printer, 76–81
  buying, 81
  connecting, 56, 100
  grounding, 101
  installing/uninstalling, 141
  manufacturers, 80, 81
  networking, 79
  paper-handling capability, 79
  purpose of, 28
  resolution, 78
  sharing, 79
  speed, 78
  supplies, 77–78, 81, 243–244
  types
    color, 80–81
    inkjet, 76, 77–78, 81, 243–244
    label, 247
    laser, 77, 78, 79–80
    in multifunction device, 77
    and UPS devices, 97
Printer Command Language, 80
printer languages, 79–80
printing
  fonts, 79
  labels, 247
  photographs, 80–81, 90, 241
PrintShop Deluxe, 246
privacy
  and Web browsers, 277–280
  and Windows Update, 148
privileges, account, 142, 143
Prodigy, 84, 268
Professional Edition, Windows XP, 24, 192
program crashes, 22, 173, 195
programs. *See also* software
  adding/removing, 136–137
  associating files with, 158
  closing, 175–176, 195
  creating shortcuts for, 164–165
  scheduling to run automatically, 181
  starting, 27
  switching among, 132
  updating, 138–139, 146–147
  working with, 166–176
protocols, 187, 260
PS/2 ports, 57, 73
PubMed, 313

Q

QPS Que drives, 53, 193
Quick Launch Toolbar, 133
QuickCam, 286

Quicken
  legal forms software, 318
  personal finance software, 248–249
QuickTime, 228
Quit command, 176

R

Radio Shack, 101
radio station Web sites, 304–306
RAM. *See* memory
Rambus, 48
random access memory. *See* memory
ratings, game, 253–254
RCA jacks, 235
RD-RAM, 48
Reader Rabbit, 256
README files, 222
Real files, 92
real-time strategy games, 254
RealOne Player, 226
RealVideo files, 237
Recycle Bin, 112, 114, 136, 198
Red Book audio, 229
Redo command, 168
refresh rate, monitor, 66
refurbished computers, 33
Regional options, Control Panel, 144
registration, software, 223
Registry, Windows, 136
removable storage, 52–54
repetitive stress injuries, 94, 95, 105
Replace command, 169
Residential Gateways, 186, 187–188
resolution
  digital camera, 90
  monitor, 64, 65, 66
  printer, 78
Restart command, 194–195
restore points, 197–198
Retrospect, 193
Return key, 70
reverse directories, 309
reviews
  hardware/software, 16, 214, 256
  ISP, 269
right-clicking, 125
RIMM, 47
RJ-11 connectors, 57
RJ-47 connectors, 58, 185

RobotFilms, 308
role-playing games, 255–256
routers, 186–188, 201
Roxio, 54, 193

S

S-Video jacks, 235
Safe Mode, 111
SafeKids.com, 274, 275
safety, Internet/online, 271–274, 275
San Jose Mercury News
    computer column, 214
    Web site, 303
SanDisk, 240
satellite, accessing Internet via, 85–86
Save As command, 172, 174
Save command, 171
Save icon, 171
scam artists, Internet, 276–277
scanners, 77, 86, 88–89, 100
Scheduled Tasks program, 180–181
screen savers, 135–136
screens. *See* monitors
Scroll Lock key, 71
ScrollPoint mouse, 74
SCSI interface, 50
SD-RAM, 47
search engines, 9, 263, 295–298
Search tool, 152–153
searching
    documents, 169
    hard disk, 152–153
    help system, 145, 146
    newsgroups, 10
    World Wide Web, 9–10, 263,
        295–298, 318
SecureMate, 240
Select All command, 72, 169, 172
serial numbers, hardware/software, 12
serial ports, 56
Shared Documents folder, 159
shareware, 218
Shareware.com, 218
Shields Up utility, 201
Shift key, 70
shortcuts
    adding/removing from desktop,
        113, 114
    for files/folders, 164–165

    for menu commands, 128, 172
    for programs, 164–165
Show Desktop icon, 133
Sierra Home, 246
SIMM, 47
simulation games, 255
slang, chat, 287
sleep mode, 140, 205
SmartMedia cards, 91, 240
SMC Networks, 186
software. *See also* specific categories and
        programs
    activating, 180, 220
    categories, 211
    choosing, 212–215
    copyright considerations, 219–220
    getting help with, 8–18, 215
    installing/uninstalling, 9, 222–223
    manuals, 8, 9
    operating system *vs.* application, 19
    registering, 223
    reviews, 16, 214
    rules for buying, 221
    serial numbers, 12
    tutorials, 9, 18
    with used computers, 33
    Web sites, 13, 218, 219
    where to get, 216–220
Software Information and Industry
    Association, 220
SohoWare, 186
Sonique, 228
Sony, 91, 236
SOS KidProof, 273
sound cards, 28, 57
sound controls, 137–138
Sound Recorder utility, 179–180
speakers
    adjusting volume, 137
    plugging in, 57
    purpose of, 28
special interest groups, 318–319
special needs, configuring Windows for,
    144, 178
speed
    bus, 45
    cache memory, 44–45
    CPU, 43–44
    hard disk, 45
    modem, 83, 84–85
    mouse, 125
    printer, 78

spell checkers, 170
spiders, 263
Split-Up.com, 318
sports games, 255
spreadsheet software, 211
Sprint Broadband, 85
spy ware, 231
Stand By command, 205
standby mode, 140
Staples, 219, 247
Starband, 86
Start menu, 115–122
   accessing from keyboard, 70, 72
   adding Favorites to, 290–291
   adding shortcuts to, 164–165
   Help option, 8
   Log Off command, 205
   organization of, 115–116
   purpose of, 26–27
   Restart command, 194–195
   Turn Off Computer command, 204
static electricity, 102, 103, 104
stereo store, buying PC from, 30–31
stickers, 247
StickyKeys options, 144
storage media, 51, 52, 54
Store4Power, 97
stretch breaks, 105
Studio DV, 237
Studio Online, 92, 235
surfing, Web, 294–295
surge protectors, 96, 100
Switchboard, 309, 310
Symantec
   Anti Virus Research Center, 200
   Norton Anti-Virus, 200
   tech support, 13
system requirements, 9
System Restore program, 196–198
System Tools accessories, 180–182
system unit, 29

T

tabs, dialog box, 130
Tagged Image File Format, 242–243
tape cartridges, 54
Task Manager, 195
taskbar, 132–133
tax preparation software, 250–251

TaxCut, 250
Team Sonique, 228
tech support, 12–14, 215
telephone directories, 309
Telocity, 84
text boxes, 130
text editors, 182
TFT screens, 36, 63–64
themes, desktop, 134–135
TheStreet.com, 315
thin film transistor screens. See TFT screens
Thumbnails option, View menu, 162
.tif file extension, 242
TIFF files, 242–243
Time options, Control Panel, 144
toolbars, 130–131, 133, 291–292
Tools menu, 161
ToolTips, 131
top level domains, 297, 298
Toshiba, 13
touchpads, 35, 39
Tour, Windows, 146
trackballs, 39, 75
training, computer, 17–18
travel Web sites, 310–311
Travelocity, 311
Trip.com, 311
Trojan horses, 198–199, 201
troubleshooting
   guides, 8, 9
   startup problems, 111
TrueType fonts, 79
TurboTax, 250–251
Turn Off command, 204, 205
tutorials, hardware/software, 18
TV Guide Web site, 308–309
TV news Web sites, 304

U

Ulead, 237
ultralight PC, 36–37
Undo command, 72, 168–169, 172
Unerase feature, 198
uninterruptible power supply, 96–97, 100
universal serial bus. See USB
Update, Windows, 11, 101, 138–139, 146–148
UPS devices, 96–97, 100

URLs, 262, 297
U.S. Copyright Office, 232
USB
    contrasted with FireWire, 58
    and mouse, 73
    ports, 37, 53, 56
USB 2.0, 57
Used Computer Mall, 33
user accounts
    adding/changing, 142–143
    assigning privileges, 143
    purpose of, 121–122
    security considerations, 143
user groups, 14–15, 16
Utilities, Norton, 198
Utility Manager accessory, 178
utility programs, 179–180, 201, 211

V

Vaio Digital Studio PC, 236
version numbers, software, 12, 138
VGA monitors, 65
VGA ports, 56
video
    capturing, 235, 236
    distributing, 237–238
    editing, 236–237
    file format for, 92
    playing, 225
video adapters, 63
video cameras, 92–93, 234–235
video-editing software, 92–93, 236–237
Video Studio, 237
VideoWave, 237
View menu, 160, 162–163
Virtual Dr., 11
virus-protection software, 200
viruses, 147, 198–200
vision-impaired, configuring Windows for, 144.
    See also Accessibility Wizard
Volume Control accessory, 179

W

Wall Street Journal Web site, 214, 303
Washingon Post Web site, 303
.wav files, 137, 229
Web addresses, 262, 297
Web-based email, 284–285

Web browsers. See also Internet Explorer;
    Netscape
    and cookies, 279–280
    and ISPs, 268
    and newsgroups, 264
    privacy considerations, 277–280
    purpose of, 262
Web cams, 91–92, 286
Web sites, 262–263
    adding to Favorites list, 290
    blocking access to, 273–274
    creation of, 262–263
    finding, 9, 263, 295–298
    for specific information/product
        addresses, 309
        computer books, 17
        computer courses, 18
        computer magazines, 16
        computer memory, 48
        drivers, 11, 101
        games, 252
        greeting cards, 247
        health/medical, 312–314
        law/lawyers, 317–318
        maps/directions, 310
        money/banking, 314–317
        movies, 307–309
        news, 302–306
        online tax-preparation, 250–251
        phone numbers, 309
        refurbished computers, 33
        shareware/demo software, 218
        software, 218–219, 273
        special interest groups, 318–319
        tech support, 13
        travel, 310–311
Web surfing, 294–298
WebMD, 312, 313
WebTV, 7
White Pages services, 309
WiFi technology, 185–186
WinAmp, 228
Windows. See also Microsoft; specific
    Windows versions
    accessories, 177–182
    Address Book, 211
    Clipboard, 168
    Explorer, 151–152
    Media Player, 19, 224–226
    Messenger, 285–286
    Movie Maker, 236–237
    Registry, 136
    Tour, 146
    Update, 11, 101, 138–139, 146–148

windows, closing *vs.* minimizing, 176
Windows 3.1, 20
Windows 95, 20–21, 23
Windows 98, 20, 21, 23, 24
Windows 2000, 20, 21, 22–24
Windows Me, 20, 21, 23, 24
Windows Millennium Edition, 21. *See also*
    Windows Me
Windows NT, 21, 22
Windows XP
    activating, 180, 220
    best way to get, 25
    compared with Windows 2000, 22–24
    configuring for networking, 188–190
    Control Panel, 134–144
    desktop, 26, 112–114
    help system, 145–148
    Home Edition, 24, 192
    memory requirements, 22, 46–47
    multi-user function, 25, 121–122
    new features, 25–27
    Professional Edition, 24, 192
    and program crashes, 22
    software compatibility, 212–213
    Start menu, 8, 26–27, 115–122
    startup problems, 111
    system requirements, 23
    taskbar, 132–133
    update feature, 11, 101, 138–139,
        146–148
    upgrade considerations, 23
    wizards, 148
Wintel machines, 7
wireless Internet service, 85
wireless LANs, 185–186
wizards, 148
    Accessibility, 144, 148, 177
    CD Writing, 153
    Compatibility, 213
    File Transfer, 180–181
    Maintenance, 148
    .Net, 300–301
    Network Place, 301
    Network Setup, 189–190
    New Connection, 270
    Passport, 300–301
    XP Connection, 270
WMA files, 225, 228
word processing software, 211
WordPad, 182, 212
workplace, computer, 104–105

World Wide Web. *See also* Web sites
    creation of, 262
    searching, 9–10, 263, 295–298
    surfing, 294–295
WorldNet, AT&T, 268
worms, 198–199
wrist rests, 94–95

X

X button, in dialog box, 130
xBox, 252
Xerox printers, 80
XP. *See* Windows XP
XP Connection Wizard, 270

Y

Yahoo
    email service, 282, 285
    for kids, 295
    maps, 310
    people search, 309
    portal, 295
    shopping, 219
    Web directory, 263
Yahoo Internet Life, 16
Yahooligans, 295
Yellow Pages services, 309

Z

ZDNet, 214, 218
Zip Disks, 53, 193
Zone Labs, 201, 276
ZoneAlarm, 201–202, 276

PEACHPIT PRESS

Quality How-to Computer Books

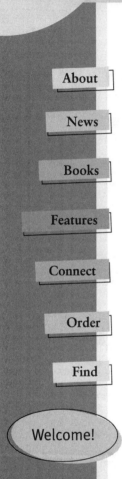

About

News

Books

Features

Connect

Order

Find

Welcome!

Visit Peachpit Press on the Web at www.peachpit.com

- Check out new feature articles each Monday: excerpts, interviews, tips, and plenty of how-tos

- Find any Peachpit book by title, series, author, or topic in Books

- See what our authors are up to on the News page: signings, chats, appearances, and more

- Meet the Peachpit staff and authors in the About section: bios, profiles, and candid shots

- Use Connect to reach our academic, sales, customer service, and tech support areas

Peachpit.com is also the place to:

- Chat with our authors online
- Take advantage of special Web-only offers
- Get the latest info on new books